GOVERNOR
CHARLES ROBINSON
OF KANSAS

CHARLES ROBINSON, 1892
Courtesy of The Kansas State Historical Society

GOVERNOR
CHARLES ROBINSON
OF KANSAS

Don W. Wilson

THE UNIVERSITY PRESS OF KANSAS
Lawrence, Manhattan, Wichita

Library of Congress Cataloging in Publication Data

Wilson, Don W.
    Governor Charles Robinson of Kansas.

    Bibliography: p.
    Includes index.
    1. Robinson, Charles, 1818–1894.
I. Title.
F685.R648 1975   978.1′03′0924 [B]   75-6875
ISBN 0-7006-0133-3

FOR

Gayle, Todd, and Jeffrey

WITH MY LOVE

Preface

For more than a century most historians of nineteenth-century Kansas have portrayed Charles Robinson's public career as secondary to the roles of James Lane and John Brown. Robinson's significance has been overlooked except for his involvement with the free-state controversy of Kansas' Territorial period. His convictions and actions—particularly those of his later years—have been maligned or misunderstood. The purpose of this study is to present a balanced interpretation of Robinson's life and activities and to shed additional light on a controversial figure whose active career encompassed nearly half a century of early Kansas history.

Robinson's early career from 1854 to 1861 centered around the struggle to make Kansas a Free State; it was highlighted by a personal battle with James H. Lane for control of the movement. This contest for power between Lane and Robinson continued through Robinson's term as governor of Kansas. From his service as Republican governor in 1861 until he became the Democratic candidate for governor in 1890, Charles Robinson's political career mirrored the turmoil faced by a state politician with strong personal commitments. In his later years, for example, Robinson came to reject the Republican party's stand on monetary policies, the tariff, prohibition, labor, and agricultural issues. His rejection of key Republican issues, in turn, led him to become active in every significant third-party movement in Kansas from the Civil War period through the Populist revolt. Though he was a candidate for numerous high state and national offices in the last thirty years of his life, he was unable to compromise his convictions in order to secure votes, and, therefore, he never gained the broadly based support that he needed in order to win a major election. An outspoken reformer, Robinson easily alienated large interest groups who did not conform with his views. Nevertheless, as an advocate of suffrage for women and Negroes, regulation of railroads, and liberalized currency laws, and as an opponent of prohibition, Charles Robinson was a major figure in Kansas politics during the period.

As a private citizen, Robinson made outstanding contributions to public and higher education. He was one of the founders of the University of Kansas, and he served as a member of its Board of Regents for many years. In 1887 he began a two-year term as superintendent of Haskell Indian Institute, making it one of the leading Indian industrial schools in the country during his incumbency. He promoted intellectual development within the state as a founder of the Kansas Liberal League and as an active leader in the Kansas State Historical Society. The wide range of his activities and interests, combined with what many of his contemporaries considered radical political and philosophical views, made Charles Robinson a colorful and significant figure in Kansas throughout the last half of the nineteenth century.

This study has been based primarily upon Robinson manuscripts located at the Kansas State Historical Society, the University of Kansas, and the Kansas City, Kansas, Public Library. I have also used related manuscript and newspaper collections at the Kansas State Historical Society.

The preparation of this book involved the help and encouragement of many people. I, however, take full responsibility for any errors in factual or historical judgment. Not everyone can here be acknowledged for his assistance, but some individuals must be mentioned. I am indebted to Professor Burton J. Williams, of Central Washington State College, for his encouragement and for his deep knowledge of Kansas history, which greatly contributed to the content of this study. Appreciation must be extended to Professor William D. Aeschbacher, of the University of Cincinnati, whose direction, guidance, and patience aided in bringing the project to completion. To Robert W. Richmond and John E. Wickman special acknowledgments are given for assistance and advice received by me over past years.

Contents

1

To Kansas
via California

Charles Robinson's life was one that dealt with new frontiers and bold ideas. He combined many careers—doctor, newspaper editor, politician, speculator, farmer, and educator. In each of these he was at least moderately successful, and every role that he undertook revealed a strong crusading spirit. The causes that he championed were as numerous as the careers that he followed. As a doctor in New England he experimented with new medical techniques. As a newspaper editor in California he championed squatters' land rights. In the mid 1850s his name was almost synonymous with the free-state movement in Kansas. He was identified with most major educational, political, and intellectual movements that occurred in the first forty years of Kansas Territorial and state history. From early manhood he was an idealist, but possessed with a Yankee twist of practicality. This study is an examination of Charles Robinson—his careers and crusades, his ideals, and the times in which he lived.

Charles Robinson, like many of the idealistic crusaders of the mid nineteenth century, was a product of rural New England. His wife, Sara T. D. Robinson, maintained that the Robinson family was established in New England by John Robinson, a passenger on the *Mayflower* who became a resident of Plymouth.[1] Other sources, however, have disputed this claim. John Speer, editor of the Kansas volume of the *U.S. Biographical Dictionary* of 1879, wrote: "In fact, thinking that craft unseaworthy, he [the first Robinson] had waited some sixty years for a safer boat."[2]

The Robinson family settled in Massachusetts, and most of Charles's ancestors were farmers. In 1808 Jonathan Robinson, father of Charles, married Huldah Woodward of Hardwick, Massachusetts, and the young couple settled on a modest farm near her home. To Jonathan and Huldah were born ten children—six boys and four girls. Charles, the third son, was born on July 21, 1818.

The story of the childhood and family of Charles Robinson was written by his wife in the later years of her life. Charles himself was close-mouthed about his early life and his parentage. In an age when it was popular to trace one's ancestry, it was unusual to find a man of Robinson's prominence so reluctant to disclose the experiences of his youth. Sara's accounts of his boyhood, many of which were written after his death, indicate that he was raised in a thrifty and religious home. He attended the Congregational church regularly. Apparently he had an interest in music, for he sang in the church choir and played clarinet in the Hardwick band.

Two of his early teachers appear to have had considerable influence on him during his formative years. His early classroom instruction took place in a one-room schoolhouse only a few hundred yards from the Robinson home. For several terms he was taught there by William B. Stone, a student at Amherst College who supported his own schooling by teaching in the winter. Stone, a brother of Lucy Stone's, an advocate of women's rights, later married Charles's sister Samantha. After Samantha's death he married another sister, Phoebe, in 1842. She died in 1852, and Stone then married Martha, a third sister of Charles's.

Following this initial formal education, Robinson was sent to Hadley Academy in Hardwick, three miles from the family farm. Here young Robinson came under the instruction of a Universalist preacher named Goldsburg, who apparently altered his new student's traditional Congregational viewpoint. Robinson began to question Congregational beliefs, and eventually he left that church.[3] He never again held a church membership.

2

He considered his personal religion above the confines of a church, and he later developed and wrote down his own philosophy. It aligned him closely with what many late-nineteenth-century Universalist spokesmen were expounding. He believed that the "laws of God and Nature are one of the same" and that since his creator had given him a body, an intellect, and a moral nature, it was his own responsibility to examine and probe all things. He would hear all sides and select only what stood the test of reason.[4]

By the time that Charles Robinson was eighteen he was qualified to be admitted to Amherst Academy. After two years at that school he developed a severe eye inflammation, which forced him to quit. One can speculate that this affliction is what led him to begin studying medicine under Dr. Amos Twitchell, a physician in Fitchburg, Massachusetts. Later he attended medical lectures at Pittsfield, Massachusetts, and in 1843 Berkshire (Massachusetts) Medical School granted him a degree in medicine. He started practicing his new profession in Belchertown, Massachusetts, that same year.

Robinson had been in Belchertown only a short time when he met Sarah Adams of Brookfield, Connecticut, whom he married in the late summer of 1843. Sarah was not a strong woman physically. Two children were born to Charles and Sarah, but both died in infancy. Sarah died in early January, 1846, shortly after the death of their second child.

In 1846, following his tragic losses, the young doctor moved to Springfield, Massachusetts, where he and Dr. J. G. Holland opened a private hospital. Little is known about the following two years except that Robinson suffered a physical breakdown, which forced him to give up his practice. Travel and change were prescriptions frequently given to cure a variety of illnesses in the nineteenth century, so Robinson decided to take a long trip and to change his life style. A good opportunity presented itself when he was asked to become physician for a group of Massachusetts men who had formed a stock company (the Congress and California Mutual Protective Association) for the purpose of traveling to California in pursuit of gold. He described the party, which left Boston on March 19, 1849, as one "composed

3

of men of all classes and professions, including tradesmen, clerks, manufacturers, mechanics, farmers, and laborers."[5]

The group of fifty-one men went to Pittsburgh, Pennsylvania, by railroad and canal. There a steamboat, the *Ne Plus Ultra*, was engaged to take them all the way to Kansas City, Missouri.[6]

By the time that the party arrived at the western border of Missouri on April 10, dissension was rampant within the organization. Robinson later wrote of the state of affairs:

> Like all joint-stock companies, made up of all classes and characters of independent, intelligent Yankees, no sooner was the journey commenced than the officers in control were subjects of suspicion, jealousies, innuendoes, reflections, and open charges of incapacity, inefficiency, crookedness, theft, and robbery. The farther removed from home and home influences, the louder the complaints, until on landing at Kansas City a general mutiny prevailed. No settlement of difficulties could be reached without a division of the party and a consequent division of the tons of supplies. Accordingly, two parties were organized, and a committee of three, of which the Doctor was one, was appointed to divide the "plunder." This quarrel and division, with the purchase of teams, consumed some four or five weeks of time, or till the first week in May.[7]

Thomas F. Dana was chosen captain of the splinter party, which consisted of fourteen men, including Robinson. The remainder of the party proceeded under the direction of John Webber, Jr., of Boston.

Robinson's group departed from Kansas City, Missouri, on May 10. As they traveled through what is now eastern Kansas, Robinson was so impressed with the surrounding countryside that he recorded in his diary:

> May 11, 1849.—Our course to-day has been over the rolling prairie, and we passed along without difficulty. The prairie seems to be an endless succession of rolls, with a smooth, green surface, dotted all over with the most beautiful flowers. The soil is of the most rich and fertile character, with no waste land. The feelings that come over a person, as he first views this immense ocean of land, are

indescribable. As far as the eye can reach, he sees nothing but a beautiful green carpet, save here and there perhaps a cluster of trees; he hears nothing but the feathered songsters of the air, and he *feels* nothing but a solemn awe in view of this infinite display of creative power.[8]

As the journey proceeded, Robinson's observations on the land gave way to accounts of hardships encountered by the party. The Dana group reached Fort Kearney (Nebraska) on June 3. Even before they reached that point they had realized their error of taking too much baggage and had thrown away nearly five hundred pounds of bread and bacon along with large quantities of flour and beans. After leaving Fort Kearney, the party again fragmented. Robinson now found himself in the company of only two other men. All were on horseback, using pack animals for their supplies. "After a journey of some three months," Robinson later wrote, "fragments of the Boston party began to arrive in California, and a small detachment, including Dr. Robinson, stopped [August 17] on Bear Creek for the purpose of washing out the precious metal."[9]

Robinson tried his hand at mining for only about two weeks before turning to other ways of making his livelihood. In the fall of 1849 he left Bear Creek and went to Sacramento, a boom town and a principal supply center for the gold region. The town then consisted of several buildings constructed of rough-hewn lumber, a few built of clay, and many tents. Robinson opened a restaurant in Sacramento early in the winter of 1849. More and more of his time, however, was absorbed by a land-issue crisis in California. By the spring of 1850 he was involved full time in leading a movement to reform the land system in California.

After the United States had acquired California as a result of the Mexican War, new settlers were faced with an established policy of land ownership that was alien to them. California had been under an irregular government that was characteristic of a remote and sparsely settled province. Land ownership was based upon grants that the various governments of the province had made to settlers. By the treaty of 1848 between Mexico and the United States, the validity of all such grants was guaranteed.

Yet the precise definition of individual titles was often questioned by unsympathetic emigrants who were unused to the system. In addition, the surveying methods that were used in setting the boundaries of the grants left the way clear for numerous disputes.

Captain Johann Augustus Sutter, whose name is closely associated with the gold discoveries in 1848, owned eleven leagues of land under a grant from Juan Alvarado, a former governor of California. Part of this grant covered the land where the town of Sacramento had developed. Initially, people who wanted lots assented to Sutter's claims and recognized his title by purchasing land from him. But as new settlers arrived, they began to question the legality of the grant. A major factor in the growing dissension stemmed from the fact that many of the newcomers were accustomed to squatter practices that were common in other parts of the American West—the right to settle on vacant land had become to them traditional and inalienable. In Oregon, for example, squatter sovereignty was the guiding principle in settling the land questions of a new territory.

By the spring of 1850 the issue of squatters' rights became a major source of dispute in Sacramento. On April 23 the Sacramento *Transcript* carried an advertisement announcing for sale a pamphlet entitled "Translation of the Papers Respecting the Grant Made by Governor Alvarado to Mr. Augustus Sutter." This publication, according to the advertisement, showed that the Sutter grant did not extend any farther south than the mouth of the Feather River and, therefore, that it did not include Sacramento City. Numerous meetings were held by agitated squatters, and at one point each man voted himself a lot, causing a great stir among those who were the owners under the Mexican grant. The squatter movement, already active, was given further impetus by the pamphlet.

Shortly after the pamphlet was published, a group of squatters and recent emigrants formed a settlers association for the protection of all squatters. Charles Robinson attended the organizational meeting, which took place after a squatter had been evicted by a mob from a vacant lot in Sacramento. At the meeting, Robinson made a forceful speech describing and pro-

6

testing similar evictions. He concluded his speech by proposing the adoption of the following resolution:

> Whereas, the land in California is presumed to be public land, therefore,
> *Resolved*, That we will protect any settler in the possession of land to the extent of one lot in the city, and one hundred and sixty acres in the country, till a valid title shall be shown for it.[10]

The resolution was received with great enthusiasm; and before the meeting had adjourned, Robinson had been chosen president of the association.

Thus organized, the settlers' association employed a surveyor and issued to their members "squatter titles," which were simply receipts given by the surveyor certifying that the land had been mapped within the limits of the town of Sacramento. To this the land owners reacted by forming a Law and Order Association and then by printing notices in the newspaper, stating that they intended to defend property obtained under the Sutter titles by force, if necessary.[11]

The squatter movement grew in strength under Robinson's leadership, and his efforts were recognized even by opponents of the movement. One observer wrote:

> Doctor Robinson added to his idealism the aforesaid Yankee shrewdness, and to his trust in God considerable ingenuity in raising funds to keep the squatter association at work. He wrote well and spoke well. He was thoroughly in earnest, and his motives seem to me above any suspicion of personal greed. He made out of this squatter movement a thing of real power, and was, for the time, a very dangerous man.[12]

Robinson's strategy was to have the issue brought into federal court, where he believed the squatters would receive a fair hearing and possibly would secure judgments in their favor. Realizing that if the affair came to open warfare, the amount of public sentiment that was aroused would depend on where the blame for the first violence was placed, he counseled the association to use legal methods to settle the disputes, if possible.

Further, he suggested that, should violence erupt, the association should let the "land speculators" clearly be the aggressors, so that public opinion would be behind the squatters. Many members of the association, however, grew impatient with Robinson's methods. In the second week of August, 1850, a squatter's case came before the judge of the county court in Sacramento. The judge ruled that the squatter's case was one of simple trespassing and therefore that the question of title could not be properly entered as part of the evidence at all. An appeal, made by the settlers' association, was promptly dismissed. The squatters were furious. Several days later, with tension high on both sides, Robinson led a delegation of squatters to a meeting with the mayor of Sacramento. Robinson explained the squatters' position and requested the mayor to use his influence in order to prevent further arrests by city officials until the issue could be brought before the state Supreme Court. Robinson left the meeting assured of the mayor's promise to cooperate, but that evening two more members of the association were arrested for trespassing.

On the next day, August 14, the conflict came to a head. Thirty armed squatters gathered with Robinson at one of the disputed lots. A few minutes later the mayor, the sheriff, and a posse arrived at the scene. The mayor ordered the squatters to lay down their arms and submit to arrest. But the squatters had reached the limits of their patience. They refused, and fighting broke out, which quickly spread throughout the town. When the squatter group was finally subdued, two members of the association and one member of the posse had been killed. Charles Robinson had been severely wounded. J. H. McKune, describing the events of that day in a letter to Robinson some years later, recalled that he had found Robinson "up the stairs on a balcony attached to the Bininger Hotel with a gunshot wound. . . . the bullet had taken a course under the skin . . . lodging near the spinal column from whence it was extracted by the surgeon attending."[13]

The fight made the squatters appear to the public as lawless men resisting city authorities; so public opinion turned against them. Many fled town, and the association's attorney was threat-

8

ened with hanging.[14] Robinson was held prisoner under indictments for assault, conspiracy, and murder. Yet, when the heat of battle cooled, Robinson found that his situation was not as serious as it had appeared to be at first. After a few weeks in prison, where he recovered from his wounds, he was released on bail, and the indictments against him were dropped. As one observer of the period wrote poetically:

> The legal evidence against him was like the chips of driftwood in a little eddy of this changing torrent of California life. With its little hoard of drift, the eddy soon vanished in the immeasurable flood. After a change of venue to a bay county, and after a few month's postponement, the cloud of indictments melted away like the last cloudflake of our rainy season.[15]

Meanwhile, Robinson continued to fight for squatters' rights. First, he edited a squatter newspaper, *The Settlers' and Miners' Tribune*. Then, in the fall of 1850, he was elected a member of the California House of Representatives by prosquatter voters. In the legislature he was instrumental in getting a bill passed that restrained all illegal proceedings in land controversies and required that all parties involved in such disputes await the decisions of proper courts. Aside from squatters' rights, the major issue before the legislature concerned the extension of slavery into California. On this issue Robinson was an outspoken opponent against further extension and was a strong supporter of John C. Fremont, the only candidate for U.S. senator from California in 1850 who opposed the division of California and the extension of slavery.

In the summer of 1851 Robinson decided to return to Massachusetts. His twenty-two month career in California had been exciting and sometimes dangerous for him. The excitement and the danger continued on his return trip. Departing from San Francisco by steamer, he had been on his voyage for only a few days when the ship struck rocks off the coast of Mexico. Fortunately for the passengers, the vessel was only a quarter of a mile from shore, which made it possible for all on board to make it safely to land. Robinson finally arrived back in Fitchburg, Massachusetts, on September 9, 1851.

9

During the time that he was in California, he had corresponded with a young lady in Fitchburg by the name of Sara Tappan Doolittle Lawrence. She was the daughter of Myron A. Lawrence, a prominent Massachusetts lawyer, and she was a distant relative of Amos A. Lawrence, a well-known Boston industrialist and philanthropist. Sara was educated at the Belchertown Classical School and the New Salem Academy. From her father she had learned to love both literature and politics. By the age of twelve she was an excellent Latin scholar and could read German and French fluently. So slightly built that she appeared to be frail, Sara was nevertheless described as being "quite pretty" and as an "exceedingly agreeable young woman, very unpretending, [and] plainly dressed."[16]

Charles and Sara had first met just prior to his California venture, when she had been one of his patients. Courtship blossomed after Robinson's return to Fitchburg, and they were married on October 30, 1851. For nearly three years the couple lived an apparently sedate life in Fitchburg. He edited the Fitchburg *News* and practiced medicine on a part-time basis, while the young bride set up housekeeping. Then, in the spring of 1854, Robinson attended an antislavery meeting, which was conducted by Eli Thayer. As a young New England educator, Thayer had founded Oread Institute, a women's college in Worcester, Massachusetts. Five years later, in 1853, he was elected to the Massachusetts legislature. During this period, while Congress was still debating the Kansas-Nebraska bill, Thayer conceived the idea of forming a corporation to organize and direct emigration from New England to Kansas and, by making investments in the Territory in the form of mills, hotels, and other capital improvements, to attract migration from all parts of the North. Robinson listened to Thayer's plan; later he wrote his impressions: "No man could listen to him without partaking of his spirit, neither could any person, after listening, entertain any doubts of the feasibility of his plan, or of his ability to put it in successful operation."[17] Shortly after the meeting, Robinson offered his services to Thayer.

The Massachusetts Emigrant Aid Company was chartered on April 26, 1854, more than a month before the passage of the

Kansas-Nebraska Act, with a capital of $5,000. Among the largest subscribers were Amos A. Lawrence, Eli Thayer, and Charles Francis Adams—son of John Quincy Adams—who was the vice-presidential candidate for the Free-Soil party in 1848.[18] Early in May, 1854, Thayer and Lawrence summoned Charles Robinson to Boston to discuss the question of emigration to Kansas. The meeting ended with Robinson and Charles H. Branscomb, a young lawyer from Holyoke, Massachusetts, accepting a commission to visit the new Territory called Kansas on behalf of the company for the purpose of observing conditions and selecting possible sites for settlement.

The two men left Boston late in June, reaching the village of Kansas (Kansas City, Missouri) early in July. Robinson continued up the Missouri River to Fort Leavenworth, while Branscomb went up the Kansas River to Fort Riley. Each observed the character of the country, noted locations for possible settlement, and investigated Indian land titles. Late in July they returned to Boston, where Robinson began to write a description of the Territory for a company pamphlet. Published under the title *Organization, Objects, and Plans of Operations of the Emigrant Aid Company*, the pamphlet reflected Robinson's impressions of Kansas from both his 1849 trip and the one just completed. It was widely distributed to prospective emigrants until March, 1855, when it was replaced by Dr. Thomas H. Webb's *Information for Kansas Emigrants*.

Before Robinson's return, the company's first party of twenty-nine emigrants departed from Boston, and on August 1, 1854, they reached the present site of Lawrence, a location that had been selected by Branscomb as the first desirable site along the Kansas River. At a meeting of the company's trustees on August 7, 1854, Robinson was appointed a general agent for Kansas Territory at a salary of $1,000 a year, plus a 2½ percent commission on all sales and receipts. He left Boston on August 29, 1854, leading the second party to the Wakarusa Settlement, as the small colony at present-day Lawrence was then known.

Emigration to Kansas in 1854 was slow, mainly because of the shortage of land available for settlement. Nearly all of the accessible portions of Kansas and Nebraska, as defined by the

11

bill that organized the Territories, were included in Indian reservations on which settlement by whites was forbidden. One white man who had a personal knowledge of Kansas in the spring of 1854 estimated: "All the school and missionary stations at that time, including missionaries, teachers, traders, mechanics, squawmen, etc., . . . as about 1200 men, women, and children. About one-half of this number were single men. There were no settlers upon the public lands prior to 1854."[19] Yet as early as 1852 agitation began in Missouri to open more land in the area to white settlement. With the passage of the Kansas-Nebraska Act in 1854, a large number of emigrants gathered along the Missouri border. New treaties were negotiated between the federal government and the Indians, moving them either south into Indian Territory or farther west. By the fall and winter of 1854 more immigrants were moving in, establishing actual settlements in the new land.

The first large influx of settlers and land speculators into Kansas Territory came from western Missouri. As in any large migration to a newly opened land area, motives were nearly as diversified as the people who journeyed there. The ones that have been widely publicized and proclaimed in traditional interpretations were the efforts to make Kansas a Slave State or a Free State. The evidence suggests that other motives were more important, at least in the early stages of settlement. As one Missourian wrote home after living in Kansas a few months:

> The rush from this state [Missouri] to Kansas Territory is not so much to secure a foothold for slavery there as to secure a fortune, not-withstanding what the newspapers say about it. No, most who go from here are young men in want of farms, and slavery, to say the least, is a secondary matter with them, if indeed they are not opposed to its introduction into Kansas, which is certainly the case with many.[20]

Many people knew, although this fact was ignored by the newspapers, that the emigration companies in most cases were not entirely crusading organizations. They were designed to be profit-making ventures. Certainly the motives of the founders of the New England Emigrant Aid Company, the largest of them all, were quite mixed. Thayer himself declared that he hoped to make money out of it. As he later admitted: "The enterprise was intended to be a money-making affair as well as a philanthropic undertaking. . . . In all my emigration schemes I intended to make the results return a profitable dividend in cash."[21] Those who purchased tickets from the company were never questioned on their beliefs concerning slavery. As one of the emigrants from New England expressed it: "We went to Kansas to better our conditions, incidentally expecting to make it a free state."[22]

These same motives applied to Charles Robinson. His writings and previous commitments in California proved that he was concerned over the slavery issue, but there can be little doubt that he considered his position as a Kansas agent for the Massachusetts Emigrant Aid Company to be an opportunity to combine genuine humanitarian principles with personal economic profit, as his subsequent career showed. Nor, in light of the motives of the founder, is there reason to suggest that his employers did not endorse his thinking. From the time that he joined the company until he resigned in the fall of 1856 he maintained the backing of the principal officers of the company in all of his activities. In 1857 Amos Lawrence wrote to a correspondent, "Governor Robinson is more reliable than any (other) man who has gone to Kansas, so far as my experience with him and others has enabled me to form an opinion."[23]

Robinson not only had the complete confidence of his employers, he was essential to the success of the company. As a Kansas agent he had custody of the company's property, and he was responsible for selecting settlement sites for subsequent parties. Altogether, six parties of the Emigrant Aid Company traveled to Kansas in 1854, with a total of 579 individuals appearing in the official rosters of the company.[24]

Samuel C. Pomeroy, a native of Northampton, Massachusetts, and a graduate of Amherst College, shared Robinson's heavy responsibilities as financial agent for the company. He had previously attained some distinction as an antislavery politician while serving in the Massachusetts legislature. According to his own statement, Pomeroy decided to go to Kansas after

13

some of his friends persuaded him to associate himself with the Emigrant Aid Company. He declared that he was interested not only in the agricultural and commercial possibilities of the Territory but most of all in keeping slavery out. Whatever his primary motivation, he was undoubtedly a valuable man to the company in many ways. An effective public speaker, he frequently returned to the East as a lobbyist for the Emigrant Aid Company cause. But while he contributed in public relations, he proved to be detrimental in financial matters. As an agent for the company, Pomeroy was a poor manager. His accounts were always in a chaotic condition, and as one scholar of the period has expressed it, "Mr. Pomeroy was reckless with drafts."[25]

Robinson located the company's headquarters after the arrival of the second party. Upon examination of the site selected by the preceding party, he discovered that most of the people were still living in tents on the hill along the Kansas River. Looking over the location, he decided that a town should be laid out near the river bank. The site that was selected was occupied by one settler, Clark Stearns, and his improvement and his claim were purchased by Robinson for $500. A survey was then made for a town site, which was platted about two and a half miles by one and a half miles, although federal law allowed only three hundred and twenty acres to be held for town purposes. Company officials solved this problem by assigning different parts of the plat to individual men. Robinson held claim to a quarter section near the bank of the river. On September 18 a town company or association was organized. Charles Robinson, as president of the association, named the new town Lawrence, in honor of Amos A. Lawrence.

With the site of Lawrence definitely established, a succession of men came forth, maintaining that they had made prior claims on the land and insisting that the settlers from the Emigrant Aid Company vacate the town. The most serious dispute occurred between one John Baldwin and the Lawrence Association. He established himself within a few hundred yards of the Stearns cabin, which had been purchased by the association, and claimed one hundred and sixty acres surrounding it. Robinson's site became the first objective in Baldwin's attempt to remove

14

the settlers of Lawrence. On October 6, 1854, he sent the following note to Robinson:

> Dr. Robinson:—Yourself and friends are hereby notified that you will have one-half hour to move the tent which you have on my undisputed claim. If the tent is not moved within one-half hour, we shall take the trouble to move the same.
>
> (Signed)
> John Baldwin and Friends

To this note, Robinson, on behalf of the Lawrence Association, replied: "If you molest our property, you do it at your peril."[26] No further attempt was made by Baldwin to take the land away from the settlers of Lawrence.

Many Kansas writers have called this incident the first conflict between proslavery and free-state settlers, but it would be better represented as a common occurrence in early Kansas. There was little evidence to suggest that Baldwin espoused any cause other than his own desire for land.[27] Similar episodes occurred throughout the Territory before the federal survey was completed.

By late fall of 1854 there were nearly seventy-five hundred settlers in the vicinity of Lawrence. Most had come from the Old Northwest: Illinois, Indiana, and Ohio. The village was initially no more than a collection of tents. These were followed by "queer, grass-thatched huts, copied apparently from African kraal village models, and rude, squat, mud-plastered log-cabins, beyond which the line of territorial architecture advanced slowly and with difficulty."[28]

In February, 1855, Robinson returned East to lead an emigrant train back to Kansas in the spring. Among the party on this trip was his wife Sara. The group departed from Boston on March 13, 1855, during a driving snowstorm. They arrived in Kansas City, Missouri, on March 24, 1855. Sara remained there to buy supplies for their new home, while Charles directed a portion of the party beyond Lawrence to new areas of settlement. Upon his return, Charles and Sara left for Lawrence, arriving there on the evening of April 17. They unpacked only

15

what was necessary and arranged sleeping facilities in their partially constructed cabin "by nailing a buffalo-robe at the doorway, and arranging some articles of bedding upon chairs."[29] For the next forty years of their lives together, Lawrence would be their home.

The early months of the existence of Kansas Territory were marked by the arrival of a significant number of settlers, intent on making homes in a new land. Although this was largely a peaceful movement, the seeds of future strife had already been planted. The Kansas-Nebraska Act, which voided the clause of the Missouri Compromise that excluded slavery from most of the Louisiana Purchase, aroused a tremendous storm of opposition and inaugurated a period of intense political warfare. Charles Robinson's abolitionist views and his position with the New England Emigrant Aid Company placed him in the center of that struggle.

GOVERNOR CHARLES ROBINSON OF KANSAS

by Don W. Wilson

This biography of the first governor of Kansas is a comprehensive and balanced interpretation of a man whose career encompassed nearly half a century of early Kansas history. Robinson made important contributions to the territorial and early statehood periods, was involved in every significant third-party movement in Kansas from the birth of the Republican party through Populism, and throughout his life remained an active reformer committed to principles beyond the confines of political groups.

The story of Robinson and the times in which he lived will be useful and interesting to all students of Kansas history. The author analyzes the political effects of the Civil War and the Lincoln administration in Kansas, and also chronicles the progress of Robinson's numerous causes, including woman suffrage, anti-prohibition, farm and labor movements, and regulation of railroads.

Don W. Wilson is Assistant Director of the Dwight D. Eisenhower Library.

214 plus xii pages   *ISBN 0-7006-0133-3*   *LC 75-6875*

THE UNIVERSITY PRESS OF KANSAS

366 Watson Library / Lawrence, Kansas 66045

2

The Statehood Controversy

Kansas became an organized Territory under the provisions of the Kansas-Nebraska Act of May 30, 1854. The growth of the nation, the expansion of its population, and the movement for a transcontinental railroad had reached a point in the early 1850s that made the passage of a bill opening up the Nebraska Territory inevitable. Senator Stephen A. Douglas of Illinois, chairman of the Senate Committee on Territories, was the author of the controversial bill, which incorporated the principle known as popular sovereignty. This principle transferred to the Territory the power to make the decision on the existence of slavery within it. Acceptance of the principle required the repeal of the Missouri Compromise. The motives of Douglas in sponsoring the bill have been disputed, but most historians now believe that he was primarily concerned with opening and developing the Mississippi Valley. He thought that the slavery question was a subordinate issue, and he viewed the Kansas-Nebraska bill, which incorporated popular sovereignty, as a compromise measure that would quiet the slavery controversy. The new act, which repealed the Missouri Compromise of 1820, violated what many northerners considered a pledge between the North and the South. Once passed, the Kansas-Nebraska Act shattered the uneasy truce that had existed since 1820, and it destroyed party alignments. The Democratic party split into Northern and Southern factions, while the dying Whig party succumbed and was replaced by a new sectional party devoted to the restriction of slavery. The new law was denounced throughout the North by mass meetings, by state legislatures, and by clergymen from their pulpits. They called for political action: The formation of a new political party, the reenactment of the Missouri Compromise, and the repeal of the Fugitive Slave Law. Antislavery people in the North denounced popular sovereignty as a fraud. Opposition to popular sovereignty was summed up in remarks made by William H. Seward in the Senate on May 25, 1854:

> Come on, then, gentlemen of the slave States. Since there is no escaping your challenge, I accept it in behalf of the cause of freedom. We will engage in competition for the virgin soil of Kansas, and God give the victory to the side which is stronger in numbers as it is in right.[1]

Though the South was less vociferous than the North, it was no less interested in Kansas. There was widespread feeling among proslavery proponents that if Kansas should become free, Missouri also might be lost to an influx of free-soil settlers. To them, slavery in Kansas was necessary in order to maintain Missouri as a breakwater to the national movement of free labor to the Southwest. Southerners depended upon the proximity of Missouri to Kansas to win the state before the North could get any mass emigration under way. Missourians themselves tended to think of Kansas as a natural proslavery extension of their own state, and therefore they were staking claims in Kansas even before the Territory was organized. The action of proslavery Missourians, coupled with immediate activity by Northerners to organize emigration, caused both the proponents and the opponents of slavery to transfer their major activity to the Territory of Kansas. The organization of the free-soil settlers and the vital role that was played in it by Charles Robinson are the subjects of this chapter.

The proslavery faction had the initial advantage both in numbers and in organization. By July, 1854, thousands of South-

18

erners were reported to be on their way to Kansas, especially from Missouri, Kentucky, and Tennessee. By mid 1855 it was estimated that four out of five people in the Territory were proslavery.[2] In the first Territorial census, which was taken in January, 1855, as a preliminary step to electing a Territorial legislature, 8,601 inhabitants were counted, more than one-half of whom had come from the South. Among the minority from the North, fewer than 700 were from New England; the remainder were largely from Ohio, Michigan, Pennsylvania, and Indiana.[3] The views of these Northerners on the issue of slavery ranged from abolitionism to anti-Negro.

By the time of the March election in 1855, three distinct categories of free-soil sentiment had formed. Charles Robinson led the abolitionists, mostly New Englanders, who were opposed to slavery for humanitarian reasons. They regarded Negroes as human beings, and the institution of slavery as inhuman. Robinson typified the abolitionists' philosophy when he wrote: "This institution [slavery] is an unmitigated curse to all connected with it, intellectually, morally, physically, pecuniarily, socially, and politically." He further argued that slavery not only consigned the slave to "a hell on earth," but it compelled the master to live in it. The result was that the "whole social fabric" of the country was being destroyed.[4] The abolitionists were opposed by the "Western" attitude. Its proponents, while they were against slavery, desired to keep slavery out of Kansas because they were anti-Negro. They favored exclusion of all Negroes, slave or free, from the Territory. James H. Lane was to emerge as the leader and spokesman for this faction. A third position sought common ground among the opponents of slavery. Led by John and Joseph Speer, editors of the *Kansas Tribune* (Lawrence), this faction maintained that the question of making Kansas a Free *State* was the first priority for all Free-Soilers. They called for the two opposing groups to make the question of statehood the major issue. Conflict among proponents of these viewpoints created an atmosphere of confusion and disorganization within the ranks of the free-soil forces for the election of March, 1855, when the make-up of the legislature for Kansas Territory was first determined.[5]

The election on March 30 was an overwhelming proslavery victory. It would have been such a victory had there been no fraud in the election, but actually fraud was widespread. Many Missourians crossed the border and voted at various locations in eastern Kansas. In some cases the "visitors" swore that they were legal residents; in other cases they took possession of polling places by threatening the election judges. Of the 6,318 votes cast that day, it has been estimated that more than half were fraudulent. According to the census taken two months before, there were 2,905 qualified voters in Kansas. Outside of Lawrence, not a single precinct in the Territory contained a majority of free-soil settlers at the time of the election. By ensuring their own margin of victory, the proslavery settlers provided the Free-Soilers with a legal course of action to dispute the elections.

The reality of government by a proslavery legislature stirred the free-soil leaders to search for a means of unifying the three factions into an effective political force. Charles Robinson was one of those who realized the seriousness of the free-soil situation. He said: "There was but one hope for a free State, and that was to repudiate . . . the election."[6]

A few days after the election, Robinson led a group of antislavery leaders to the Shawnee Methodist Mission, the temporary Territorial capital, to attempt to persuade Territorial Governor Andrew H. Reeder to declare the election fraudulent. In talking with Reeder, a Pennsylvania Democrat, they discovered that although he was aware of the frauds, he was hesitant about taking any action. Not only had he been threatened with physical harm by proslavery men; he had also received instructions from Washington that the administration would look with disfavor on any trouble in Kansas. In an attempt to mollify both parties, Reeder invalidated the election in six of the voting districts and called for a special election to be held in those districts in May.[7] Consequently, Reeder lost the trust of the free-state forces by not repudiating the entire election, and he alienated the proslavery settlers by intervening at all. The announcement of a new election was met with disdain by many proslavery newspapers along the Missouri border. One editor, referring to Reeder's action in the six districts, wrote: "We learn just as we go to press, that Reeder has refused to give certificates to four Councilmen and thirteen members of the House. He has ordered an election to fill their places on the 22d of May. This infernal scoundrel will have to be hemped yet."[8]

From the conference with Reeder, it was apparent to Robinson that the governor had little control over the situation and that the free-state settlers had to organize behind the free-state cause. Three days after the meeting, Robinson dispatched a letter to Eli Thayer, warning him:

> It looks very much like war, and I am ready for it and so are our people. . . . Cannot your secret society send us 200 Sharps rifles as a loan till this question is settled? Also a couple of field pieces? If they will do that, I think they will be *well used*, and preserved.[9]

A few days later George W. Deitzler, a personal friend of Robinson's, was sent East as an envoy to reinforce the request. The needed money was raised from various sources, mostly from private individuals and church congregations, and the arms were purchased. The rifles were frequently referred to as "Beecher's Bibles," because Henry Ward Beecher's congregations had contributed a portion of the money. When the arms were ready, they were packed in boxes and labeled "bibles" in order to smuggle them past the proslavery Kansas authorities that patroled the eastern border of the Territory. Robinson also took the lead in organizing military companies in the free-state communities surrounding Lawrence.

The manner in which the March election was conducted, even more than its outcome, consolidated the free-soil sentiment. A variety of factors explain Robinson's leadership role in this suddenly active resistance against proslavery authority. As agent for the New England Emigrant Aid Company, he realized that the company's success in attracting immigrants depended on keeping at least part of the Territory free from slavery. The heavy initial investment of people and money was being threatened, and it was Robinson's responsibility as a company agent to do what he could to strengthen its position. He was being paid a relatively substantial salary to do just that. His previous

21

experiences in California also made him particularly well qualified to lead these activities. Those who have contended that his only motive was a simple dedication to the cause of freedom, regardless of his connection to the Emigrant Aid Company, appear to have oversimplified his motives.[10] Robinson's own fortunes, political and economic, were inescapably intertwined with the success of the Emigrant Aid Company and the principles of a free Kansas, at least until he could firmly establish himself in the new Territory.

To repudiate the proslavery Territorial government, a movement was launched to create a substitute government. Whether or not Robinson originated the tactic, he clearly supported it:

> When it became evident that the [bogus] Legislature would be endorsed by the territorial judiciary and the President, and that there would be no escape by election for at least two years, it was equally evident that some means must be devised to keep the settlers from abandoning the fight. While the majority of the Free-State party were antislavery from conviction, and would stand out against a slave State to the bitter end, a large minority were indifferent to the question of slavery, and had been driven to act with the Free-State party because of the invasion of their own civil and political rights. Under these circumstances it was deemed expedient to agitate the question of a State constitution. Such a movement would serve to occupy the minds of the people, attract the attention of ambitious politicians, become a rallying point for all opposed to the usurpation, and, in case of necessity, when all other means of self-preservation should fail, be used as a *de facto* government, even though not recognized by Congress.[11]

It was first necessary to form an organization through which to operate. The obvious place to begin was in Lawrence, where the concentration of New England abolition sympathizers would be most responsive to political agitation over the slavery issue. A "mass convention" was held in Lawrence on June 8, 1855, in response to a call signed by "sundry citizens." Participants in this initial meeting, including Charles Robinson, issued a call

22

for a delegate convention, five from each representative district, to meet in Lawrence on June 25, 1855. This delegate convention formally launched the free-state movement that had earlier been visualized by Robinson, declaring that all issues but freedom in Kansas should be put aside and that because of the fraudulent elections, Kansans were not bound by any acts that might be passed by the Territorial legislature, which was scheduled to meet in July. The convention also provided for the appointment of a Free State Central Committee. Although dissension was evident and ranks were divided over how the issue of slavery was to be defined, the convention was a major achievement in organizing the free-state cause.[12]

On July 2, 1855, the Territorial legislature that had been elected in March met at Pawnee, near Fort Riley. The first matter taken up by the assembly was the seating of delegates. The proslavery men, who controlled the Committee on Credentials, promptly refused to seat the six free-state men who had been elected in May in the special election that had been ordered by Governor Reeder. After barring the Free-Staters, the legislature took up the matter of the location of the capitol. Since most of the members were from border towns with interests in Missouri, they wanted the administrative center located where their strength lay. On July 4 the legislature passed a bill providing for the temporary establishment of the capitol at the Shawnee Methodist Mission, which was near the Missouri border. The governor vetoed the bill on July 6, on the grounds that the legislature was acting outside the powers conferred upon it by Congress. However, both houses promptly passed the bill over his veto and then adjourned to reconvene at Shawnee Mission on July 16.

By openly defying the Territorial governor, the legislature gave added impetus to the free-state movement. At the 1855 Fourth of July celebration in Lawrence, Robinson gave the keynote address and took the opportunity to instill greater enthusiasm for the free-state cause. He accused the citizens of Missouri of imposing laws on Kansans in order to force slavery upon the Territory. He likened the struggle to that of the conflict against England eighty years before:

It is for us to choose for ourselves . . . what institutions shall bless or curse our beautiful Kansas. . . . Let us repudiate all laws enacted by foreign legislative bodies. . . . Tyrants are tyrants, and tyranny is tyranny, whether under the garb of law, or opposition to it. So thought, and so acted, our ancestors; and so let us think and act. . . . The spirits of revolutionary heroes, and the voice of God [are] all saying to the people of Kansas, "Do your duty!"[13]

A week later another meeting in Lawrence was attended by the legislators who had not been seated by the Territorial government. All participants agreed that the present legislature was illegal and that something had to be done to repudiate any laws enacted by it; but they disagreed on the means to accomplish that objective. Charles Robinson, John Hutchinson, J. N. O. P. Wood, and others addressed the meeting. In his speech, Robinson, for the first time, recommended the selection of delegates for the purpose of forming a state constitution. He was supported by John Hutchinson. Wood, however, gave a lengthy speech against consideration of statehood, pointing out the problems of increased taxation and a consequent check on immigration. He favored armed resistance. This convention adopted the following resolution:

RESOLVED, That a mass meeting of the Free-State citizens of the Territory of Kansas be held in Lawrence on the second Tuesday of August next, to take into consideration the situation of the Territory in reference to its government. . . .[14]

When the Free-Staters assembled on August 14, 1855, Charles Robinson was named chairman of the influential Committee on Resolutions. This gathering adopted resolutions repudiating the Territorial legislature, then in session at the Shawnee Mission, and declared in favor of a state constitution. However, in order to pass the resolution calling for an election of delegates to a constitutional convention, the words "at some convenient period" were substituted for a specific date, making the resolution less effective. The conflict on timing was not based on the idea of calling a convention but on how the call should originate.

Many, including Robinson, believed that it should be called by people in mass convention. Others, such as James Lane, making his first free-state speech at this convention, thought it more important to formalize the Free State party and have it issue the call. Lane and his followers got an additional resolution adopted, calling for an election on August 25 to elect delegates to a convention at Big Springs, which would formally organize the Free State party. Several of Robinson's followers believed that the Big Springs convention had been called by Lane people for the purpose of erasing the abolitionist taint that the free-state movement had been carrying. S. C. Smith, who later participated in the Big Springs convention, saw the entire affair as an "attempt made to dethrone Dr. [Robinson] and his friends from the leadership of the Free State Party and give it to Lane."[15]

Robinson and his followers argued that for a partisan group to make the call would defeat any chance for its success. Statehood had to represent the will of the people. Thus, on the following day, August 15, yet another convention was held in Lawrence, which claimed to be entirely nonpartisan though most of the participants were from the convention that had just adjourned. Robinson was again a member of the committee that proposed the following resolution, which was adopted by the convention:

> RESOLVED, That we the people of Kansas Territory in Mass Meeting assembled, *irrespective* of party distinctions, influenced by a common necessity, and greatly desirous of promoting the common good, do hereby call upon and request all *bona fide* citizens of Kansas Territory, of whatever political views or predilections, to consult together in their respective election districts, and in Mass Convention or otherwise, elect *three* Delegates for each Representative to which such District is entitled, in the House of Representatives of the Legislative Assembly, by Proclamation of Gov. Reeder of date 10th March 1855: Said Delegates to assemble in Convention at the Town of Topeka, on the 19th day of September 1855, then and there to consider upon all subjects of public interest, and *particularly* upon that having reference to the speedy formation of a Constitution, with an

25

intention of an immediate application to be admitted as a State into the Union of the "United States of America."[16]

From these two conventions, which were entirely separate yet mysteriously the same, came two distinct developments: from the convention of the fourteenth came the call to form a Free State party; from the convention on the fifteenth came a call to establish a state government. Still, great diversities in viewpoints were clearly evident, particularly at the August 14 convention. Both conventions had passed resolutions denouncing and protesting the proslavery government, but no further action had taken place, and several of the more radical Free-Staters began to express impatience. Among these were the owners of the *Kansas Free State*, who editorialized as follows:

> The idea of re-solving and re-solving and dying for the same is one that we have never entertained. . . . To repudiate the Legislature, and the territorial government of Kansas, which is tantamount to a civil declaration of war, without taking any measures to back up such declarations, is the hight [sic] of folly. It is like the President and the Senate declaring war, and the House of Representatives refusing to make the appropriations.[17]

Free-Staters became even more unhappy when the code of laws for governing the Territory was passed by the Territorial legislature. These laws were based on the Missouri code, with the exception of the so-called Black Laws that the Kansas proslavery legislature framed independently. One of these laws, An Act to Punish Offenses against Slave Property, was aimed directly at the free-state cause. It prescribed the death penalty for anyone who hid slaves or incited insurrection among them. Another Black Law stipulated that any person who was conscientiously opposed to slavery would not be allowed to serve on any jury when the slavery question was involved. In addition, the legislature organized a number of new counties, and instead of providing for elections of county officials, it appointed proslavery men to the positions. These actions, as interpreted by most Kansas settlers, appeared to be a denial of essential rights of self-government, and it helped rally them to the new Free State party. As the Free State party developed, the followers of James H. Lane recognized him as its champion and urged him to challenge Charles Robinson for leadership of the entire free-state cause.

Lane, a Democrat, had come to Kansas in the spring of 1855 from Indiana, where he had held the office of lieutenant governor from 1849 to 1852. In that year he was elected to the United States House of Representatives, again on the Democratic ticket. He served a full term, but he chose not to stand for reelection, having decided to move to Kansas. He was no abolitionist in 1855, reportedly having made the statement that "he would as soon buy a negro as a mule, and that the question of the success of slavery in Kansas depended upon the suitability of the country to produce hemp."[18]

When he discovered that this view jeopardized his political aspirations, he underwent a "change of heart." In fact, the first public notice of Lane's arrival by the editor of the *Herald of Freedom* discussed his changing political views:

> Colonel Lane . . . who came here with squatter-phobia, of which he has been long and dangerously sick . . . and whose unfortunate constitution withstood every effort of Eastern physicians to cure him . . . is now beginning to give evidence of a speedy recovery . . . what he has hitherto denied . . . that he was deceived in imagining that squatter-phobia is a symptom of good health. We have no doubt, if our people take good care of him, that in less than a year he may be pronounced politically convalescent. If Colonel Lane adopts the Republican creed, he will make a valuable accession to the party. As yet, he has not done so.[19]

Lane was a tall, slightly built man with a dark complexion. He had a "sinister face," which was characterized by a pair of deep-set black eyes. His trademark was his clothing, which included an old straw hat, calfskin vest, a woolen shirt, worn-out pants, cowhide boots, and a bearskin overcoat.[20]

Jim Lane's greatest asset was his oratorical ability. His speeches combined dramatics and sarcasm in a way that placed him in a class by himself as a speaker. One newspaper editor reported that he had the ability to change his voice from a "shrill tenor" to a "tragic bass" in one sentence. Another reported that Lane could move an audience from laughter to tears in less than a minute.[21]

John J. Ingalls, a noted observer of the Kansas scene who later became a United States Senator, summed up Lane's character in the following manner:

> He [Lane] had an extraordinary assemblage of mental, moral, and physical traits, and, with even a rudimentary perception of the values of personal character as an element of success in public affairs, would have been a great leader, with an enduring fame. . . . He was the object of inexplicable idolatry and unspeakable execration. . . . [His foes] alleged that to reach the goal of his ambition he had no conviction he would not sell, made no promise he would not break, and had no friend he would not betray.[22]

Clearly, James H. Lane stood in sharp contrast to Charles Robinson, who was described in 1856 by George Brewerton, a correspondent of the New York *Herald*, as "tall, well made, and more than ordinarily handsome; gentlemanly, but by no means winning in his manners, with one of those cold, keen blue eyes that seem to look you through." The correspondent also said that Robinson was a man who seemed to have "strong common sense and a good brain" but no "brilliancy of talent."[23] These two men engaged in a struggle for control of the free-state movement, and their rivalry continued after statehood, becoming more and more bitter as the years passed.

Lane gained an immediate advantage through his oratory. Following the adjournment of the mass convention at Lawrence on August 15, 1855, Lane announced that he would make a major speech on the issues of the day, and that he would champion the free-state cause. An eyewitness later described the address in the following manner:

> The crowd was immense. . . . They wanted to know from his own mouth the "Grim Chieftain's" position on political questions. . . . Lane was in his best mood. He was prepared for a vituperative, sarcastic, ironical and intensely personal speech. Such the crowd usually likes, or used to

in the early days, when men were walking arsenals and crept over volcanoes. . . . No one ever afterward doubted where Lane stood. He crossed with a leap the Rubicon of radical politics and burned all his bridges behind him. He was not baptized,—he was immersed in the foaming floods of radicalism. As the whitecaps rose higher on the stormy and tumultuous political sea, Lane contended the stronger and baffled them.[24]

When on August 25, in accordance with the August 14th convention call, elections were held for delegates to the Big Springs convention, Lane challenged and defeated Charles Robinson in the Lawrence district. James Lane was selected to represent Lawrence, a town that had theretofore been considered Robinson's political stronghold.

Lane won as a "black law," or anti-Negro, candidate. The Negro question had been one of the major factors that undermined all attempts toward conciliation among the various free-state factions. Robinson, an avowed abolitionist, was opposed to any law excluding Negroes from entering Kansas if they were free. With Lane's election as a delegate to the Big Springs convention, it became clear that Robinson's philosophy was a minority one. For the majority of Kansans who opposed slavery "Free State" meant "free white state."[25] This attitude became even more obvious at the Big Springs convention.

On September 5, 1855, Lane and a hundred other delegates assembled at Big Springs. Several hundred spectators also watched the first day's proceedings as Judge G. W. Smith was elected president of the convention. James Lane was named to the powerful position of chairman of the platform committee for the proposed Free State party. His report called for Kansas to be a Free State but also for existing slave owners in the Territory to be given assurance that they would be treated fairly in order to protect them against total loss in disposing of their slaves. Another plank said that Kansas should be a free white state— that free Negroes, as well as slaves, should be excluded from Kansas. The conclusion of the document called for a complete disavowal of the abolitionist philosophy by the Free State party. This report was a clear statement of the viewpoint of the Western

29

faction, and with its adoption, two facts became apparent: (1) Robinson and his fellow abolitionists did not constitute a majority within the free-state movement; and (2) except within the Kansas River districts, anti-Negro sentiment was overwhelming among the settlers making up the Free State party.

The Big Springs convention also renewed the call, issued by the Lawrence convention, for a meeting at Topeka on September 19 to take steps toward statehood. In other actions it nominated Governor Andrew J. Reeder as the Free State party's candidate for delegate to Congress, and it set an election for the second Tuesday in October for the selection of such a delegate. Reeder had been dismissed by President Franklin Pierce from his position as Territorial governor after he had publicly protested the tactics used by the Territorial legislature in refusing to seat the Free-Staters the previous July; then he had joined the free-state cause. In summary, the Big Springs convention sanctioned the Western viewpoint on the issue of slavery, refuted the abolitionists, and committed the formally organized Free State party to a revolutionary cause by refusing to recognize the Territorial government and by advocating open resistance to Territorial laws.

The Free State party, led by James Lane, dominated the Topeka convention of September 19, 1855. The assemblage was convened for the purpose of considering the desirability both of drawing up a free-state constitution and of applying for admission to the Union under it. The legality of the proposal was debated heatedly, but finally it was agreed that the preamble to the resolutions that were adopted should state the reasons for the convention's actions. The resolutions affirmed that the free-state cause was based on the rights of assembly and petition. A course of action was then charted in the following:

> RESOLVED, By the people of Kansas Territory, in Delegate Convention assembled, that an election shall be held in the several election precincts of this Territory on the second Tuesday of October next . . . for members of a convention to form a constitution, adopt a Bill of Rights for the people of Kansas, and take all needful measures for

organizing a State Government preparatory to the admission of Kansas into the Union as a State.[26]

To implement this plan, the convention created the seven-man Executive Committee of Kansas Territory which would supervise the election of delegates and the ratification of a constitution and would direct the application for admission to statehood. James H. Lane was named chairman. Other members of the committee were Cyrus K. Holliday, Marcus J. Parrott, Philip C. Schuyler, G. W. Smith, and Joel Goodin. Two weeks after the convention, Charles Robinson was named treasurer of the Executive Committee in an effort by the members of the committee to conciliate the abolitionist wing and thus ensure maximum strength for the movement.[27] On October 1, 1855, an election called by the Territorial legislature was held to elect a delegate to Congress. The free-state people, following their adopted policy of repudiating the Territorial legislature and all of its actions, refused to participate. As a result, J. W. Whitfield, the proslavery candidate, received 2,721 of the 2,738 votes cast. The following week a free-state election was held, and Andrew Reeder, the nominee of the Free State party, was unanimously elected, receiving 2,849 votes. During the latter election, delegates were also chosen to the constitutional convention that had been called for Topeka on October 23. Robinson was elected as one of the delegates from Lawrence, even though he was the only candidate who listed his party affiliation as "Independent."[28]

Delegates to the constitutional convention assembled in Topeka on October 23. This convention, which lasted until November 11, 1855, was marked by bitter disputes over several issues. There was little accord among the delegates on the question of what kind of state constitution was to be framed. It appeared that nearly every interest group had some representatives at the convention. Those delegates who had nativist sentiments attempted to restrict voting privileges and the right to hold office to white male citizens who had been born in the United States and to certain Indians, thereby excluding all foreign-born settlers.[29] Several young representatives also tried to remove all age requirements for office holding, claiming that the statehood movement was a young man's affair.

Early in the convention, Mark Delahay, a delegate from Leavenworth, again opened the free-state issue to question. He contended that the constitution should be framed and submitted to Congress without any mention of slavery, except to provide that the matter would be determined by a referendum after admission. If the application were made in this manner, insisted Delahay, Congress would have no grounds for acting unfavorably on it, and the slavery issue would not be raised on the floor of Congress. However, his presentation was virtually ignored by the other delegates, and prohibition of slavery was placed in the Bill of Rights with little opposition. Robinson himself led a movement to defeat a resolution that was introduced to base the justification for the convention on the principle of squatter sovereignty. So far as the inclusion of a black law was concerned, the convention skirted what could have become an explosive issue by proposing that the matter be submitted to a referendum of the voters at the time they voted on the constitution.

The constitution formulated at Topeka was a somewhat radical document with a complex amendment procedure—a product of the times and the Kansas situation in which it was written.[30] It reflected the wide ideological gulf that existed between groups working under the banner of the free-state cause, and it provided insight into some of the leadership at the time. Lane saw the statehood movement as a means for advancing his political career, and, therefore, he was never overly concerned with any particular principle or doctrine in the constitution so long as the Free State party survived. Robinson's considerations were more complex. He seemed to be willing to concede to the Western viewpoint of exclusion for the sake of his basic abolitionist beliefs, even to the point of championing a constitution that went no further than to prohibit the "peculiar institution." He was also willing to sacrifice a reasonable chance of attaining statehood by leading the fight to make a document that was nearly impossible to amend, thus ensuring that the slavery provision could not be altered. Robinson was a radical on the question of slavery, but it was his moderation and his

32

counseling against radical actions during a subsequent military conflict that proved to be his political salvation.

On November 14, 1855, proslavery delegates convened at Leavenworth for the purposes of organizing the Law and Order party, or the States Rights party. It was commonly referred to as the Proslavery party. Governor Wilson Shannon, who had been appointed to replace Andrew Reeder as the Territorial executive only three months before, sanctioned the movement by attending as the delegate from Douglas County. He was named chairman of the convention. Resolutions were adopted calling for strict enforcement of the Territorial laws, labeling the free-state Topeka Constitution as treasonous, and denouncing the election of Reeder as the delegate to Congress. Emotions on both sides of the slave question ran high, and it was not long before a crisis was precipitated.

Open hostilities began when Charles W. Dow, a free-state settler, was killed by Franklin Coleman, a known proslavery sympathizer, over a disputed land claim. The body was discovered by a friend of Dow's, Jacob Branson. He organized a posse in an attempt to apprehend Coleman, who by this time had fled to Westport, Missouri, and had then turned himself in to Territorial officials at Shawnee Mission. Samuel J. Jones, the proslavery, nonresident sheriff of Douglas County, then arrested Branson for alleged threats against Coleman's friends. While he was taking Branson to jail at Lecompton on the night of November 26, 1855, a group of Free Staters intercepted Jones and forced him to release the prisoner.[31] Jones proceeded to Westport, where he wrote to Governor Shannon, reporting that open rebellion had begun and asking for three thousand men to carry out the law. Without investigating the situation, Shannon ordered the Territorial militia to report to Sheriff Jones and to assist him in the execution of the law. Nearly twelve hundred men assembled at Franklin, on the Wakarusa River, to await Sheriff Jones's orders.

In the meantime, a meeting of Lawrence citizens was called, at which Samuel N. Wood presided. Robinson, in a speech to the assembled citizens, advised "disavowal of all responsibility in the matter, dispatch of the men who were implicated out of

33

town without delay, and adoption of a strictly defensive attitude."[32] The Committee of Safety, which consisted of ten men, was appointed at the meeting. Charles Robinson was chosen commander in chief, with the rank of major general. Robinson, in turn, appointed Lane a brigadier general and gave him instructions to take command of the field forces and to make preparations to defend Lawrence. Lane held drill parades every afternoon, often using the occasion to make speeches. At such times Lane was fiery, and his remarks were designed to arouse the men to the fighting point. Robinson, on the other hand, urged people to avoid making attacks. Robinson favored an entirely defensive operation, while Lane wanted to take the offensive. On December 6 the Committee of Safety sought to open communications with Governor Shannon, dispatching G. P. Lowrey and C. W. Babcock to meet him. They were successful in getting the governor to travel to Lawrence for a meeting with Robinson and Lane. Passing through the proslavery Wakarusa camp, Shannon discovered to his dismay that a large majority of those who were gathered there had come from Missouri and were clamoring for permission to attack. He realized that it could ruin the Democratic party if Lawrence were attacked and destroyed by Missourians. The rising Republican party might go far with that kind of ammunition in the upcoming campaign.

On the following day, December 7, Shannon arrived in Lawrence to attempt to reach a settlement. After meeting with Robinson and Lane, Shannon was satisfied that the people in the town had not violated any law. An agreement, commonly referred to as the Treaty of Lawrence, was drawn up and signed by Shannon, Robinson, and Lane. In it the free-state men denied any responsibility for the rescue of Branson, disclaimed knowledge of any organization that was resisting Territorial laws, and agreed that "when called upon by the proper authority," they would assist in the execution of the laws. To make sure that the treaty was not misunderstood to mean that free-state leaders sanctioned the existing laws, a final phrase was added, which read: "We wish it understood that we do not herein express any opinion as to the validity of the enactments of the Territorial Legislature."[33]

34

The governor at once issued orders for the militia along the Wakarusa to disband. The proslavery forces were reluctant to leave, but a sudden change in the weather—a blizzard with sub-zero temperatures—reinforced the orders of the governor. Thus the "Wakarusa War" ended without a major fight. Nevertheless, it proved to be a turning point in the free-state movement. The Republicans, nationally, came to view the Kansas conflict as a basis for political capital and therefore championed the free-state cause. Within the movement, Robinson's conservative and successful guidance during the crisis gave him the advantage in the Lane-Robinson struggle for leadership. As Robinson later observed: "Those who were aware of Lane's career in Kansas, including his attempt to take the offensive at the late war, did not dare trust him at the head of the State movement."[34]

Robinson's position was further strengthened during the following month. The election to ratify the Topeka Constitution was held on December 15, 1855, and the constitution was adopted overwhelmingly by the free-state voters. The following week the Free State party convened to nominate state officers under that constitution. Lane was defeated for the gubernatorial nomination by Robinson. Lane, according to Robinson, had become "the most radical of radicals," and Robinson believed that the most influential men in Lane's defeat were the Eastern correspondents, who distrusted him.[35] The entire free-state ticket nominated at the convention was elected on January 15, 1856, including a "state legislature" and a delegate to Congress. No attempt was made at this election to open the polls in proslavery settlements. Thus, government under the Topeka Constitution was formally launched, with Robinson at its head. It became his responsibility to determine and direct the course of the movement for the next two years—a task that was complicated by national politics, the Proslavery party, and James H. Lane.

3

Free-State Governor

The year 1856 opened with a bitter blizzard—the worst on record. Thousands of plains cattle were killed, and the settlers in Kansas suffered severely from the cold. Nor was the political climate in the White House any warmer toward the Kansans. President Franklin Pierce, who had been monitoring events in Kansas with growing concern over the previous months, was in the condition of being forced to take a definite course of action. Two national developments were particularly disturbing to him, because they jeopardized his chances of being renominated for president on the Democratic ticket in 1856. First was the increased number of Free Soilers elected to the Thirty-fourth Congress. Although they were not united in a single, organized party, as a group they held the balance of power in Congress. The second factor was the success that all the free-state sympathizers in Congress had in organizing so well that they were able to alter the balance of power in the House of Representatives. Their strength was revealed in the contest for Speaker of the House in mid January, 1856. The election lasted nine weeks and finally resulted in the selection of Nathaniel P. Banks of Massachusetts, an ally of the free-state cause who was a personal friend of Charles Robinson. In effect, this broke the Democratic hold on the House of Representatives.

While this struggle was being fought in the national capital, the Free Staters in Kansas held their election and established the so-called Topeka government. The existence of two active governments in Kansas Territory, each claiming legality, placed the Pierce administration in an embarrassing position. If the president reversed his position and allowed the Topeka government to stand, his administration stood a good chance of losing all Southern support in Congress. Nor could the situation be ignored, lest the proslavery forces attempt to overpower the Free Staters by force. If any violence developed in Kansas, the administration would come under fire from the new Republican party. Faced with this dilemma, Pierce decided that decisive actions had to be taken before the political situation worsened.

The decision reached by President Pierce and his advisers was to disband the Topeka government as quickly as possible, on the grounds that it had been formed illegally. They thought that this would bring about a rapid restoration of peace in Kansas. Pierce rationalized, or perhaps he was convinced by advisers, that the Topeka government was simply a protest against the violence precipitated by a few extremists on either side of the slavery issue. He believed that once public order was restored, the slavery issue in Kansas would be permanently settled. It was in this spirit that the president sent a special message to Kansas on January 24, 1856, denouncing the Topeka government. In it he stated his intention to use the whole power of the federal executive in order to support public order in the Territory. To implement this policy, he offered Territorial Governor Wilson Shannon the use of federal troops.[1]

The burden of decision now shifted to Robinson as head of the Topeka government. What policy could be adopted in light of the president's message? A commitment had been made by the administration, and it was up to Robinson to determine a course of action by which the Topeka government could survive. There existed within free-state ranks a strong sentiment to resist by force any attempt to nullify the Topeka Constitution. But Robinson adopted the course of not doing anything that would justify armed federal intervention. The course that he advocated and actively pursued was foreshadowed in a letter of advice that he received from Amos A. Lawrence shortly after the January election. It read in part:

> Presuming that you may be severely or slightly exercised in your mind as to what course to pursue now that the President of the United States has signified this intention to use what power he has against you, I will only say that those who are your best friends would advise and urge you, if their opinion were asked, not under any circumstances to resist any legal representative of the United States, nor allow our people to do it. That would put you in the wrong before the country and more than anything else take you from the nationality which you now hold. The Fabian policy is the true one, i.e., the greatest forebearance; total discouragement of all aggression; a deadly though smiling quiet. This you must adopt. . . . You must gain time and strength.[2]

On March 4, 1856, Charles Robinson reaffirmed this "Fabian" policy in his inaugural address as the free-state governor of Territorial Kansas. In his speech to the free-state legislature he called for "wise" laws based on true principles of republicanism and squatter sovereignty. He reaffirmed the view that the Topeka government was only following precedents set by other states, yet "for the first time in the history of our country the President and his appointees characterize the movement as treasonable." Governor Robinson concluded by clearly stating the course of action that he wished pursued throughout the struggle:

> Our course as a people thus far has been distinguished for forbearance, long suffering and patience and good policy would still dictate that every honorable effort be made to establish and cultivate friendly relations with our oppressors. . . .
>
> Nothing should be done in a spirit of retaliation but rather of conciliation.
>
> Although our own rights have been repeatedly invaded and wrested from us let us show that we respect the constitution and laws of our land. . . . That until forebearance ceases to be a virtue and becomes cowardice and oppression becomes insufferable we will ever be found loyal citizens of the government.[3]

Indeed his policy proved itself by giving the Topeka government the time that Amos Lawrence had deemed necessary. Pierce's hopes for swift action on the Kansas question were dashed when the congressional seat occupied by J. W. Whitfield, the proslavery delegate from Kansas Territory, was challenged by Andrew H. Reeder, who presented credentials issued under the authority of the Topeka Constitution and signed by the Territorial Executive Committee. A bitter debate ensued. Finally, in order to settle the issue, it was proposed that the House conduct an investigation into Kansas affairs. This proposition was debated intermittently for several weeks, with the argument culminating on March 19, 1856, in the appointment of an investigating committee, the so-called Howard Committee. This special committee was chaired by Congressman William A. Howard, a first-term Republican from Michigan. The committee was authorized to conduct investigations into the Kansas question wherever it might see fit. Other members on the committee were Congressmen John Sherman of Ohio, a conservative Whig, and Mordecai Oliver of Missouri, also a Whig. The committee departed for Kansas in order to begin the investigation during the last week of March.

While the committee was journeying to Kansas, Governor Robinson and James Lane were on their way to Washington, carrying a memorial that the Topeka legislature had addressed to Congress in order to seek admission of Kansas as a state under the Topeka Constitution. The two leaders carried the document to Washington so that they could lobby for support in both the House and Senate. Through a combination of Republicans, Free Soilers, Antislavery Whigs, Know-Nothings, and Anti-Nebraska Democrats, the free-state organic bill was passed by the House of Representatives. The Senate, however, rejected it after Senator Douglas accused Lane of presenting a partially forged document, claiming that the signatures in many cases were not authentic. The proposal had almost no chance of passing, even with authentic signatures, considering the proadministration make-up of the Senate; but in Lane's mind the failure was due entirely to Douglas.[4]

The proponents of slavery in Kansas were spurred on by the

administration's willingness to use force, if necessary, to stop the free-state movement. The proslavery newspapers concentrated their attacks on Lawrence, which was considered by them to be the hotbed of abolitionism. Robinson feared that the animosity of the proslavery forces was so great that if resistance to law could be fixed on the people of Lawrence, those forces would have the excuse that they needed in order to destroy the town. This was a major reason for Robinson's urging his followers to exercise forbearance. It is impossible to determine whether or not Sheriff Samuel J. Jones intended to provoke outright resistance when he descended upon Lawrence on April 19, 1856, with a warrant for the arrest of Samuel N. Wood, a recognized Free State leader. Wood resisted arrest, other Free Staters intervened, and Sheriff Jones left town without his prisoner. Jones, in a rage, charged that the people of Lawrence had blatantly resisted Territorial law, and he requested federal troops in order to carry out his duties. The situation was critical for Lawrence citizens. H. C. Pate, a reporter, stated the problem clearly in the St. Louis *Republican* of April 30, 1856:

> There is much speculation what the Lawrence rebels will do: the writs of arrest will be in the hands of the Sheriff of Douglas county, who will be supported by the United States troops. The question is, will they resist? They have always been willing to submit to the authorities of the General Government, and if the writs were to be served by the Marshal of the U.S., there would of course be no resistance. But in submitting to arrest by Jones, they are submitting to the Territorial laws of Kansas passed by what is called the "bogus legislature."[5]

On April 23, Jones returned to Lawrence with federal troops and with warrants of arrest for all who had refused to assist him in taking Wood into custody. Unable to locate Wood, Jones remained overnight in Lawrence. During the night he was shot in the back and severely wounded by an unknown assailant who fired through the side of a tent that was occupied by Jones. The assailant escaped undetected, as much to the chagrin of the townspeople as to that of the proslavery officials.[6]

Governor Robinson, who had recently returned from Washington, deplored the action. He contended that the shooting was a plot designed either to precipitate a crisis or to disrupt the Howard Committee hearings, which were then taking place in Lawrence. On the following day, Robinson called a town meeting, where resolutions were drawn up, which read, in part, as follows:

> RESOLVED, That the attempt made in our town, last evening, upon the life of S. J. Jones, Esq., . . . was a cowardly and atrocious outrage upon Mr. Jones, and an insult and injury to the public sentiment and reputation of our town, and a crime deserving condign punishment.[7]

All attempts at disavowal and conciliation fell on deaf ears in the proslavery communities. The newspapers along the Missouri border denounced the shooting in bitter terms and clamored for revenge. "We are now in favor of leveling Lawrence, and chastizing the Traitors there congregated, should it result in total destruction of the Union," wrote the editor of the *Squatter Sovereign* on April 29, 1856.[8] Many proslavery papers placed the responsibility of the shooting, not on the individual who had fired the shot, but upon those who for the past nine months had been preaching resistance to the laws. The Topeka Constitution and its supporters, especially Robinson, were the main targets of the proslavery wrath.

A few days later, on May 5, Judge Samuel D. Lecompte's division of the United States District Court met at Lecompton to hold the spring term of court for Douglas County. A grand jury was empaneled, and the judge instructed it to find bills of indictment for treason against certain prominent free-state leaders in the county. Lecompte went on to denounce the free-state element and to tell of "the attempt on the part of men here to establish an independent Government, in opposition to the present existing one—also to assume offices of public trust, without due authority."[9]

Thus instructed, the grand jury returned indictments against several free-state leaders in Douglas County, including Charles Robinson, James Lane, G. W. Brown, George Deitzler, S. N. Wood, and Gaius Jenkins. Warrants for their arrest were given

41

to a United States marshal, who, in turn, issued a proclamation calling for "law abiding citizens of the Territory . . . to be and appear at Lecompton as soon as practicable, and in sufficient numbers for the execution of the law."[10] When John Sherman, a member of the Howard investigating committee, learned that these warrants had been issued, he urged Robinson to leave the Territory as soon as possible on the pretext of delivering a copy of the committee's report to Washington, D.C., in order to place it in the hands of Speaker Nathaniel P. Banks.

Governor Robinson and his wife promptly departed for Westport, Missouri, where they boarded a steamboat.[11] Although they thought that they would be safe once they were out of Kansas Territory, the Robinsons were surprised by fifteen proslavery men at Lexington, Missouri, some forty miles east of the Kansas border. These men arrested Robinson for fleeing from a federal indictment, and they placed him under heavy guard. Mrs. Robinson was allowed to proceed to Washington and, subsequently, to Boston, where she eloquently reported the plight of her husband and the free-state cause to sympathetic congressional leaders and to officers of the New England Emigrant Aid Company.

Governor Robinson, in the meantime, was escorted back to Westport, where he was restrained under heavy guard until May 22, because, according to his captors, "Lawrence would be attacked and they wanted him to remain in Westport until after it was done."[12] Several other free-state leaders, including Gaius Jenkins, G. W. Brown, and George Deitzler, had been arrested on similar charges and had been confined at "Uncle Sam's Bastile on the Kansas prairies," which was near Lecompton.[13] James Lane and S. N. Wood had managed to avoid arrest and had traveled East in order to rally support for their cause.

The citizens of Lawrence, without their aggressive leaders, were thrown into fearful disorganization—a situation that well suited the plans of Sheriff Jones. Early on the morning of May 21, 1856, W. F. Fain, a deputy United States marshal, rode into Lawrence with a posse. Several arrests were made, and the citizens of Lawrence followed Robinson's policy of nonaggression against federal authorities by not making any protest. Later

42

in the afternoon, however, Sheriff Jones, who had fully recovered from his wound in the back, arrived with a posse. He made one arrest without meeting any opposition. Then the Sheriff ordered his men to line up in front of the Free State Hotel, and he called on Samuel C. Pomeroy, an agent of Emigrant Aid Company, to surrender all the arms that were in the building. Pomeroy refused, stating that the Sharps rifles were private property over which he had no jurisdiction. Pomeroy's reply failed to satisfy Jones, and he called on the Eldridge brothers, owners of the hotel, to have all the furnishings removed within two hours. The Free State Hotel was the particular object of interest to Jones, because proslavery leaders generally believed that it had been built and equipped as a fort. While the sheriff's men were waiting, some of them were assigned to destroy the offices of both of the free-state newspapers. Stores were broken into, and the then-vacant dwelling of Charles Robinson was burned to the ground. Promptly at five o'clock the Free State Hotel was destroyed. To Sheriff Jones, revenge was sweet. "This is the happiest day of my life," Jones reportedly declared. "I determined to make the fanatics bow before me in the dust and kiss the territorial laws." Watching another round being fired into the hotel, he added, "I've done it, by God, I've done it!"[14]

Two days after the raid, Robinson was sent to Leavenworth. There he remained until June 1, 1856, at which time he was taken to Lecompton and placed with the other free-state prisoners.

As expected, the Lawrence attack prompted retaliation. Few, however, could foresee how severe it would be. John Brown, the major figure involved in the retaliatory action, had settled in Kansas in 1855, bringing with him a consuming hatred of all proslavery men. Although he professed a divine inspiration to destroy slavery, his actions following the "sack of Lawrence" were probably inspired by a blind desire to strike terror into proslavery men.[15] While difficulties centering around Lawrence were mounting during April and May, 1856, communications with other free-state communities had been kept open. When the threat of attack became apparent, messengers were sent from Lawrence to different parts of the Territory, asking for aid. In response to this call, the free-state men of Osawatomie and of the Pottawatomie Creek settlements in Franklin County set out toward Lawrence. John Brown, Jr., was recognized as the leader of all the forces that were descending on Lawrence from a southerly direction. Near the crossing at Marais des Cygnes a messenger intercepted the force to report that Lawrence had been destroyed. A second messenger met them near Prairie City with instructions not to continue to Lawrence, as federal troops were now there and food was scarce. The forces made camp and remained in that area on May 23, 24, and 25.

All did not remain, however, according to James C. Malin, who gives the following account of the activities of John Brown, Sr.:

> On Friday afternoon, May 23, John Brown, Sr., with five sons and two other men, started back toward Potawatomie creek on an unknown mission. The remainder of the expedition did not start until Sunday afternoon, when a federal army officer found them south of Palmyra and ordered them to disperse. Sunday night was spent at Ottawa Jones's on Ottawa creek, and during the night John Brown, Sr., and his party rejoined the expedition.
>
> In the meantime, news came from the vicinity of Dutch Henry's Crossing on Potawatomie creek that five pro-slavery men had been called out of their cabins on Saturday night and murdered with swords; [James] Doyle and two minor sons, [Allen] Wilkinson and William Sherman. On Monday morning, after the arrival of the elder Brown, men in the camp recognized one or more horses belonging to the murdered pro-slavery men.[16]

This horrible massacre set off the beginning of a border war, which did little for either side of the Kansas cause as far as public support was concerned.

These two events—the Lawrence raid and the Pottawatomie massacre—heightened the fears and emotions of all Kansas settlers. With most of the free-state leaders either imprisoned or out of the Territory, all orderly activity on the part of the free-state movement ceased. During the ensuing three months, several "battles" occurred between roving bands of free-state and proslavery forces. Henry C. Pate, from Westport, Missouri, who was a participant in the "sack of Lawrence," still had a detachment of the posse with him near Franklin when he learned of the Pottawatomie massacre. This proslavery force immediately broke camp and set out to capture John Brown. When Brown learned that Pate's posse was coming, he rounded up volunteers to reinforce his small party. With twenty-eight men, Brown set out to meet Pate, finding him on June 2, encamped less than a mile from the small town of Black Jack. The Battle of Black Jack had lasted less than three hours when Pate surrendered. "I had no alternative but to submit or to run and be shot," Pate reported to the *Missouri Republican*. "I went to take Old Brown, and Old Brown took me."[17] The capture of Pate received wide publicity, and proslavery groups, bent on vengeance, formed into companies along Kansas' eastern border.

The events in Kansas throughout May and June took on added national importance since the Democratic and Republican nominating conventions were to be held in the summer of 1856. The capture of Robinson, the sack of Lawrence, and the Pottawatomie massacre were subjects of discussion as the Democrats convened on June 2 in Cincinnati. President Pierce's hopes for renomination suffered from the inability of his administration to maintain order in Kansas. He had failed to restore the peace that he had called for in January, and the Topeka government still remained intact. Resentment against him grew as the delegates caucused, and a growing conviction spread that the party would need a new nominee to win. As a result, James Buchanan of Pennsylvania was nominated.

The Republicans met on June 17 at Philadelphia. They arranged a coalition with antislavery Americans (Know-Nothings), and John C. Fremont was nominated for president. His selection tied the Republican party to the free-state movement, thus strengthening Robinson's position in Kansas. Early in February, Robinson had written a letter to Fremont, in which he recalled some of their common experiences in California and suggested that Fremont be a candidate. On March 17 Fremont replied to Robinson, stating that he favored the Free State party.[18] Robinson turned this letter over to the editor of the

Herald of Freedom, who published it and called for Fremont to become a presidential candidate. Other papers such as the New York *Tribune* and the Cleveland *Herald* took up the cause, so the Fremont campaign began with the Free State party attached to him and, thereby, to the Republican party. This arrangement was not one-sided. The Topeka government, which personified the national antislavery impulse, was the only major issue on which the otherwise incongruous antiadministration faction could unite.

Territorial Governor Wilson Shannon now faced a difficult situation. He had received instructions from President Pierce to maintain the laws firmly and fairly—a task that was becoming more and more difficult. Proslavery groups along the Missouri River boarded incoming vessels when they docked at Kansas City and Leavenworth, questioned passengers about their politics, and took weapons from free-state sympathizers. An organized force of proslavery sympathizers known as the Kickapoo Rangers, who were led by former U.S. Senator David Rice Atchison, moved across the river from Missouri and set up an encampment on Kansas soil. Meanwhile, John Brown continued his activities. After the Battle of Black Jack, he conducted other raids in Douglas and Franklin counties. On June 4 Governor Shannon ordered out federal troops, as other outbreaks of disorder in eastern Kansas made the situation even more complex.

By mid June, Lt. Col. Philip St. George Cooke, commander of the Second Dragoons at Fort Riley, reported that the Kansas dispute had changed in nature, because the emotional situation had attracted lawless men who regularly resorted to banditry and murder. Another officer, Maj. John Sedgwick, observed that disorders were increasing daily, and he believed that either a full-scale civil war would erupt or the bands of the "vicious" would increase their stealing and killing.[19] By the use of federal troops, however, an uneasy peace was restored in Kansas until August, at which time the so-called Lane Army of the North, a force of antislavery sympathizers who were intent on winning the conflict, began to move into Kansas from Iowa. Whether this was an excuse or a cause, it reignited hostilities in Kansas.

The Pierce administration now realized that its policy was

not working at all, and drastic measures were taken in order to try to salvage a Democratic victory at the polls in November. The longer the conflict raged in Kansas, the stronger the Republican party became. Shortly after the outbreak of new disorders in August, President Pierce replaced Governor Shannon with John W. Geary. Geary was instructed to restore peace in the Territory at almost any price. Pierce also decided to release the free-state prisoners that were being held at Lecompton on charges of treason. After this news had arrived in Kansas, Robinson, who had said or written little while he was imprisoned at Lecompton, sent a letter on August 16 to several free-state leaders who had been directing raiding parties in southeastern Kansas. He urged caution for the good of the cause, advising them as follows:

> We have heard of your good deeds and so far as we understand matters, highly approve of your course. But now is the rub. It is easy to commence operations, but difficult to stop at the right time and in the right way. If the enemy will keep quiet, we think you can afford to rest where you are and try *negotiation* provided the other party is willing. . . . If possible we think our friends should be at peace while the new governor takes his seat and give a chance for justice and peace to reign if he wills it.[20]

When Governor Geary arrived in Kansas on September 7, 1856, he took immediate steps to restore order by calling out federal troops and by disbanding the Territorial militia. Three days later, on September 10, Judge Lecompte announced his decision to postpone the treason cases of the political prisoners at Lecompton, on the grounds that it was not possible to gain a fair trial under the present state of "excitement in the country." Thus, four months after Robinson had been apprehended, the tents on "Traitor Avenue" were taken down, and he and other free-state prisoners were freed.[21]

A few days after Robinson returned to Lawrence, he learned that the town was in danger of being attacked by a force of about twenty-seven hundred proslavery men, who were gathering because they were angered by the release of the free-state leaders. Robinson hastily arranged a meeting with Geary, after which

Geary, backed by federal troops, persuaded the invaders to disband. After September 16, 1856, Lawrence was not seriously threatened again, and peace rapidly returned to Kansas. By the use of regular troops and by enrolling both free-state and proslavery men in a new federal militia, Geary was able to break up the guerrilla bands. By November he had won the confidence of the leaders of the Topeka government and had become quite friendly with Robinson and Pomeroy.

In late September, Robinson resigned his position as a Kansas agent for the New England Emigrant Aid Company in order to devote himself completely to the politics of the Territory. This was done upon the advice of Amos A. Lawrence, who had assured him in a letter that should Robinson decide to do this, the company would make good any loss of income while he engaged in the task. On October 3 the Executive Committee of the New England Emigrant Aid Company received Robinson's letter of resignation and passed the following resolution:

> Voted, that the resignation of Dr. Charles Robinson, as Agent of the Co., in accordance with his wish as expressed in his letter of September 14, 1856, be hereby accepted to take effect October 3, inst.
>
> Voted, that in consideration of the valuable services rendered by Dr. Robinson, from the date of the first organization of the Co. to the present time, his salary be continued for six months from this date, at the rate of one thousand dollars per annum.
>
> Voted, that Dr. Robinson be requested to continue his correspondence with the Executive Committee as heretofore, and to communicate with them at such times as he may deem expedient in regard to all matters that concern the cause of Kansas. . . .
>
> Voted, that the Executive Committee cannot lose their connection with Dr. Robinson without expressing their entire confidence in the uprightness and integrity of his character, and their deep conviction of the value and importance of his service to the great cause of freedom in Kansas.[22]

The leaders of the Topeka government held strong hopes for a Republican victory in November, 1856, which they believed would enable the government to be recognized and statehood to be achieved. Buchanan, however, narrowly won the election, thus giving the Democratic party a respite and proslavery Kansans a new hope for making Kansas a slave state. Governor Geary, who was now committed to the Topeka cause, met with Robinson after the election and outlined a plan whereby Kansas would be admitted to statehood under the Topeka Constitution and whereby he himself, as an administration Democrat, could then be elected governor of the state. Geary believed that he could secure the backing of the administration if Robinson would relinquish his governorship and go to Washington to reconcile the Republicans.[23] Both Geary and Robinson believed that the leaders of the Democratic party would accept the arrangement in order to align Kansas with the Democrats and salvage what they could from an embarrassing situation. It was also assumed that the Republicans would be content with having saved Kansas from slavery. Robinson, although he never expressly said so, was probably willing to step aside for Geary, because if the plan succeeded, he would be in the prime position to become a U.S. Senator from Kansas.

Early in January, 1857, Robinson gave to Geary his letter of resignation as governor under the Topeka Constitution. Then he departed for Washington to lobby for the plan, arriving in the capital on January 14. He quickly came to the conclusion that the Topeka Constitution had little chance of succeeding in the new session of Congress.[24] Neither the Republicans nor the Democratic administration would accept his and Geary's plan. When newspapers learned of the plan and of Robinson's apparent cooperation with the Democrats, mass meetings were held in Topeka and Lawrence to censure him. Robinson learned of the discord while in Washington, and he was deeply disturbed by it. He wrote his wife:

> I see by the papers that some of the people of Kansas are holding meetings to censure me. That is right. It would not do to allow anyone to have any influence in favor of Kansas if they can help. . . . Thank God their censure cannot fix guilt upon me, and if it will aid them by depriving me of power to serve them I am well pleased

to have it so. Politically . . . I want no man's favor and personally I care as little for it as anyone well can. I expect to please myself as well as I can and hope to do some good in the world and this is all I can expect to accomplish in this short life.[25]

Governor Geary, however, did not abandon the free-state cause. He openly opposed the Territorial legislature and, eventually, the Pierce administration. In February, 1857, a bill was passed that provided for a convention to frame a state constitution; it was to meet in Lecompton on the first Monday of the following September. The act stipulated that delegates to the convention would be apportioned among counties on the basis of a special census of voters, which was to be completed by sheriffs under the supervision of local county officials. In this manner the apparatus for taking the census and for registering the voters was entirely in the hands of county officials who had been appointed by the proslavery legislature. The election of delegates was scheduled for June, 1857. The bill was vetoed by Governor Geary, but it was promptly passed over his veto. Geary then traveled to Washington, where he personally protested the action to President Pierce, arguing that the failure of the legislature to insist on the submission of the question of a constitution to a popular vote was a breach of legislative responsibility. When Pierce failed to back Geary, criticizing him for previous acts of sympathy toward the free-state cause, Geary had no recourse but to resign. His resignation became effective on the day that President Buchanan was inaugurated, March 4, 1857.

The new Territorial governor appointed by President Buchanan was Robert J. Walker, a successful lawyer and politician from Mississippi. He arrived in Kansas on May 24, 1857, and he made his inaugural address at Lecompton three days later. His views on slavery, as expressed in his inaugural remarks, did nothing to alleviate the fears of the antislavery people. He said:

> There is a law more powerful than the legislation of man, more potent than passion or prejudice, that must ultimately determine the location of Slavery in this country; it is the isothermal line; it is the law of the thermometer, of

latitude or altitude, regulating climate, labor and productions, and, as a consequence, profit and loss.[26]

Walker was further hampered in his efforts to gain free-state trust, because Acting Governor Frederick P. Stanton, earlier in the month, had issued a proclamation setting forth the apportionment of delegates to the Lecompton convention. The census for the apportionment was not taken in any of the counties where free-state sentiment was strong. Of an estimated twenty thousand voters in Kansas, only about seven thousand were registered. Thirty-seven of the sixty delegates were to be elected from the counties bordering Missouri, thereby assuring proslavery control of the convention. T. Dwight Thatcher, editor of the Lawrence *Republican*, urged that all free-state men ignore the election. He contended that no Congress would accept a constitution that was based upon a representation in which half the state had no part.[27] This advice was endorsed by a convention of free-state men which was held in Topeka just three days before the scheduled election. On election day only two thousand votes were cast, less than one-tenth of the estimated adult population, and proslavery candidates won handily.

The convention assembled at Lecompton on September 7, and it remained in session for four days. After electing permanent officers and choosing committees, the convention adjourned until October 19, to await the outcome of an early October election for the Territorial delegate to Congress and for members of the Territorial legislature. Governor Walker made repeated assurances that this election would be fair and impartial.

The Free State party experienced a crisis in leadership after Robinson's participation in Geary's abortive plan for statehood in January. This was reflected by the difficulty it had in reaching a decision about free-state participation in the October elections. Robinson, who was consistent with his "Fabian" policy, urged that a political solution should be attempted if there were any chance of avoiding the open hostilities that had plagued the Territory in 1856. These views he made known at a Free State convention held in Topeka on July 15 and 16, 1857. He was opposed by Lane, who led a contingent of the party that opposed participation in elections and favored the use of force in stopping the movement for the Lecompton Constitution. The Topeka convention came to a close without any agreement having been reached. This convention illustrated the apparent decline of the Topeka government; it also made clear the division within the party.

One participant in the convention contended that Robinson's actions during the previous winter had "disheartened the people, so that they lost confidence in him and in the movement." The observer stated, however, that Robinson was not the only one who was to blame; he had to be joined by James Lane and the Lawrence *Republican,* who had made equally harmful blunders:

> Col. Lane boasted in his public speeches that the Constitutional Convention at Lecompton would be driven into the Kaw river by violence. . . . The *Republican* boasted that old Capt. [John] Brown would be down on Gov. Walker and Co., like an avenging god. . . . Whatever was intended, much more was threatened than could possibly have been performed unless there was an extensive conspiracy.[28]

The question of participation in the election was finally resolved at another Free State convention, which met at Grasshopper Falls (the present-day Valley Falls) on the last Wednesday of August, 1857. The conservative policy finally carried, after an address by Robinson in which he stated: "I have no doubt we shall be triumphant. From the census returns I am satisfied there is not a district in the Territory in which we have not a large majority of voters. If we are defeated by fraud, we shall be in a position to show up the fraud."[29]

Thomas J. Marsh, a special agent of the New England Emigrant Aid Company, wrote a report on August 27, the day after the second convention, in which he said:

> The [Grasshopper Falls] Convention was well attended, all portions of the Territory was [*sic*] represented. . . . And notwithstanding the very able speech of Judge Conway in opposition to voting [in October], upon the question being taken, the only dissenting vote was the Judge himself. They

52

voted to go into the election with all the powers they have, and for all the offices.[30]

The election resulted in a free-state victory. The candidate for delegate to Congress, Marcus J. Parrott, won by a decisive margin. Some fraud was attempted, but Governor Walker threw out the election returns from two voting areas, and the antislavery party ended up with large majorities in both houses of the Territorial legislature. After a three-year struggle, the Free State party had finally triumphed.

The Proslavery party now realized that its last chance for establishing slavery in Kansas resided in the Lecompton constitutional convention. The convention reconvened on October 18, despite protests from free-state newspapers. The constitution that it drafted and adopted, which provided for the existence of slavery, was not submitted to the people for a vote. Instead, it was sent directly to Congress, in the hope that the Democratic administration could force its acceptance. Already defeated in Kansas in the sense that the proponents of slavery were out of power, the document, while voted down in Congress, nevertheless disrupted American politics and increased sectional tensions.[31]

The movement that favored the Topeka Constitution faced even more serious difficulties. The effectiveness of its leadership, which had suffered severely during the first months of 1857, deteriorated further after the October election. Robinson, who had been under suspicion since January, devoted less time to politics as the year wore on. The economy and land values were booming in Kansas. At the height of the political conflict just prior to the election, Robinson wrote his wife that he was "tired of this turmoil." He went on to state that what he really wanted to do was "spend my time cultivating a part of my claim and have no other business except to buy and sell property and loan money if I have any to loan."[32] Lane also was unable to muster the support that he had possessed in 1856. His unbridled radicalism and his frequent public threats of violence only served to make him equally suspect. Perhaps the greatest factor in the growing apathy to the Topeka Constitution was the prosperous economy and the relative peace in Kansas by the end of 1857. In 1857 over a hundred thousand emigrants—mostly from Ohio and Missouri—arrived in the Territory, which set off an unprecedented boom in land values.

Statehood was still four years away, but the Free State party had won. In that victory the Topeka Constitution, despite its failure to gain congressional acceptance, had played a significant role; it had been the cause that held the party together. And, as Robinson learned in 1857, even with the defeat of the Lecompton Constitution, the chances that the Topeka Constitution would succeed in the next Congress were negligible. Schuyler Colfax of South Bend, Indiana, a friend and advisor to Robinson, suggested that perhaps another course would have to be pursued in order for Kansas to be admitted as a free state. He wrote, in the spring of 1857:

> These two years will probably decide whether Kansas will enter the Union with a slave or Free Constitution; and evident that it is that your excellent Topeka Constitution cannot receive a majority, or anything near a majority, in either House, a grave responsibility is devolved on its friends in Kansas—a responsibility which friends and defenders elsewhere must share.

Colfax concluded that the Topeka Constitution would not command more than eighty-five votes in the next Congress.[33]

In assessing Robinson's role as governor and as leader of the movement, it must be recognized that he displayed many qualities of effective leadership: courage, a strong commitment to the cause, and consistency. His "Fabian" policy of peaceful resistance faced many challenges, failing only during the summer of 1856 while he was imprisoned. Though the Territory went through times of great turmoil, much credit can be given to Robinson for the avoidance of outright civil war in Kansas between 1855 and 1858. Thus, at the end of 1857, convinced that the threat of slavery in Kansas had been averted, Robinson turned his back on politics, and for the next two and one-half years he concentrated on the development of his own speculative ventures in railroads and land.

4

The Economy
of Territorial Kansas

The civil and political conflicts of early Kansas have received the most attention from historians of this period, but there were other important parts of Kansas' Territorial development. Many settlers were involved or interested in political issues to some degree, but all faced the necessity of earning a living—a task that was complicated by what was a new environment for most of them and by a lack of currency in the Territory. Economically, the Territory and its settlers first experienced a complex period, which was marked by difficulties with land titles and a lack of transportation. This was followed by a brief "boom" in land values and a large amount of immigration. The Territorial period then closed in a period of drought and depression. Weather, politics, and national financial distress had their effects on the Kansas economy, but the major problem was the lack of production of marketable items. Only by opening new avenues of trade could the settlers acquire and maintain a level of capital that would provide them with a solid economic base.[1]

In addition to the obvious problem of getting a start, Kansas settlers faced a complicated transportation situation. The long distances to markets and the paucity of navigable rivers in Kansas made it difficult for residents in the interior of the Territory to compete with the agricultural producers of the Mississippi

Valley, who had both water transportation and a rapidly expanding and developing railway system at their disposal. Until inexpensive means for quickly transporting farm products to markets were developed, Kansas products were of little value except for home consumption, and home consumption brought no currency into the Territory. Even in years of large crops, the low prices offered for Kansas corn coupled with high prices for Eastern manufactured goods to create a constant drain on the available currency in Kansas. This problem was constant throughout the Territorial years. John J. Ingalls observed in a letter in 1859: "Affairs in the territory seem to be brightening a little, but even now the prostration seems almost perfect. Want of money is the great difficulty." More than a year later he reported that conditions were unchanged, explaining: "The trouble is there is nothing here to attract money. The actual exports of the country—corn, pork and hides—has not yet been enough to pay for the whiskey that is drank every month, and men are living on what they had, or the charity of their friends."[2]

One immediate difficulty for settlers who attempted to make a living by farming was the acquisition of land. When Kansas became a Territory, not a single acre of land was officially open for white settlement. The land in Kansas in 1854 belonged to several Indian tribes, and it could not legally be settled or claimed until Indian titles had been quieted. Thus, in 1854 and 1855, settlers were not allowed to use land claims as collateral for loans, nor were they sure that they could perfect or clear their claims on land. It is not surprising, then, to find that many settlers rejected farming and turned to speculation. While this practice was not uncommon in the settlement of other Territories, the number and amounts of funds involved were especially significant in Kansas. Historian Paul W. Gates has written: "Kansas was conceived, staffed, promoted, and quarreled over by speculators to such a degree that one can almost say speculation in land, town lots, the location of county seats, railroad terminals and routes, and of the capital, was the principal business of its people."[3]

While he was an agent for the New England Emigrant Aid Company and afterwards, Charles Robinson was involved in many speculative ventures. He was initiated early into the complex land situation when he became embroiled in a dispute over the Lawrence town site, which involved land granted by treaty to the Wyandot Indians. He discovered that, to gain legal title for the Emigrant Aid Company, he had to deal with the Indians. In an attempt to provide land quickly for settlement in the Territories of Kansas and Nebraska, Congress had responded to the Wyandots' request that a new treaty be negotiated with them, and had made a new treaty on January 31, 1855. The leaders of that Indian nation had realized that with the passage of the Kansas-Nebraska Act their reservation, which was cradled between the Missouri and Kansas rivers, was in a good location for settlement and that they would be under pressure from the white settlers.

Also in 1842, the Wyandots had been granted thirty-five sections of land, a potential claim of 22,400 acres, but these grants were not tied to any particular sites. They were called "floating" grants or "Wyandot floats."[4] The new treaty initiated the processes of dissolving tribal government and of partitioning the lands. The Wyandot nation relinquished all rights that it had been granted in previous treaties. The most important provision of the treaty stipulated that

> each of the individuals, to whom reservations were granted by the fourteenth article of the treaty of March seventeenth, one thousand eight hundred and forty-two, or their heirs or legal representatives, shall be permitted to select and locate said reservations, on any Government lands west of the States of Missouri and Iowa, subject to the pre-emption and settlement . . .; and the reservees, their heirs or proper representatives, shall have the unrestricted right to sell and convey the same, whenever they may think proper.[5]

Lands that were claimed in Kansas Territory under these floats included the town sites of Lecompton, Topeka, Lawrence, Manhattan, and Kansas City, Kansas. Robinson purchased the William L. Tennery float in an effort to support the Emigrant Aid Company's claim to the Lawrence town site. Other claimants in the area still challenged the company's ownership rights, and it took nearly a year to work out a satisfactory compromise. It was not until 1860 that the town-site claim was completely cleared. Similar disputes arose over other Wyandot floats throughout the Territorial period.

In 1856 Robinson became involved in another town-site venture on land owned by the Wyandot Indians. During the initial stages of the Kansas conflict, free-state settlers and land agents found themselves at an economic disadvantage, because all towns along the Missouri River were controlled by pro-slavery men who would discourage Free Staters from entering the Territory. In addition, Robinson, like most men from east of the Mississippi, believed that control of river towns was required for the transportation and commercial development that the Territory needed. Thus, he and other free-state leaders did not hesitate to act to establish a free-state town along the Missouri River when they were approached by Abelard Guthrie with a plan to build and develop one. This would provide a Kansas port of entry for free-state immigrants, and they could subsequently utilize the town as a market. The site selected was named Quindaro after Guthrie's wife, a Wyandot Indian who was the original owner of the land. A town company was organized, and officers were chosen. They were: Joel Walker, president; Abelard Guthrie, vice-president; Charles Robinson, treasurer; and S. N. Simpson, secretary.[6]

A survey was completed in December, 1856, and within the month the town was plotted on the west bank of the Missouri River, six miles above the mouth of the Kansas River. By May, 1857, a weekly newspaper, the *Chindowan*, reported that trees had been removed from several acres of the town-site, nearly forty houses had been constructed, a school had been opened, and "sixteen businesses are being erected."[7] Throughout 1857, Quindaro grew faster than any town on the Missouri River. Shares in the town company sold well, and New Englanders invested heavily in the project, mainly due to Robinson's influence. Business lots near the river sold for $500 to $750 each. By 1858 there were prospects that Quindaro would become a city. It had a mayor and a council, which met weekly. There were by this time two hotels, two prosperous churches, and a stage line, which provided daily mail and passenger service to the interior towns of the Territory. Town promoters boasted that it had a population of one thousand people, with all branches of business being represented.[8]

The growth ended, however, nearly as fast as it began. When the new county of Wyandotte was organized in 1858 and the town of Wyandotte, rather than Quindaro, was made the county seat, the fortunes of the river boom town began to wane. Another factor contributing to the downfall of Quindaro was the Panic of 1857, which moved into the West and cut off the Eastern investments that were so important to the town. Finally, the town's fortunes suffered when the free-state movement won control of the legislature, and it was no longer the only free-state port of entry. The larger, more established trading towns of Leavenworth and Wyandotte, which was soon to become Kansas City, Kansas, quickly became free-state, equal-rights towns. As its income stopped and its capital was drained, the town company was unable to meet expenses. Abelard Guthrie lost everything; and Robinson, who had invested nearly $15,000 and owned twenty shares of stock in the company and forty acres of land adjoining the town, lost heavily.[9]

Although Quindaro retained some population for several years, it, like many other small towns in eastern Kansas, was destined to die. Charles M. Chase, a correspondent for the Sycamore, Illinois, *True Republican and Sentinel*, who visited Quindaro in 1863, wrote that he only found one family there—a poor man and his crazy wife, who were living in an abandoned hotel. In 1873 he revisited the place and wrote the following report:

> Quindaro was, but now she is not. Governor Robinson thought to make it *the* point west of St. Louis on the Missouri River. He interested a Massachusetts colony, who emigrated, laid out the town, and began building. . . .
>
> Governor Robinson Avenue was graded back into the bluff 75 rods, where it stopped, leaving a perpendicular embankment 20 feet high. . . . The lots are there, today, and so is the governor's avenue, but it is covered with a fine growth of cottonwoods. The buildings have tumbled down, and the solitary family even have abandoned the place.[10]

The rise and fall of Quindaro not only served as an indication of Robinson's interest in town development, it later provided a basis for criticizing him as a business man. Robinson, who did not suffer as severe a financial setback as Abelard Guthrie, became the object of Guthrie's enmity, and Guthrie blamed all his misfortunes on Robinson. Apparently, there had been earlier disagreements between the two men, for Guthrie recorded the following in his diary in February, 1858: "Every transaction I have with Chapin, Robinson, and Smith but the more convince me that they are dishonest men, and it shall be my constant effort hereafter to get rid of them."[11] When the collapse finally came, Guthrie's anger increased, and in 1859 he brought suit against Robinson in district court for damages. The case was referred to three referees, who decided in Robinson's favor. Guthrie was highly incensed with the decision, and for years he carried on a personal campaign to discredit Robinson.[12]

It was while Robinson was trying to develop Quindaro that he first became interested in railroad promotion. He came to realize the vital role that railroads would play in the development of the state. The Pacific Railroad had been built as far west as Jefferson City, Missouri, when Quindaro developers joined with George Park of Parkville, Missouri, to connect with the Hannibal and St. Joseph Railroad. Railroad promoters from Quindaro and Park City constituted one of three major Kansas groups that hoped to build a road into Kansas. Robinson worked closely with Robert S. Stevens, an influential Kansas Democrat. A second group, headed by Samuel C. Pomeroy, was centered around the city of Atchison; it obtained charters for three railroads in 1859, intending to build west from Atchison to Topeka, then to Fort Riley and on to Pikes Peak. A third group was headed by William H. Russell, a banker and a partner in the freighting firm of Russell, Majors and Waddell. Also included were Andrew J. Isaacs, Hugh Boyle Ewing, and Thomas Ewing, Jr., the last two being sons of former Senator Thomas Ewing of Ohio. They promoted the Leavenworth, Pawnee and Western Railroad, which was designed to run from Leavenworth to Lawrence and then to Fort Riley by way of the north bank of the Kansas River.[13]

All three groups had problems in common—any success that they might achieve would depend on Congress's resolving the Indian land question and on a favorable government subsidy. Thus, during congressional sessions in 1858 and 1859, representatives from each of the rival interests converged on Washington for the purpose of securing land grants and the right to purchase trust lands. Robinson, because of his experience in land speculation in 1857, proved to be a capable lobbyist.

In January, 1857, Robinson had signed a two-year contract with Joseph Lyman, treasurer of the Kansas Land Trust in Boston, to serve as land agent for the company. His salary was set at $1,000 per year. In addition, the contract stipulated that he would receive one-quarter of the profit at the end of the two years.[14] Thus, throughout 1857 Robinson bought land for Eastern investors. In September, 1857, he asked for further business, informing an officer of the Kansas Land Trust that he could lend money on good security at the rate of 5 percent per month.[15] At the end of 1857 Robinson reported that he personally had accumulated property worth around $44,000.[16]

Financial prospects, however, dimmed for most promoters, including Robinson, in 1858. The effect of poor crops in 1857 reached a critical stage in the early winter of 1858. The newly appointed governor, James Denver, concluded that the place was "cursed of God and Man" and that it would require all the powers conferred upon him to "prevent them [the settlers] from cutting each others throats."[17] Kansans faced, in 1858, the direct effects and backwash of the panic of 1857. As the hard times spread throughout the East, relatives and friends of Kansans were no longer able to send cash or supplies, nor did they have funds to invest. A letter to Hiram Hill of Massachusetts from Abelard Guthrie suggested the bad state of economic affairs in Kansas:

> I am constrained by unprecedented hard times to call upon you for the balance due on the property. . . . I have refrained asking you for the money while the times were harder in the East than here, but now the case is reversed

and we are without money and credit. We cannot beg, borrow, or collect debts—there is no money in the country.[18]

A similar fate struck other developments. Railroads, particularly in Kansas, had little chance of being constructed until better times returned. Most land grants to finance construction failed to pass Congress in 1858; among those was one for the Quindaro, Parkville, and Grand River Railroad. Despite the failure of that road, Robinson continued to use his influence for other railroad development in the Territory, for he saw railroads as a major solution for the area's economic ills. In early 1859 he wrote a letter to the editor of the *Herald of Freedom* stating that "Kansas, although more beautiful and desirable on some accounts, has probably less commercial advantages than any state in the Union. Her lands, so rich and beautiful, must lie unimproved and comparatively valueless without the means of getting their products to market."[19]

In the same article, Robinson pointed out that in an ordinary season, corn sold for twenty-five cents a bushel at the Missouri River ports but was worthless in Lawrence because of the cost involved in transporting it to those ports. Thus, he argued, if no railroads were built in the near future, only the area along the river would increase in value, while interior lands would never rise in value above the price of grazing land. He also used the same reasoning in discussing the future development of Kansas towns:

> The river towns will increase in importance, as all articles of export must be carried to them by the farmer, while the interior towns will lose even their present trade. . . . [W]ithout the early construction of a system of railroads Kansas would experience a stagnation of business that would be ruinous alike to all departments of industry.[20]

Robinson blamed the failure to obtain land grants for railroads on the interference of "political demagogues," specifically M. F. Conway, the Kansas Territorial delegate who was elected under the Leavenworth Constitution. It is interesting that Robinson blamed, not the Proslavery party or the Democrats or even the Buchanan administration, but rather the Kansas antislavery radicals—the very men who were attempting to gain domination of the Republican party in Kansas, which was about to be organized at Osawatomie.[21] The fact that Robinson had placed the blame on his former allies could be cited as an indication of the trend of his subsequent political career. His choice of political parties would depend upon circumstances and issues. Charles Robinson was not averse to placing blame where he believed it belonged, regardless of party, philosophy, or economic situations.

In this light, it was not out of character for Robinson to switch his railroad support. Reluctant to give up anticipated personal financial gains, but realizing that the Territory needed railroads, Robinson decided to work with the strongest railroad group in order to salvage what he could for both himself and the town of Lawrence. The bitterness of the railroad fights among the leading towns, along with some of the strategy, was reflected in a letter that he wrote to Sara in 1859:

> I have to fight the Lawrence battle entirely alone. Leavenworth men are unwilling to make Lawrence a point on the road South. We shall make it a point West. I shall try to fasten the Southern road also at Lawrence. Were it not that I have, with Stevens, the advantage of the fellows, Lawrence would not have a single road if they could help it. The friendship of the other towns, whether Leavenworth or Kansas City, will not do to count on. Lawrence must fight its own battles for they will be fought by other towns. I hope to be able to make Lawrence a point in both roads before we get through.[22]

At this juncture it had become increasingly apparent that the Leavenworth, Pawnee and Western Railroad had the most support among the people in the Missouri Valley and that it was in the strongest position for bargaining. In March, 1859, after he had been approached by Thomas Ewing, Jr., Robinson agreed to make up a purse of between $10,000 and $15,000 in Lawrence property to secure aid from important lobbying groups. Such a purse was necessary, according to Ewing, to keep alive any possibility of obtaining passage of the land grant that was necessary for railroad construction.

Robinson, R. S. Stevens, and S. N. Simpson were negotiating for Delaware Indians lands in the eastern part of Kansas Territory. Thomas Ewing, Jr., and John P. Usher, who later became secretary of the interior in Lincoln's administration, supported the treaty efforts in Washington. On May 30, 1860, a treaty with the Delawares was finally signed. It provided for 80-acre allotments to members of the tribe, and then authorized the sale of the remaining lands to the Leavenworth, Pawnee and Western Railroad. These lands, amounting to nearly 225,000 acres, were to be sold at their appraised value, but for not less than $1.25 per acre. Title to one-half the land was to be given to the railroad after it completed construction to a point twenty-five miles west of Leavenworth, and title to the remainder was to be given when construction was complete to the western boundary of the reserve—fifty miles in all.[23]

Despite this piece of success, scarcity of capital still left unresolved the question as to how the speculators were going to pay for the land. Thus, instead of offering to pay the Delawares in cash, they proposed to pay them in bonds on the company, which were secured through a mortgage of 100,000 acres of the total land transaction. This left the speculators with the right to sell nearly 125,000 acres, provided that the construction schedule was maintained.

To secure additional support for the treaty in Washington, numerous other land commitments were made. One was a commitment of 2,320 acres of bottom land in the Kaw Valley near Lawrence, which was quitclaimed to Martha Robinson, sister of Charles Robinson. It was on this land that Charles Robinson later built his large estate. This transaction occurred in several stages between 1862 and 1873.[24] The final title was granted by the Union Pacific Railroad Company, which later took over the land holdings of the initial railroad, the Leavenworth, Pawnee and Western. Transactions were carried out in Martha Robinson's name through Charles Robinson, who had her power of attorney. Charles paid all taxes upon the land until September 19, 1885, when "in consideration of one dollar" he purchased from his sister all the land.[25]

Even with all his speculative activities during the late Territorial period, Robinson suffered the same economic plight as his contemporaries. He was hard hit by the drought of 1860 and the "Kansas Famine" that followed. The drought actually commenced in June of 1859. From the nineteenth of that month until November, 1860, not enough rain fell in Kansas "to wet the earth at any one time, two inches in depth." Before the close of the summer of 1860 "the ground was so parched that it broke open in huge cracks, the winds blew from the south like a blast from a furnace, vegetation was destroyed, crops were a total failure, and wells and springs were dry."[26] Conditions were grave by the fall of 1860, and numerous relief projects were begun. At least one plan called for the charities of the East to channel funds into the construction of the Atchison, Topeka and Santa Fe Railroad in order to provide jobs for those in distress. Robinson opposed this plan, suggesting that more capital, not charity, was the answer:

> [Thaddeus] Hyatt is making a great fuss over the starving Kansas and is proposing to turn the charities of the East into the Atchison, Topeka and Santa Fe Railroad Co. How much good they will do for the poor who cannot go 20 to 100 miles to work for 15¢ a day remains to be seen. Mr. Nute wrote to me asking our condition, and I told him if we could get money to be loaned on good security we would need no other assistance.[27]

Less than a month later, Charles wrote to his wife, who was visiting her family in Massachusetts, and reported that starvation was staring the whole population of Kansas in the face: "How long we can hold out I cannot say."[28] It was reported that nearly thirty thousand people left Kansas Territory between mid 1859 and the end of 1860.[29] Perhaps even Robinson would have left had he not been elected as the state's first governor in an election held on December 6, 1859.[30] A return to Massachusetts would certainly not have disappointed Sara, who frequently made known her dislike of Kansas and who, on a number of occasions, spent several months at a time visiting her family in Massachusetts. At one point her brooding about her life in Kansas prompted a harsh response from Charles, which contrasted greatly with his usually tender correspondence of nearly forty years:

> I think your feeling of want of usefulness would be in a measure removed if you did not isolate yourself from the human family with the exception of a few chosen friends who need no improving. If the people are as bad as you think, it would seem that it is just the place for you to do good. You think some people aristocratic or exclusive but I know of no one more exclusive than yourself; I do not know whether from your pride of character or circumstance or something else. For myself I am aware that I could find more leisure for reading, etc., in another part of the country, but I am doubtful about it being right to shut myself out of a business and other connections just to gratify my desire for personal ease and happiness. . . . I have not written this in a complaining mood, but I thought you were looking on the wrong side of things.[31]

Robinson, however, was now more committed than ever to Kansas affairs. Although his political career appeared to have come to an end in 1858, when he withdrew from politics in order to concentrate on business, he was again in the political arena by 1859. While Robinson made business connections in 1858 and 1859 that bore fruit in later years, his political inactivity provided James Lane with an opportunity to gain additional strength on the state scene.

5

Governor of the State

Three years elapsed between the triumph of the free-state forces and the admission of Kansas to the Union. After the autumn of 1857 the question was not whether the Northern or Southern influence would dominate, but, rather, which faction of the Free State party would dominate. The formation of the Republican party did not significantly alter this situation. Only the name of the party was changed—not its make-up. The radical element of the old Free State party, those who advocated violence and outlawry as necessary courses of action in order to make Kansas a Free State were led by James Lane and T. D. Thatcher, editor of the Lawrence *Republican.* They continued to battle against the conservative element, which was led by Charles Robinson and George W. Brown, editor of the *Herald of Freedom.* Robinson and Brown were the leading spokesmen for carrying out all agitation and necessary action within existing laws. This period of Kansas history can only be understood in the light of this factional conflict.

Lane's political power rested in the Republican party organization in Kansas. Like the Topeka Constitution, the Free State party had fulfilled its special mission in keeping slavery out of Kansas. It was expendable once that question had been settled. A convention of free-state settlers was held in Lawrence as early as November 11, 1857, to discuss the question of discarding the old Free State party in favor of the National Republican party. The change was too sudden for many of the regulars of the Free State party, and the plan was abandoned at that time. On May 18, 1858, another convention to consider the same question was held at Osawatomie, with nearly one thousand people in attendance. The forenoon of the first day was devoted to the guest speaker, Horace Greeley, who was well received by the delegates. In the evening a permanent organization was formed and committee assignments were made. It appears that both wings of the old Free State party were represented on all committees. Oscar E. Learnard, a free-state conservative and a Robinson supporter, was elected president of the convention. Learnard later wrote that the office was a reward for his having encouraged the conservative element to attend the convention.[1] Among the leading members of the radical, or Lane, wing who achieved prominent positions were D. W. Wilder, T. D. Thatcher, and W. A. Phillips. James Lane and Charles Robinson did not appear—which probably enabled the party to organize smoothly and to avoid the outright appearance of a struggle for power between the two factions of the old Free State party.[2]

With the establishment of the Republican party in Kansas, the Free State party ceased to exist. The Lane and Robinson factions remained in the new party, however, and friction between them continued throughout the remainder of the Territorial period. According to historian G. Raymond Gaeddert, the Republican party at the close of the 1850s "was divided into two hostile factions whose conflict would be intensified by every political breeze that might sweep the Kansas prairies."[3]

In May, 1859, the Democrats, in an attempt to rally many of the old free-state settlers back into the Democratic fold, ceased to support the slavery issue. But the Republican party kept most of the former members of the Free State party in its ranks. In the first test—the election of delegates to the Wyandotte constitutional convention, which was held on the first Tuesday of June, 1859—35 Republicans and 17 Democrats were elected.[4] Neither Robinson nor Lane was a candidate in this election. In fact, there were few experienced leaders present when the delegates convened in Wyandotte on July 5, 1859. Various explanations have been offered for their absence. According to one leader, "Constitution-making, like the grasshopper, had become a burden."[5] A more plausible explanation was that the experienced leaders who had participated in framing previous free-state constitutions did not wish to prejudice the electorate or Congress when the Wyandotte Constitution was submitted for approval.

The drafters of the Wyandotte Constitution incorporated in it the important constitutional trends of the time, but they made few innovations. The model selected by the framers was the Ohio Constitution of 1851. The governor was given the veto power and the authority to grant pardons, to fill vacancies, and to convene and adjourn the legislature. Suffrage was given to all white males who were citizens of the United States or who had declared their intention of becoming such. Another important provision limited the amount of indebtedness that the state could incur—a limit that could not be changed except by a direct vote of the people.[6]

The election to ratify the Wyandotte Constitution was held on October 4, 1859, and for the first time in Kansas, "all parties cast a full, free and independent vote." Of the nearly sixteen thousand votes cast, over ten thousand favored adoption. Endorsement of the constitution stimulated many candidates to seek office, and among those who were prominently mentioned for governor were Cyrus K. Holliday of Topeka, the Reverend H. P. Johnston of Leavenworth, and Charles Robinson of Lawrence.[7] Interest outside the Territory was also running high. One H. Wilson of Massachusetts wrote to Robinson, admonishing him:

> Our friends in the East are not a little anxious about your new state. Don't, for God's sake, let the Democrats carry it. You must look to the matter. They are stronger than I wish to see them. I think it was a mistake to organize the Republican party before coming into the Union, but you decided otherwise, and now do not be defeated.[8]

The Republican Central Committee issued a call for a state convention to meet at Topeka on October 12, 1859, to select a slate of candidates. A major battle, however, was fought two days before, at the Douglas County convention in Lawrence, between the Robinson and Lane forces. The Topeka *Tribune* reported that an arrangement was made there, whereby it was agreed that "in consideration of the friends of Lane voting for Robinson for governor, the friends of Robinson should go for Lane for United States Senator."[9] George W. Brown, however, wrote that the agreement only called for Lane's support in getting some Robinson men to the Topeka convention and that it did not commit Lane and his followers to support Robinson at Topeka.[10] It appears that Robinson did not attend the county convention and that he was not aware of any agreement at that time.

The Topeka convention opened October 12, 1859, with an estimated five hundred Republicans in attendance. Robinson was nominated for governor, and he defeated the Reverend H. P. Johnston on the first ballot by a vote of 43 to 34. The other candidates who were nominated were: J. P. Root, lieutenant governor; J. W. Robinson, secretary of state; George S. Hillyer, auditor; William Tholan, treasurer; B. F. Simpson, attorney general; Martin R. Conway, representative to Congress; and Thomas Ewing, Jr., Chief Justice.

Robinson's Democratic opponent was the incumbent Territorial governor, Samuel Medary. John Brown's ill-conceived action at Harper's Ferry on October 16 and 17, 1859, provided the Democrats with a campaign issue; it also placed the Republicans on the defensive. Medary denounced the Republicans as abolitionists and supporters of John Brown. The Republican candidates tried to convince the electorate that the Democratic party was composed of holdovers from the proslavery "border ruffians." Sol Miller, editor of the White Cloud *Chief*, wrote of the campaign: "Money was squandered freely, slanders were circulated unsparingly, and local prejudices were worked upon incessantly."[11] After the hard-fought campaign, the returns of the election, which was held December 1, 1859, showed that the entire Republican ticket had been elected. Robinson polled 7,908 votes to Medary's 5,395. With the Wyandotte Constitution ratified and state officers elected, settlers still had to wait more than a year before Congress acted to make Kansas a state.

On February 21, 1860, Senator William H. Seward introduced a bill to admit Kansas as a state under the Wyandotte Constitution, but the Democrats were unwilling to add another Republican state prior to the 1860 presidential election. When the bill came up for a vote, Senator Robert T. M. Hunter of Virginia moved to postpone it, and the motion carried. Reaction in Kansas varied at the news of the defeat. While some concerned Kansans thought of calling still another constitutional convention, most of the people were willing to give Congress another chance.[12] The presidential election would be over by the time the next Congress convened, and the major obstruction would thereby have been removed.

The delay was welcomed by Lane, who used the year to great advantage in building his political strength. In the election of 1860 Lane was an ardent supporter of Abraham Lincoln. He had met Lincoln in 1859, when the presidential aspirant visited Kansas as a guest of his old friend Mark W. Delahay. After Lincoln's nomination, Delahay went to Springfield to receive instructions for campaigning. Lane followed him East and was also an active campaigner for Lincoln, especially in Indiana and Illinois. Lincoln's election to the presidency not only smoothed the way for the admission of Kansas into the Union, but it later gave Lane a sympathetic national administration to support him in political battles in Kansas.[13]

The Republican victory prior to the convening of the Thirty-sixth Congress of the United States on December 6, 1860, made for an explosive atmosphere when the question of Kansas' admission was introduced by Senator Jacob Collmer of Vermont on December 11, 1860. Again it faced strong Democratic opposition. Debate continued from December 11, 1860, until January 21, 1861. On that day, the senators from Mississippi, Alabama, and Florida withdrew, South Carolina's senators having withdrawn the previous November. After the secession of these Southern states, the vice-president called up the unfinished business of the bill concerning Kansas' admission. It was passed on January 21. The House concurred on January 28, and President Buchanan signed the bill on January 29, 1861.[14]

The news of statehood was received in Kansas with unparalleled jubilation, according to the announcement in the Lawrence *Republican:*

> Two days ago Lawrence was electrified by the announcement of the admission of Kansas to the Union. She had been a Virgin Territory so long, we feared the fate of all overripe maidens; but as some women, like fruit, are sweetest just before they begin to decay, Kansas, in her maturity, was more attractive than in her youth. . . . Let men shout till the welkin rings; let women smile till the prairies blossom and the birds sing as though it were not winter.[15]

Throughout the new state the hardships that the people were enduring were briefly interrupted by cannon firings, bonfires, speeches, and resolutions. For, despite the merrymaking and jubilation, the child had truly arrived "bawling and hungry."[16] It was little consolation that Charles Robinson would assume the state's highest office "with more prestige than a Governor ever had since the days when Isaiah sang his peon [*sic*] over young Hezekiah's accession."[17] On February 9, 1861, when word was officially received from Washington that Kansas had been admitted to the Union, he was sworn into office by Caleb S. Pratt, county clerk of Douglas County. As his first official act, Governor Robinson issued a proclamation calling the legislature to convene at Topeka on Tuesday, March 26, 1861.[18]

A controversy immediately erupted over the time lag in convening the state legislature. Robinson said that vacancies in the legislature had to be filled in a special election. His opponents, however, accused him of delaying the call for personal reasons. One newspaper editor was severe in his accusations and listed several reasons for the delay: "We understand the Governor wants to be Commissioner of Indian Affairs. He wants Mr. Lincoln to make all his appointments before our legislature meets. . . . This dodge is to kill off all Senatorial appointments. He is hostile toward Lane."[19] While all the reasons stated were true to some degree, the first was perhaps the primary one—Robinson did have designs on the office of Commissioner of Indian Affairs.

In the early winter of 1860, Robinson had traveled to Washington, ostensibly to attempt to secure relief for drought-stricken

Kansas in the form of an appropriation from Congress. Finding time to lobby for some of his own railroad interests, he reported his progress to his business associate, Thomas Ewing, Jr., of Leavenworth. Ewing replied on November 22, 1860. His letter contained an indication that both Robinson's and Ewing's interests encompassed more than relief and railroads. Ewing wrote to Robinson that he needed to talk matters over privately and that Robinson should not commit himself about any Kansas affairs, "for I have some big plans afoot and they may be embarrassed by unlucky appointments."[20] A few weeks later, Robinson wrote to his wife that he had accompanied Eli Thayer to Montgomery Blair's house and that Blair had informed Robinson that he would support him for Commissioner of Indian Affairs. Robinson went on to say that no one who was being considered for the position of secretary of the interior would be likely to turn down his request for a commissionership. "Unless men lie beyond all comprehension I don't see how I can fail of the appointment." The next day, Robinson left for Kansas with everything looking *"first rate."*[21] Such reports evidently pleased Mrs. Robinson, who was vacationing with her mother in Belchertown, Massachusetts. Since she had not enjoyed her first years in Kansas, she left little doubt about where she preferred to live, writing:

> I sometimes thought that I may have done wrong in favoring—perhaps urging you to advance your claims for an office in Washington. One can walk safely there, live as pure a life as in the most retired place and the light coming from a position at Washington would be a beacon to many more than in the latter circumstances.[22]

Meanwhile, Ewing prepared to go to Washington in order to further espouse Robinson's cause, thinking that if Robinson were appointed commissioner, he himself could win the senatorial contest. If Robinson failed to receive an appointment, Ewing forecast that his own bid for office would probably be defeated by a combination of Lane and Pomeroy.[23] Robinson was concerned about attempts by his archenemy, James Lane, to destroy his influence in Washington. In a letter to his wife on January 11, Robinson wrote that Lane was undertaking a "personal fight on me." But he concluded that he could "by paying a little attention to the matter make him smell worse than ever."[24]

Nevertheless, it was Lane's proponents who led the attack on Robinson's decision to postpone the convening of the legislature until March 26. Led by the pro-Lane Leavenworth *Herald*, Lane's forces argued that the governor had no right to make a move toward filling any vacancies until the legislature had informed him that they existed. Defenders ably countered that since the situation was not specifically covered in the Wyandotte Constitution, the clause empowering the governor to "convene the Legislature and do all things else necessary to complete the active organization of the state" more than justified the governor's action.[25]

While the Lane-Robinson feud got warmer, the national conflict between the North and the South drew closer. Only three days after taking office, Governor Robinson appointed a close friend, George W. Deitzler, to serve as the Kansas delegate to the Virginia Peace Convention—a conference of representatives from twenty-one states, which met in Washington, D.C. Robinson himself departed a week later for the capital on a personal political mission. Robinson had observed in January that a strong movement was under way "for the purposes of destroying my influence at Washington."[26] In addition to countering such influences, he also made a final effort at securing the post of Commissioner of Indian Affairs. Upon his arrival in Washington, Robinson learned that President-elect Lincoln had promised the position to William P. Dole of Illinois. Robinson's failure to obtain the position brought the charge from several of his enemies that the governor was "not in favor with the new administration."[27]

A disappointed Robinson returned from Washington in time to convene the legislature in Topeka on March 26. Topeka was then a town of only eight hundred people, so the state government had poor accommodations. The governor's office and the Senate occupied a downtown building known as Museum Hall. The House of Representatives met in the Congregational church. Desks in the legislative chambers consisted of "small tables, covered with the meanest cotton velvet," scattered around the room. Throughout the session a fierce wind blew, which did little to alleviate the legislature's situation. One observer vividly described the atmosphere:

> Pipes were blown from our mouths; tobacco quids sent whirling from annoyed cheeks; . . . hedges transplanted; bumble bees confused and gophers taken bodily from their holes. We found Topeka full of dust and politicians. . . . If a man spits in Topeka while maintaining the usual altitude, the fluid salivation is carried by the wind and deposited all over the good clothes of his companions.[28]

Factional politics were quite evident as state officers and legislators gathered in Topeka. Along with the lawmakers there were candidates for the position of United States senator. Local politicians had reached the understanding that one United States senator would be elected from north of the Kansas River and one from south of it.[29] Frederick P. Stanton and James Lane were the leading candidates from south of the river; Thomas Ewing, Jr., Marcus J. Parrott, and Samuel C. Pomeroy were the principal rivals from the north. Governor Robinson supported Stanton and Ewing. They were both conservative Republicans, and all three shared mutual interests in the Leavenworth, Pawnee and Western Railroad.

Robinson had hoped to defeat Lane's candidacy through the position of Commissioner of Indian Affairs, from which he could control local political patronage. For this reason, Robinson had held off convening the legislature as long as possible, but his plan did not go undiscovered. A correspondent of the St. Louis *Missouri Republican* wrote in February:

> If the State Legislature is called at an early day, Lane will certainly be elected Senator, so the Governor announces his intention of not convening it before spring, no doubt devoutly hoping some combination may be formed before that time to defeat his enemy.[30]

When he discovered what Robinson was planning, Lane made an agreement with Marcus J. Parrott for political cooperation.

At first, Pomeroy preferred to act independently, counting on his work with the Kansas Relief Committee in 1860 to give him the necessary support. But when the Lane-Parrott combination broke apart over a resolution that would have allowed each house to elect senators separately, a new Pomeroy-Lane combination was effected.

The legislature, in joint session, proceeded to elect the United States senators on April 4. The procedure that was agreed upon stated that as the secretary of the Senate called the roll, members should rise and announce their choices for two candidates. The same procedure was then to be followed by the Clerk of the House, after which the Speaker of the House and the President of the Senate would announce the results. Mass confusion reigned for more than two hours. One observer was reported to have remarked: "Of the 98 members, 58 changed their votes from one to six times; the record shows 297 votes, of which 76 occurred in the Senate, and 221 in the House, being an average of a little more than three to each member."[31] The vote for Lane fluctuated between forty-nine and sixty-four. Robinson observed that before and during the election "every appliance was used . . . , such as bribery with money and bribery with promise of office, flattery, threats, and every weapon that promised to procure a vote."[32] When the voting had finally ceased and the results had been announced, Lane had fifty-five votes; Pomeroy, fifty-two; Parrott, forty-nine; and Stanton, forty-nine; there was also a scattering of votes for Isaac, Kingman, Delahay, Conway, and Huston. It was declared that Lane and Pomeroy had been elected.

Lane's victory proved to be a mortal blow to the Robinson faction of the Kansas Republican party. The office of senator carried with it most of the patronage power in the state. It also placed Lane close to the Lincoln administration. Among Robinson followers there was little doubt of the significance. George W. Brown lowered the American flag above the *Kansas State Journal* building to half-mast the day after the election.

After the election, the governor and the legislature settled down to business. Robinson had little time for personal political battles. He was beset with office seekers; border warfare resulting from jayhawking activities threatened to erupt in southern Kansas; and the Union was on the verge of civil war. It was under difficult circumstances, therefore, that Robinson began the task of setting the government in motion.

In his first message to the joint legislature, on March 30, 1861, Robinson briefly traced the history of the Territory. He reported that the indebtedness of the new state was, at the minimum, more than $100,000, and he called upon the federal government either to reimburse the people of Kansas for debts incurred in the holding of several constitutional conventions or to pay taxes on federal land within the state. He also recommended that the legislature soon "provide for an apportionment of the members of the legislature, and for submitting the question of the permanent location of the capital to vote of the people." Other specific actions suggested for starting state government were: the establishment of a common school fund, to be provided for by selling a portion of the school lands; the creation of a state court system; immediate funding of the legitimate Territorial debt; the reduction of membership in the House of Representatives from sixty-eight to forty-five, and in the Senate from twenty-three to fifteen; and, finally, the formation of a codifying commission to revise existing laws. Reaction to the message was generally favorable—that it was "just what it ought to be coming from the Governor of a new and poor, but a free and enlightened state."[33]

The governor's first priority, however, was to get the new state ready for war. Two days after the firing on Fort Sumter on April 14, Robinson received a letter from his friend and advisor George Deitzler, urging him to take immediate action and warning him of the potential danger to Kansas: "Why not telegraph the President that Kansas will furnish 1,000 or more troops if required? Secession flags are being raised all over Missouri. We must be ready for war."[34] On the seventeenth of April, Governor Robinson wrote to President Lincoln, stating: "Kansas will furnish 1,000 men for the enforcement of the laws, if desired."[35] Kansans were mostly pro-Union and were often emotional in their sympathies. On April 18 the steamboat *New Sam Gaty*, out of St. Louis, arrived at the former proslavery town of Leavenworth, flying a rebel flag. A large crowd gathered at the levee and forced the captain to take down the flag. By the end of April, Union military companies had been formed in nearly every Kansas county.

With the outbreak of civil war, a new dimension was added to the Lane-Robinson political fighting. Who would control the military patronage in Kansas? Traditionally, the chief executive of the state controlled the calling of troops and the commissioning of officers in the state militia. But Lane, a former officer in the Mexican War, was not a man to stand by and let Robinson use his power to gain political strength. Three days after President Lincoln issued his first call, Lane organized the Frontier Guard. This was a group of approximately one hundred men from Kansas who were either officeholders, members of Congress, or individuals who were in Washington seeking political appointments. Lane offered the services of this group to the secretary of war, and from April 11, 1861, until May 3, 1861, this quasi-military force guarded the president in the White House. One observer provided this vivid description of the Frontier Guard as it began its active duty:

> At dusk they filed into the famous east room, clad in citizens' dress, but carrying very new, untarnished muskets, and following Lane, brandishing a sword of irreproachable brightness. Here ammunition boxes were opened and cartridges dealt out; and after spending the evening in an exceedingly rudimentary squad drill, under the light of the gorgeous gas chandeliers, they disposed themselves in picturesque bivouac on the brilliant-patterned velvet carpet. . . . Their motley composition, their anomalous surroundings, the extraordinary emergency, their mingled awkwardness and earnestness, rendered the scene a medley of bizarre contradictions.[36]

The contribution made by Lane and his Frontier Guard was a small one so far as the immediate situation was concerned, but it did mark the strengthening of a political acquaintance with the president that provided Lane with some prestige and influence in his battles with Robinson.[37]

Meanwhile, Governor Robinson and the legislature were

attempting to create the laws that were vital to state government. Much rivalry between towns and special interest groups was evident in the legislative body. Among the first items to be decided were the locations of various state institutions. A minor dispute arose over the location of the penitentiary, but ultimately it was located at Lansing. A more controversial bill was the one concerning the permanent location of the state capital. While the constitution called for the legislature to submit the question to popular vote, the consideration of several bills was required before a solution could be found. The final bill, which was prepared by Andrew Stark of Linn County, passed the House on May 20, 1861. In the Senate it was considered along with the bills to locate the penitentiary and the state university, and several attempts were made to connect the three decisions in the interest of certain towns. The final act provided for an election to be held November 5, 1861, and annually thereafter, if necessary, until one location received the majority of all votes cast.

The site for the state university was discussed in both sessions of the legislature during the Robinson administration without a solution being reached. The first legislature wanted to locate it at Manhattan, but Robinson vetoed that bill and was accused of doing so because he preferred Lawrence. He justified his action by stating that the bill was unfair because it was based upon a proposed donation of land which other communities had not had an opportunity to make and that it was untimely because the state had no funds available for a state university. The legislature attempted to override the veto but could only get thirty-eight of the fifty-eight votes that were needed.[38]

The judicial system of the state was set up by a series of acts, beginning with one establishing district courts, which was approved by Governor Robinson on April 25, 1861. They were made courts of record and were given jurisdiction in all cases in which jurisdiction had not been previously granted to justices of the peace. The Supreme Court was organized, and its jurisdiction was defined, in an act approved May 21, 1861, although it did not hold its first regular session until January, 1862.

Justice courts and probate courts were organized in acts passed on May 22, 1861, and June 3, 1861, respectively.[39]

The first legislative session also implemented acts setting forth the powers and duties of state officers, passed legislation retaining the civil and criminal codes adopted by the Territorial legislature of 1859, provided for the organization of new counties, and authorized bond issues that were designed to help Kansas out of its financial difficulties.[40]

Not all the work of the first session, however, involved the critical needs of creating a state organization. After the initial flurry of public-interest bills, a few private-interest bills were introduced, one of which drew the governor's first veto. The bill was written "to prevent injury to dogs."[41] Perhaps bills such as this prompted one correspondent to write, some time after the legislature had been in session:

> Life at the capitol is rapidly growing weary, stale and unprofitable. No moving incident by flood or field occurs to diversify the monotony of existence, and the days drag slowly by between legislative halls and beer saloons, between bed and board, morning devotions and evening sacrifice.[42]

The first legislature adjourned on June 4, 1861.

The remainder of Robinson's first year in office and, in fact, his whole administration, saw a continuing struggle with his arch rival, Senator James H. Lane, over control of patronage and political power. There was hardly a middle ground as Kansans strongly favored either Robinson or Lane. In May of 1861 the Leavenworth *Conservative* wrote: "On all public questions there is the Robinson version and the Lane version."[43]

After disbanding the Frontier Guard in early May of 1861, Lane returned to Kansas, while rumors ran rampant about a possible invasion from Missouri. Robinson reacted to the rumors by issuing a proclamation calling for all male citizens of the proper age in Kansas to organize themselves into military units and report to General Lyman Allen at Lawrence for the purpose of defending the state from a possible invasion.[44] Lane urged aggressive action against Missouri, advising that there should be armed occupation of border towns on the Missouri side if that state should secede. He assured his constituents that he would serve in any capacity, "from drill master up."[45]

The crisis passed when the Confederate Army under Calib Jackson, which was traveling west through Missouri toward Kansas, swung south into Arkansas. The political turmoil, however, did not subside. Lane returned to Washington at the end of June. Having ingratiated himself with Lincoln, he asked for and secured authorization from the War Department to organize two or more Kansas regiments. On the same day, Lincoln wrote to the secretary of war, requesting that Lane be appointed a brigadier general of volunteers.

A few days later, Lane publicly notified Kansas of his appointment, and he appealed to men of his and adjoining states to join the Kansas brigade. He further announced that all regiments organized under this authorization would be allowed to elect their own officers by popular vote, a plan that was deliberately intended to undermine the governor's authority and prestige.[46] Robinson countered Lane's announcement by appointing F. P. Stanton as the senator from Kansas, to succeed Lane. Robinson did not wait for a resignation, which Lane had no intention of giving. Robinson based his action on the provision of the U.S. Constitution that prohibits the occupancy of two offices simultaneously. Therefore, on July 12, 1861, Senator Solomon Foot of Vermont presented the credentials of F. P. Stanton as the senator to replace Lane. Lane rose to defend himself, by claiming that so long as his commission had not been recorded nor his oath filed, he had not accepted the position. The Judiciary Committee finally decided to give Lane a further hearing and to defer action until the Senate adjourned. This left Lane free to continue his military plans. He subsequently organized three regiments, which were known as Lane's Brigade.

Lane returned to Kansas in mid August, 1861, proceeding directly to Fort Scott to assume command of his brigade. Shortly after his arrival, he announced that the town of Fort Scott was vulnerable to attack, and he set the men to work on a new fortification twelve miles away, which he named Fort Lincoln. During the following two months, Lane destroyed Missouri border towns that had welcomed secession. On September 22 Lane's army entered Osceola, a Missouri border town with a population of two to three thousand people. After confiscating all that his army could carry in the way of food and equipment, Lane ordered that the town be destroyed. The courthouse, along with its records, and all but three houses were burned to the ground.[47]

Governor Robinson denounced Lane's activities. He labeled the destruction of Osceola an act of plunder, robbery, and arson. Lane was furious at Robinson for making the charges. He wrote President Lincoln on October 9:

> I . . . succeeded in raising and marching against the enemy as gallant and effective an army, in proportion to its numbers, as ever entered the field. . . . Governor Charles Robinson . . . has constantly, in season and out of season, vilified myself and abused the men under my command as marauders and thieves.[48]

Then Lane made a series of public speeches in which he assailed Governor Robinson. In one notable speech in Leavenworth, he professed that his cause was one that was being carried out only for the welfare, defense, and protection of Kansas. Then he denounced Robinson in the following manner:

> When I was here last, I said I would co-operate with Robinson in any measures necessary for the defense of Kansas. Did I not? ("Yes," "Yes"). When 12,000 rebels assailed us in Southern Kansas, I asked Gov. Robinson to call out the militia. He did so, and the only reply Robinson made was that Cols. Johnson, Ritchie, and others—as good as we have—*had no commissions.*
>
> But now we have the evidence of his treason. Shall I go into detail? Shall I tell you how these men have done everything against you, nothing for you? I cannot get a force, I cannot ask for a gun. . . . [49]

The speeches and appeals against Robinson were part of a more direct attack against Robinson on which Lane was working. He disclosed his plan for unseating the governor at a meeting of the Republican State Committee held in Topeka on

October 16, 1861. The day before the committee met, the Leavenworth *Daily Conservative* announced that a public petition had been circulated and signed by more than three thousand voters in Kansas, demanding an election of state officers. It read as follows:

> We, the undersigned citizens, suffering in common with others from the impotency or malice of the present State Executive, and earnestly desiring a State Government that will, in a patriotic and energetic manner, defend our people from invasion—knowing that by the plain and emphatic provisions of the State Constitution the term of our State officers expires on the first day of January, and that the legislature enactment continuing the State officers beyond that time is null and void, and that there is not sufficient time, before the election, to hold a Nominating Convention, do respectfully pray your honorable body to nominate a full State ticket of efficient Union men, without reference to their political antecedents—men who will conduct the State Government with reference to the good of the whole country, and not upon mere personal grounds.[50]

The following day the committee met and nominated a full State Union Ticket, which was headed by George A. Crawford, a Lane Republican from Bourbon County, for governor.

The Lane faction based the call for an election upon Article I, Section 1, of the Wyandotte Constitution, which stated that officers should hold office for the term of two years from the second Monday of January after their election. Since the first election had been held in December, 1859, they argued that the terms of the present state officers would expire on the second Monday of January 1862.

The campaign that followed was short. Crawford traveled from town to town in an effort to gain votes. Robinson, on the other hand, ignored the election, resting his case on the law and the proper interpretation of it. In the election, which was held on November 5, 1861, the State Board of Canvassers, composed of Governor Robinson, H. R. Dutton, and Charles Chadwick, refused to report the results for the disputed offices. The only recourse for Crawford was to appeal to the Kansas Supreme

Court. On January 14, 1862, the decision was handed down; it upheld Robinson by declaring that "the election for governor in 1861 was illegal."[51]

Thus, Lane's scheme to have Robinson removed from office had failed, and the governor had survived his first year in office. His record was not particularly impressive, though it must be pointed out that few men have ever assumed the office of governor under more unfavorable circumstances than did Charles Robinson. National political turmoil, a state economy that was on the verge of bankruptcy, and strong political opposition on the state level were some of the major factors in 1861 which contributed to making Charles Robinson's governorship one of the stormiest on record in Kansas. His political battles with Lane accomplished little for either the state or himself. It had been a year of trial and turmoil, and, unfortunately for Kansas, it was but a prelude to the second year of Robinson's administration.

6

The Triumph of Lane

The Civil War created new problems in Kansas, and it complicated old ones. The major internal problem was the financial
condition of the state. Governor Robinson later wrote: "At the
admission of the State into the Union not a dollar was found in
the Treasury nor a gun or a pound of ammunition in its
armory."[1] Kansas had not recovered from the drought and
famine of 1859–1860 before the war started. Externally, settlers
in western Missouri threatened to invade. To the west and south,
Kansas faced another threat of invasion from Indians who were
sympathetic to the Confederacy, particularly the Cherokee and
Osage tribes.[2] Settlers in southeastern Kansas were also threatened by organized bands of thieves and outlaws, which raided
settlements on both sides of the Missouri-Kansas border in the
name of either the Confederate or the Union cause. Governor
Robinson placed the blame for many of these "jayhawking" activities on men who attached themselves to Lane's Brigade. He
was supported in his accusations by Maj. Gen. H. W. Halleck,
who wrote the following letter to Gen. George B. McClellan on
December 19, 1861:

> The conduct of the forces under Lane and [Col. Charles]
> Jennison has done more for the enemy in this State than
> could have been accomplished by twenty thousand of his

own army. I receive almost daily complaints of outrages committed by these men in the name of the United States, and the evidence is so conclusive as to leave no doubt of their correctness. It is rumored that Lane has been made a brigadier-general. I cannot conceive of a more injudicious appointment, . . . it is offering a premium for rascality and robbing generally.[3]

In January, 1862, Governor Robinson explained to the legislature why he was unable to protect the settlers along the border. The previous legislature had granted no appropriations for arming, equipping, or maintaining an adequate state militia. Because of this, he had not been able to respond to the hundreds of calls for assistance. He claimed that he had made attempts to organize a militia, but that he had been unable to furnish it with provisions. The governor also reopened the question of Lane's holding the office of U.S. Senator and the rank of brigadier general simultaneously. He argued that since Lane had received an appointment as brigadier general and since it had been confirmed by the Senate, there was a senatorial vacancy for the legislature to fill in its 1862 session.[4]

Robinson lost both of his contentions. The U.S. Senate reconsidered the question of Lane's position on the fifteenth of January, 1862. The original motion stated that Lane was not entitled to his seat. But a motion made to strike out the word "not" carried by a vote of 24-to-16. Senator Lane was again free to continue his military plans.[5]

The governor fared no better with the Kansas lawmakers. In March, 1862, he again warned the legislature of the danger faced by the settlers along the eastern border. Most of the federal troops in Kansas had been ordered South to reinforce the Union Army in Arkansas. The governor's words were:

It is for the legislature to decide whether, in any emergency, the Executive shall have the means to protect the State, or whether it shall be left powerless, as during the past year. The responsibility is entirely with you gentlemen. My duty is accomplished when I have informed you of the condition of the State.[6]

A bill was introduced in the House to provide an appropriation for the protection of border settlers, but it failed to pass.

Control of finances and military patronage were obviously the factors at the heart of the Robinson-Lane conflict. Robinson challenged Lane's position in the Senate in an attempt to keep him out of the state military arena. General Lane was never subtle in either military or political affairs, and his efforts to thwart Robinson were always obvious. He used any available influence to strip Robinson of authority, and the Kansas legislature was one of his most useful tools. He had enough supporters in the legislature to attack Robinson's administration, even enough to bring impeachment charges against the governor and other elected officials.

Shortly after the admission of Kansas to the Union, the critical financial situation had prompted the legislature to issue bonds. It voted two issues, $150,000 in 7 percent bonds and $20,000 in 10 percent bonds. The bill authorized Austin M. Clark and James M. Stone of Leavenworth to negotiate the sale of the bonds. When Clark and Stone failed to sell them within seventy days, the legislature passed a supplementary bill, which authorized the governor, the secretary of state, and the auditor, or a majority of them, to sell $100,000 of state bonds for not less than 70 cents on the dollar.[7]

The state had difficulty in finding a buyer for the bonds. Governor Robinson wrote and telegraphed Eastern brokers, but he received no offers. The famine of 1860, which had brought business nearly to a standstill, had impaired the state's credit. Potential investors also feared that Kansas might yet be compelled to join the Confederacy because of the influence of Missouri. Kansas was not the only state with financial problems. Minnesota, Wisconsin, and Iowa were selling some of their bonds at forty cents on the dollar. In this situation, the treasurer of Kansas, H. R. Dutton, went to New York to sell the bonds, but he found no buyers. On his way back to Kansas, Dutton stopped at Buffalo, New York, where he met Robert S. Stevens of Lawrence, a business friend of Governor Robinson's, who was on his way to Washington. Stevens bought $31,000 worth of the 10 percent bonds from Dutton for 40 cents on the dollar. Stevens also took $29,000 worth of the 7 percent bonds to Washington, after giving Dutton a receipt for them. When he arrived in Washington, Stevens sold $26,000 worth of the 10 percent bonds to Caleb B. Smith, secretary of the interior, at 95 cents on the dollar. As Stevens had paid only 40 cents on the dollar, he made $14,300 profit in the transaction and thus became interested in obtaining more Kansas bonds.[8]

When Stevens returned to Kansas, he met with the state officials to discuss the purchase of more bonds. The secretary of state and the auditor reasoned that they had the right to sell $50,000 worth of the 7 percent bonds at 40 cents on the dollar and the $100,000 worth of state bonds that were covered by the Supplementary Act at 70 cents on the dollar. Accordingly, they arranged with Stevens to sell the $50,000 worth of the 7 percent bonds at 40 cents and $37,000 worth of the 10 percent bonds at 70 cents on the dollar. When the proposition was presented to the governor, he agreed to sign only $29,000 worth of the 7 percent bonds for sale to Stevens. These were sent to Washington with Stevens.[9]

At the same time, Senator Samuel Pomeroy wrote to Secretary of State J. W. Robinson that there was a chance to sell the state bonds, and he asked Robinson to send all that were available. Pomeroy was acting on information that he had received in a conversation with Secretary Smith, Stevens's customer. Secretary Robinson and the state auditor, George Hillyer, gathered up the available bonds and departed for Washington at the end of October, 1861. When they arrived, Pomeroy advised them that negotiations should be left in the hands of Robert Stevens, who should be made agent of the state.[10] Accordingly, an agreement was drawn up which read in part as follows:

> The undersigned, Executive officers of this State, authorized by law to dispose of, and sell, the seven percent bonds, . . . do hereby constitute and appoint Robert S. Stevens, Esq., an agent to sell and dispose of said Bonds, giving him, the said Stevens, full power and authority to negotiate, dispose of, and sell the entire issue of said $150,000 of said Bonds, for the benefit of the State of Kansas, hereby ratifying . . . all . . . and whatever said Stevens may do in the premises.[11]

The agreement allegedly contained the signatures of Charles Robinson, J. W. Robinson, and George S. Hillyer, but J. W. Robinson had signed the governor's name. Although Governor Robinson had discussed the matter with J. W. Robinson and Hillyer before they had departed for Washington, he testified that he had not authorized anybody to use his official signature. Rather, he said, he had told them that "any arrangement for the sale of bonds that they might make *according to law* [he] would approve of."[12]

Stevens, on the strength of this agreement, began negotiations with officials of the Department of the Interior, who expressed willingness to purchase the bonds with money from a fund held in trust for certain Indian tribes. On December 14 the secretary of the interior wrote to the president, informing him that the United States was holding in trust $40,000 for the Kaskaskia Indians and $15,000 for the Iowa Indians, which, according to the treaties of 1854, the president might invest. The secretary asked the president for his opinion on investing the money in Kansas bonds, which were offered at 85 cents on the dollar. The president answered that he would concur if the Kansas delegation would acquiesce in the sale and if the secretary of the interior thought that it was a safe investment.[13] Both Pomeroy and Congressman Conway immediately signed a letter of approval. Lane hesitated because of Stevens's connection with Governor Robinson. By paying Lane's secretary $1,000, Stevens was able to obtain Lane's signature. Lane at first denied ever having signed the paper, but later he admitted that he might have signed it without reading its contents.[14]

The transaction was completed on December 18, 1861. According to later testimony, Senator Pomeroy advised the state officers to accept 60 cents on the dollar for the sale of the bonds. The state officers believed that if they failed to sell the bonds to the federal government, they would lose their last chance for a sale. Both Hillyer and Secretary Robinson claimed that they did not know that Stevens was getting 85 cents on the dollar, or a 25 cent profit.[15]

Believing their task accomplished, J. W. Robinson and Hillyer returned to Kansas in Late December, 1861. Hillyer, on the return trip, was so pleased that he reportedly commented, "Won't the people of Kansas think we are kings?"[16]

But the jubilation was short-lived. On the sixth day of the new legislative session the state representative from Nemaha County proposed the following resolution:

> Resolved, That the Governor of the State be requested to communicate to this House any information in his possession, relating to the sale of the $20,000 war bonds, authorized to be issued by the act of May 7, 1861; and also in relation to the sale of $150,000 of bonds authorized to be issued under the law passed May 3, 1861, setting forth—first, by whom sold; second, when sold; third, to whom sold; fourth, at what price sold.[17]

Lane had also returned to Kansas, and his knowledge of and involvement in the bond sale made him a key figure in presenting this resolution. He may have returned to Kansas to consult with his constituents, as he claimed, but the evidence points to the fact that he intended to use the bond sale for another attack on Governor Robinson. John J. Ingalls wrote his father about his views on the situation shortly after the news of the investigation was made public.

> He [Lane] knew of this fraud on the part of our officials. There is no doubt that he participated in the profits; but his audacity is volcanic. The people detest Governor Robinson, and Lane, in order to divert attention from his own ridiculous failure, and at the same time gain additional reputation as the friend of the masses reveals this speculation and urges the impeachment as a duty owed to the State. . . . I had a long conversation with him yesterday in which he told me that the failure of his [military] Expedition was owing to the malignity of Governor Robinson; a statement so ridiculous to anyone who knows the facts, that it could receive no reply. He sat on the side of the bed in his room, whittling an oak stick with a full pen knife, looking like the last remnants of an humble petition. Baffled, beaten, disgraced, there were none so poor to do him justice.[18]

Governor Robinson referred the resolution of the State

House of Representatives to George Hillyer and John Robinson. Upon receiving their reply to the questions, the House appointed a special committee to investigate the matter. Two weeks later, the special committee, charged with determining whether or not state officers were involved in speculating with official funds, unanimously asked the House to adopt this resolution of impeachment: *"Resolved,* That Charles Robinson, Governor, John W. Robinson, Secretary of State, and George S. Hillyer, Auditor of the State of Kansas, be and they are hereby impeached of high misdemeanors in office."[19]

When the announcement reached the public, emotions ran high, and sentiment was overwhelmingly against the three state officials. In areas where there was a particularly strong Lane following, editorial sentiments reflected political fanaticism:

> Kansas, so recently a pauper, is robbed by its highest officers. Kansas, depleted by unprecedented drouth, has a pickpocket for governor. Kansas, so true to freedom, has state officers who are only true to robbery. Unless the legislature impeaches and removes these scoundrels from office it will be the religious duty of the people to hang them. And it will be done.[20]

Within two weeks the lower house had drawn articles of impeachment for each of the accused. Eight articles of impeachment were reported for the secretary of state, and seven for the state auditor; both reports were accepted without opposition. In the case of Governor Robinson, five articles of impeachment were reported, and they were adopted by a vote of 53-to-7. The specific charges against Governor Robinson considered by the Senate were:

1. That Governor Charles Robinson, contrary to the law which authorized the issuance of the $20,000 worth of war bonds, signed and issued such bonds to the extent of $40,000;
2. That he, together with J. W. Robinson and Hillyer, conspired with Robert Stevens in the fraudulent sale of the seven per cent bonds;
3. That he, and the other two state officers, knew that the bonds could be sold for 85 per cent par value;

4. That he consented to the sale for 60 per cent par value, when he knew that such sale was contrary to the laws of the state of Kansas;

5. That he officially approved the said sale, and thereby committed an high misdemeanor in office.[21]

The Senate sat as a court of impeachment on February 24, 1862. The prosecution, however, asked for more time, since much of its case depended on depositions from people outside of the state. As a result, Secretary Robinson's trial was scheduled for the first Monday in June, that of Hillyer for Thursday of that week, and Governor Robinson's for the second Monday in June.

Sentiment against the state officers ran exceedingly high among the legislators. According to one member of the House, "It required greater courage to vote 'no' on the question of the impeachment of Gov. Robinson, in the face of the crowd in that old hall, . . . than it did to face an army in battle array."[22]

His forces having been set in motion against the state officers, Lane returned to Washington, D.C., where he continued his campaign to obstruct and discredit the Robinson administration. On April 6, Lane lodged a protest from the "Citizens of Kansas" with Salmon P. Chase, secretary of the treasury, and E. N. Stanton, secretary of war, in an effort to withhold all payments of money due the State of Kansas. It read:

> The undersigned, citizens of Kansas, protest against the payment of money due the State of Kansas for expenses in organizing Volunteer Troops for the Service of the United States, to the present State Treasurer of Kansas, or to any of the officers of the present State Government, or Agent of the same, for reasons deducible from the following statement of facts.[23]

The protest went on to outline the charges of impeachment against the officers, claiming that the state had been robbed of $48,000. It concluded with a request that all payments be withheld:

> The almost entire want of confidence on the part of the people of Kansas in their present State Government, thus

impeached and dishonored in the persons of its highest Executive Officers, induces the undersigned to protest against the payment of any money to the State, till the people shall have elected State Officers in whose integrity they have confidence and to whom their interests can be safely committed.[24]

This was signed by nine individuals, including Lane and three of his close political associates—Mark W. Delahay, William Weer, and Sidney Clarke.

Once the document had been made known, R. S. Stevens sent a dispatch to Robinson, asking him to come to Washington immediately to attempt to clear up the matter. Robinson left Kansas on April 8, hastily writing a note to his wife about his trip. By April 17 he had still not succeeded in freeing the funds that were due the state, but he commented, "I intend to make the fur fly here unless I am permitted to get my business done without hindrance from Lane. He is endeavoring to levy black mail upon everybody."[25]

By April 27 he wrote that his task was nearly completed and that he would return to Kansas just as soon as he had made a quick trip to New York State to look after some personal matters. The quick trip to New York turned into a long stay at Buffalo, however, when Robinson contracted smallpox. It was the end of May before he returned to Kansas.[26]

Shortly after Robinson's return, the Senate reconvened as a court, in accordance with its adjournment resolution of February 28. Between the time of the first adjournment and June 4, when the trial actually began, elections had been held and five new pro-Lane senators had been seated in positions that had been declared vacant. When Lane's tactics first became apparent in February, Sol Miller, editor of the White Cloud *Chief*, informed his readers of what was happening:

> Hitherto, all efforts to oust certain members have failed. But Gen. Lane, instead of attending to his duties in the Senate, is . . . laying the wires to punish his ancient enemy, Gov. Robinson. A great deal of caucusing and manipulating has been observed going on for several days past, and this afternoon the fruits began to be visible. One of the noisiest

anti-Lane Senators suddenly resigned, and another absented himself from his place. The Senate straightway went to work and filled the place of the resigning Senator, by putting in a man of the desired stripe. It is the general impression that the resigned Senator and the absentee have made a good thing of it.[27]

By the time of the trial, Lane had a majority of the senators in his camp. John W. Robinson's case was tried first. Following the opening arguments by the prosecuting managers, depositions were read and witnesses were called. The managers argued that there had been a conspiracy on the part of the officials in an attempt to defraud the state. Counsel for the defense stressed the state's need for money, arguing that the legality of the entire transaction hinged only upon how one interpreted the three statutes of May and June, 1861, which authorized the original bond issues. Arguments ceased on June 13, and the court voted upon the eight articles of impeachment against John Robinson. When the votes were counted, the members of the Senate had sustained the charge in the first article of impeachment, that the state had been defrauded out of its money with the full knowledge and consent of the secretary. He had, therefore, betrayed a trust held by him as an officer of the state. The vote on the first count was 17-to-4. He was not found guilty on any of the other counts. Nevertheless, the vote to remove him from office was 18-to-3 in favor of removal.[28]

The trial of Auditor Hillyer was brief. Since the two officers had cooperated in the selling of the bonds, his case paralleled that of John Robinson, and no new evidence was introduced. The auditor was only found guilty of article one, by the same vote count as was John Robinson, and similarly, he was removed from office.[29]

Governor Robinson's trial commenced in the late afternoon of June 16. Interest, however, was not high, and it was one of the shortest impeachment trials on record, lasting less than two hours. Counsel for the managers spoke only ten minutes, while the counsel for the defense, Wilson Shannon, spoke for five minutes. In Shannon's summary, he said that no claim of complicity had been advanced by the opposition and that all the testimony proved that the governor was not engaged in the transaction. The result was a complete acquittal; only three votes were cast for conviction.[30]

Governor Robinson was justly exonerated, but Lane's followers remained staunch in their efforts to carry on Lane's plan to destroy Robinson politically. The Emporia *News* stated that although the court had failed to convict Governor Robinson, he would stand convicted in the estimation of the people. The editorial went on to suggest that perhaps the matter should be taken before the next session of the Kansas Supreme Court.[31] Supporters of Robinson were equal to the occasion. The editors of the Lawrence *State Journal* proclaimed that the Emporia *News* was seriously ill:

> The *Emporia News* . . . has, within a few weeks back, been seriously taken with the Lane-Phobia, a disease which used to be quite prevalent in the country, but which lately has been gradually dying out. . . . The *News* of last week contains a full report of Lane's great humbug speech in New York. And after Gov. Robinson has been fairly and triumphantly acquitted by a court, composed, in greater part, of his political enemies, it, like a dog returning to his vomit, recharges the Governor with the crimes, of which the court, by an almost unanimous vote, declared him innocent.[32]

Governor Robinson believed that both J. W. Robinson and George Hillyer were victims of a scheme directed toward him. When all avenues for them to retain their offices had been closed, the governor appointed John Robinson, a medical doctor, as a surgeon in the Union Army, and he commissioned Hillyer as a first lieutenant and quartermaster of the Thirteenth Regiment. Neither man survived the war.[33]

Nor did Governor Robinson politically survive the impeachment proceedings. Though Lane had known that there was not enough evidence to convict the governor, his purposes were served by creating the scandal and holding the trial. Governor Robinson was allowed to complete his term, but enough seeds of doubt had been planted in the minds of the electorate to ensure that he would not be reelected. The impeachment proceedings placed Robinson on the defensive, and there he remained for the next several years.

In the few remaining months of his term, however, the governor continued to fight Lane in his efforts to control military patronage in the state. The quarrel reached a climax in August, 1862, in connection with the commissioning of the officers of the newly formed Eleventh, Twelfth, and Thirteenth Kansas regiments. The three regiments were raised under the president's call for troops of July 2, 1862. Secretary of War E. M. Stanton appointed Senator Lane as recruiting commissioner for the Department of Kansas. Lane, in his recruiting proclamation of August 4, 1862, stated: "Those who join this army will designate the men who will command them." Governor Robinson informed Lane that while he was willing to approve of the company officers' being elected, he reserved the right to designate the field and staff officers of the regiments.[34] Lane, therefore, asked Secretary of War Stanton for instructions. Stanton replied to Lane a few days later with the following message: "In reply, you are enacted to report the names of the officers selected to the War Department. The Governor will be requested by the Department to commission them. Upon his refusal, the President will issue commissions."[35]

Governor Robinson, in the meantime, sent Maj. T. B. Eldridge to interview the secretary of war and to inform him of the problems that Lane was creating. The letter that Robinson sent to Stanton through Eldridge read in part:

> Genl. Lane claims full power over recruiting in Kansas. He ignores the State Government, has had no communication with it and is as hostile to it as Jeff Davis is to the Federal Government. Having heard nothing upon the subject of recruiting from the War Department, I desire to learn precisely what authority Genl. Lane possesses and what is desired of the State Executive. . . . I have endeavored to do everything in my power to aid the government in subduing this whole rebellion. . . . No Governor, I dare say, has been so harassed, annoyed, and insulted as I have been by Genl. Lane.[36]

Major Eldridge reported to Robinson on August 28 that he had met with Stanton and had been informed that Lane indeed had full authority to recruit in Kansas.[37] On the same day, Stanton wrote to Robinson: "The extent of that [Lane's] authority and how far the action of General Lane comports with it you can judge as well as anyone else." Enclosed in the letter was a copy of Lane's appointment, which gave him authority "to raise and organize one or more Brigades of Volunteer Infantry, . . . to establish camps, to provide for the maintenance of discipline and the supply of troops with the munitions of war." Stanton concluded his letter to Robinson with an expression of regret that there was trouble between the executive of Kansas and General Lane "at a time when all men should be united in their efforts against the enemy."[38]

The letter from Stanton irritated Robinson greatly. He refused to sign the commissions, and he publicly justified his decision by pointing out that the state executive had the authority to name all officers of state volunteers, that it was a right guaranteed by the Constitution, by the laws, and by the orders of the War Department. When the secretary of war informed Robinson that if the state executive did not commission the officers soon, the War Department would, Robinson curtly replied: "You have the power to override the constitution and the laws, but you have not the power to make the present Governor of Kansas dishonor his State."[39] In the end, the officers were commissioned by the War Department.

With his term of office coming to a close, Robinson became increasingly bitter toward the Lincoln administration. Shortly after leaving office, he wrote to Amos A. Lawrence, expressing his opinion that Lincoln was a "poor weak man" who was used by "demagogues" such as the secretary of war, a "despotic demagogue who would sacrifice the rights of citizens and the country itself to subserve his ends." He concluded that "if Gen. Lee would take the President and Secretary of War prisoners, leaving [Vice-President Hannibal] Hamlin or someone else at the head of the government, I think we should be the gainers."[40]

It is doubtful that President Lincoln actually was aware of Senator Lane's and Secretary Stanton's involvement in the military affairs of Kansas. When Robinson's successor, Governor

Thomas Carney, was faced with a similar situation, he went directly to President Lincoln. The president, in turn, wrote the following letter to Senator Lane on April 27, 1863:

> The Governor of Kansas is here, . . . complaining of the military interference of General Blunt in the late election at Leavenworth. I do not know how, if at all, you are connected with these things; but I wish your assistance to so shape things that the Governor of Kansas may be treated with the consideration that is extended to governors of other states. We are not forcing a regimental officer upon any other governor against his protest.[41]

Had Governor Robinson gone directly to the president several months earlier, Lane's activities might have been curtailed, and some of Robinson's problems might have been avoided.

The state elections of 1862 occurred while Lane was serving as recruiting commissioner for Kansas, and the Lane-Robinson feud carried into the elections. The Republican party held its convention at Topeka on September 17, 1862, and nominated Thomas Carney, a Leavenworth merchant, for governor. Carney was a native of Ohio who had moved to Kansas in 1858. He was supported by Lane in his bid for the nomination. In a speech at Atchison on September 20, Lane praised Carney as a financier and businessman of talent who would redeem "the credit of the state, which had been so seriously injured by the present officers."[42] With regard to the entire Republican ticket, the *Kansas State Journal* commented: "Lane nominated it, Lane owns nearly all the nominees, and Lane says that the people of Kansas shall vote no other ticket. It is a Lane ticket."[43]

Opponents of Lane, including Robinson and his supporters, bolted the ticket and met in Lawrence on September 29, 1862, under the banner of the Union party. The justification for the revolt was expressed as an "uprising" of the people "whose every notion of honor, integrity, and common decency" had been violated. The report of the convention stated that the delegates were in accord on two basic principles—the country had to be saved and the state had to be saved. The former had to be saved from "the dispoiling depredation of Southern traitors, the latter from intrigue and corruption, and the usurpation of blatant demagogues."[44] A series of resolutions passed by the forty delegates from eleven counties called for a united effort to stop the threat of rule by "powerful demagogues." A resolution supporting Robinson was passed, stating that no policies of the current administration were being questioned.

The Emporia *News*, a pro-Lane paper, had a vitriolic editorial on the new political organization, entitled "Union Ass Convention," which read, in part:

> The great Union Convention came off at Lawrence last Monday . . . and it was a Union Convention, sure enough. It was composed in a large degree of sore-headed Republicans, . . . proslavery Democrats, of the old Border-Ruffian stripe, Robinson Democrats and Republicans, milk-and-water Democrats, played-out fogy Democrats, "dead-as-nits" Democrats, Democrats who laugh at every Union defeat and get drunk for joy at every Rebel victory, Robinson men, sour-stomached and dissatisfied Republicans and Abolitionists, who think their plan is the only one that can save the country; and perhaps some other species of conglomerated political fossils whom we have not got down—including the friends of the present State Government.[45]

For governor the Union convention nominated W. R. Wagstaff, a former state legislator and a Democrat. John J. Ingalls of Atchison was the nominee for lieutenant governor, and Marcus J. Parrott of Leavenworth was the nominee for congressman. Two days later the Democratic convention assembled at Topeka and resolved to support the candidates nominated by the Union party.[46]

The ensuing campaign was hard fought, but the majority of Kansans voted the Republican ticket. The result was regarded as a "Lane triumph."[47] The newly elected state officers assumed their responsibilities without ceremony on January 12, 1863. Charles Robinson later wrote that he

> gladly delivered up the executive chair to his successor, Governor Thomas Carney. Enough had been seen and experienced of the management of the war in the West, permitting the most brutal and inhuman outrages, all to

gratify personal greed, malice, or ambition, to disgust any person not entirely given over to subsisting upon human misery.[48]

Robinson's departure from the office marked his absolute break with the Republican party. Lane's triumph was complete. In later years, Robinson was criticized for abandoning the Republican party. Sol Miller, an ardent Republican and a widely quoted Kansas editor, was his strongest critic:

> Gov. Robinson had only to patiently wait, to hold his friends together, and to give Lane a dig in the ribs whenever the opportunity, but expecting to be worsted for a few years. . . . [He] had only to wait, making his fight within the Republican party, and when the time came, as it eventually must, that Lane played out and went under, Robinson would have become the great leader of the Republican party of Kansas—the party would have instinctively turned to and rallied around their first governor.[49]

Charles Robinson was bitter when he left office. He had suffered two years of frustration. While he could take some satisfaction in the knowledge that forces had been set in motion that would enable the state to outgrow its political turmoil and economic strife, the feud with Lane had done nothing to enhance his career. Had their personalities been slightly different, the state might have derived more benefit from the abilities of these two leaders. As it was, Kansas suffered politically throughout another decade from the effects of the Lane-Robinson conflict.

7

Politics and Reform

During the last thirty years of Charles Robinson's life in Kansas he was a political maverick who frequently changed his party affiliations and political connections. And as he maneuvered from party to party, he embraced new causes, which, in many instances, were politically inexpedient. Always a reformer, Robinson now abandoned the pragmatic political philosophy that had enabled him to compromise and bend when he was leading the free-state struggle. By the mid sixties he was a radical reformer. He believed that social and political conditions in Kansas should conform more closely to the ideals of the Declaration of Independence and to the imperatives of man's conscience and the moral law. Robinson applied that spirit to Kansas reform in the 1860s, 1870s, and 1880s. He was involved in every major reform movement that occurred in Kansas between 1865 and 1890. In every cause he championed—woman suffrage, Negro rights, financial reform, opposition to prohibition, and opposition to monopolistic business practices—the theme was always evident. Robinson had a strong faith in man and in man's ability to perfect his institutions. Robinson spelled out his philosophy when he wrote: "Man was designed to be perfect in all his parts, physically, mentally, and morally—he is capable of infinite progressivism and happiness, and he is governed by fixed laws perfectly adapted to his condition."[1]

Since most of the reform efforts were political in nature, Robinson aligned himself with whatever party or group held views nearest his own. His constant shifting, together with his continual opposition to a strong Republican party in Kansas, kept him from holding a dominant position in Kansas politics. The tradition of party regularity has always been a strong force. Still Robinson remained active, he was influential in the state and at times in the nation, and he continued to be a potent force in Kansas political activities and reform movements.

The first noticeable application of Robinson's liberal philosophy was evident on the issue of Negro rights in Kansas. On December 17, 1863, less than a year after he left office, he was invited to speak before a convention of freedmen, which was scheduled to meet in Leavenworth on January 1, 1864. He was asked by the Colored Citizens Committee of Leavenworth to give his views on amending the Kansas Constitution by striking the word "white" in the fifth and eighth articles of the document, thereby extending the franchise to "colored citizens" of Kansas.[2] Although he was unable to attend the meeting, Robinson sent a letter outlining his views and requested that it be read before the assembled delegates. He wrote, in part:

> I can see but one side to the proposition in question. The white and colored people have a common origin, are endowed alike with intellect, with moral and religious natures, and have a common destiny. If this proposition is correct, it follows from necessity that both alike are entitled to equal civil, political, moral, and religious rights, according to the principles laid down in the Declaration of Independence by our ancestors, and according to the immutable laws of God himself, who is no respecter of persons.
>
> No valid argument can be produced against the right of suffrage for the colored man. *Prejudice* has suggested various objections, such as ignorance, vice, etc. But if the Japanese and Hindoos, who know nothing of our language, customs, or institutions, can become sufficiently enlightened in five years to vote, surely the native colored man, after a

pupilage of twenty-one years, ought not to be excluded on account of ignorance. . . .

In closing, permit me to congratulate you and the friends of universal freedom upon the general good conduct of the late slaves now in Kansas. Considering their former conditions and disadvantages, their deportment is truly praiseworthy. Crime among them is comparatively rare, while most are proving to be honest, truthful and industrious. They do not, like some, whose advantages have been superior to their own, interpret liberty to mean license, and become a curse to society.[3]

Robinson restated the same concept to include woman suffrage when, in an undated manuscript answering his own rhetorical questions, he wrote: "Who are the governed? All for whom laws are made. Do the laws apply equally to blacks and females? Then should not they have a voice in the government?"[4]

It is interesting to note the difference between Robinson's attitude in 1855, when the issue of voting rights was being debated by the Topeka constitutional convention, and his stand a decade later. In 1855 he had sacrificed Negro suffrage in order to ensure the abolition of slavery in Kansas. In the mid 1860s Robinson was firm in favoring Negro suffrage despite the political advantage that might have resulted from a different stand.

Robinson championed suffrage for women and Negroes when he came back to the Kansas political scene in 1866. He had taken little part in the 1864 state elections, concluding, after the results were known, that it would have been hopeless to try. "It is claimed they spent $6,000 in this [Douglas] county to carry it for Lane," reported Robinson, "the *Sheisters* are in a working majority in this state, and I think here Lane is a true representative of the people."[5] Perhaps some of Robinson's bitterness left him when Lane ended his own life on July 1, 1866. James Lane had been charged, in 1865, with financial irregularities while serving as a United States senator. As a result of the charges and subsequent scandal, he shot himself.[6] News of the suicide prompted S. C. Smith, a long-time friend of Robinson's, to encourage him to get back into politics, so that he could "go to the Senate to fight against [President] Johnson."[7] Others also suggested that Robinson consider running for political office again, for on November 9, 1866, Robinson wrote to Samuel N. Wood, stating that he had supposed himself through with politics entirely, but some of his friends were urging him to run for the United States Senate.[8] The Kansas legislature of 1867 was required to elect two senators, because, in addition to the Lane vacancy, Senator Samuel Pomeroy's term had expired. The support expected by Robinson failed to materialize when the legislature convened in January, 1867. Pomeroy was reelected, and Edmund G. Ross was chosen to fill the unexpired term.

Even though the legislature failed to make Robinson a U.S. senator, the defeated candidate remained vitally interested in the 1867 session. Gov. Samuel J. Crawford, in his annual message, advocated the submission of two constitutional amendments to the people. One would have provided for Negro suffrage and the other would have disenfranchised persons who had been enemies of the government during the rebellion. The legislature accepted the governor's recommendations and then added a third —woman suffrage. A special election was scheduled for November 5, 1867, and Robinson actively campaigned for the adoption of the two suffrage amendments.

The campaign to enfranchise women and Negroes began in late 1866 with the formation of the Lawrence Impartial Suffrage Association. Robinson was named president of the organization; working closely with him was Samuel N. Wood.[9] After the amendments had been approved by the legislature for submission to the voters, a statewide Impartial Suffrage Association was formed, with Gov. Samuel Crawford as president and Lt. Gov. Nehemiah Green as vice-president. The influence of the Lawrence group was plainly evident, as Sam Wood was named corresponding secretary and Charles Robinson was elected to the state executive committee.[10] While Negro suffrage was favored by the association, its main emphasis was on female suffrage.

Initially the organization attempted to give equal support to both franchise amendments, and it distributed widely a circular that read:

We are satisfied that an argument in favor of colored suffrage is an argument in favor of woman suffrage. Both are based upon the same principle. It is the doctrine of our fathers "that governments derive their just powers from the consent of the governed." We "white" men have no right to ask privileges or demand rights for ourselves that we are not willing to grant to the whole human family. There never has been, and never can be, an argument, based upon principle, against colored or woman suffrage."[11]

The 1867 campaign was a bitter one. Editors of leading newspapers took sides, and name-calling became prevalent. The first lines from an article in the Emporia *News* gave supporters of the amendments an indication of the type of editorial opposition they could expect: "Next to the grasshopper humbug, in point of damage to the State, is this question of Female Suffrage. It is the most impudent, uncalled-for proposition ever crammed into the throats of the people, by a shystering legislature."[12]

To counter such attacks, national advocates of woman suffrage came to Kansas in the spring of 1867, among them Lucy Stone and her husband, Henry B. Blackwell, who spoke widely throughout eastern Kansas. Robinson, who knew Lucy Stone well, because one of his sisters was then married to her brother, escorted them to several lectures in Lawrence and surrounding towns. He reported to Sam Wood on April 15 that "the cause is prospering finely." He concluded that the people in both Leavenworth and Lawrence would vote for the propositions the following November, but warned that some of the ministers in Lawrence were speaking out on the female-suffrage question, appearing "to be against it or lukewarm."[13]

The favorable reaction that was evident in Lawrence and Leavenworth was not as apparent in other Kansas towns. C. V. Eskridge was carrying on a strong campaign against the female-suffrage amendment in Emporia. In an article that he wrote for the Emporia *News*, Eskridge claimed that granting such rights would ruin the entire family structure and would eventually affect all of society. He warned that the end results would be that a man's children would be taken from his control and that his wife would become common property. He concluded with the following prophecy:

> I tell you fathers, mothers, sisters, brothers, husbands and wives, this is the tendency of this proposition, and into this it would finally run, just as surely as the revolt of angels ended in their consignment to the bottomless pit.
>
> Then these petticoated old Eves, whom kiln-dried lightning would glance from, and whose faces would prevent a dog from biting them, would rollick in the general demoralization of society. . . . "O, happy state! Now souls each other draw, For *love* is liberty and nature law."[14]

Bitter personal attacks were levied against Sam Wood in particular. He was charged with being interested in woman suffrage in order to defeat Negro suffrage. The editor of the Topeka *Weekly Leader* attacked Wood, saying that Wood wished only to profit financially through his position as corresponding secretary of the association. The editor did not believe that women even wanted the vote: "Nowhere in the state have the women organized, or published addresses or given an intimation they desire it, but it is chiefly being done by demagogue men—shysters of the Sam Wood stripe who have a penchant for handling funds raised for such purposes."[15]

Charles Robinson did not escape the charge of participating in the campaign for personal gain. An article in the Emporia *News* in October called attention to the fact that most of the names appearing on the executive committee of the Impartial Suffrage Association were distinguished by the title "ex" before their name, such as "ex-Governor" and "ex-Judge." "No wonder they go for female suffrage," argued the writer. "Next time it will be something else. Anything, Good Lord, to get into office again."[16]

Despite the criticisms, both Wood and Robinson worked vigorously. During the summer months the Reverend Olympia Brown and Bessie Bisbee lectured in numerous Kansas counties. In September and October, suffrage meetings were addressed by Susan B. Anthony and Elizabeth Cady Stanton. Miss Anthony's brother Daniel was a distinguished Kansas newspaper editor in Leavenworth. Thus, his participation in the Kansas campaign was not unexpected. In addition to these recognized feminist leaders, the singing Hutchinson family and George Francis Train, the eccentric promoter and author, participated in the fall meetings.

The use of advocates with national prominence and the efforts to combine the two franchise amendments into one moral cause were not enough. Kansas was not yet ready to accept either woman or Negro suffrage; it was still harnessed with the anti-Negro attitude that had characterized its Territorial era. Results of the November 5 election were 10,483 for granting the franchise to Negroes, and 19,421 opposed. The woman-suffrage amendment was defeated by an even greater margin. Some people attempted to blame the woman-suffrage issue for the defeat of the Negro-suffrage amendment. A typical comment appeared in the Emporia News: "We believe that had the 'side issue' been out of the way, and had the Republican party been united upon the manhood suffrage issue, it would have carried the state."[17]

The following week the Emporia News attacked almost every major supporter of woman suffrage in a poem entitled "Who Killed Female Suffrage?" Robinson was prominently mentioned:

Who'll be the looker on?
I, says Governor Robinson,
With my grave clothes on,
I'll be the looker on
The watcher of Female Suffrage.[18]

Robinson's own disappointment was evident in a letter that he wrote to Susan B. Anthony less than a month after the election. He explained that he had based his hope for victory on the old-school, liberal-thinking, antislavery men and women scattered about the state—people who he believed would have been motivated by something "besides claptrack and bluster."[19]

In a still later letter to Elizabeth C. Stanton, Robinson re-iterated his reasoning about the defeat of the amendment; this time he pointed to Sam Wood and George Francis Train as the two major causes for defeat:

It is very remarkable that Miss Anthony and yourself should be so magnetized by him [Train] when everyone

107

else seems to regard him as an egotistical clown. . . . In my judgment the telegram to Train and carrying out of the program therein announced has had the effect I predicted, viz., to create a general disgust. . . . What will be done in Kansas in the immediate future I am unable to predict. Mr. Wood, the "distinguished citizen," had made his announcement that he is to make a party issue, etc. which I think is not helpful to us. If some people could be content to move with the rank and file until they had been elected Major Generals, the army would be more efficient. If we make a party issue, it should be decided upon a convention of our friends, and not appear to be the policy of one man, however "distinguished."[20]

The issue of Negro suffrage was settled with the adoption of the Fourteenth Amendment; and after its poor showing in the 1867 election, the female-suffrage question ceased to be an active political issue for a time. Nevertheless, Charles Robinson remained actively interested in these issues. He attended the National Suffrage Convention in 1868, and he was an official delegate from Kansas to the convention of 1872.[21]

The Kansas political scene was quiet for a time, but as the state elections of 1870 approached, Robinson again became involved in politics. His name was associated with a loosely-knit group of reformers, known as the Purifiers, which wanted to unseat incumbent Congressman Sidney Clarke. Robinson was not a candidate for Congress, but he placed himself squarely with the anti-Clarke faction and made several speeches against Clarke. He accused Clarke of taking bribes from land-speculation companies. When editor John Speer of the Lawrence *Tribune* defended Clarke, Robinson noted in a letter to his wife that "the *Tribune* is assailing everybody that opposes Clarke in the most contemptible manner. . . . There never was such a low set as Speer and Clarke before the people. I think they will be badly beaten."[22] His prediction proved to be accurate, for when the Republican state nominating convention met at Topeka on September 8, 1870, Clarke was defeated for the nomination by D. P. Lowe of Fort Scott. Bonfires were set in Lawrence that evening in celebration. The Purifiers had severely undercut the regular leadership of the Republican party in 1870.

In 1872 many of the same persons who were in the Purifiers camp became involved in the organization of the Liberal Republican party in Kansas. On April 10, 1872, a Liberal Republican convention was held in Topeka for the purpose of completing the state organization and selecting delegates to the national convention at Cincinnati. Democrats and Independents were well represented at the state convention, which was called to order by Marcus J. Parrott. Former Gov. Samuel J. Crawford was chosen as convention president. Charles Robinson's name appeared prominently in the convention proceedings. The group was addressed by Gov. B. Gratz Brown of Missouri, who was subsequently nominated for vice-president at the national convention. More than one hundred delegates were then elected to attend the convention.

The Liberal Republican convention met on May 1, 1872, and nominated Horace Greeley and B. Gratz Brown to head the national ticket. Charles Robinson made several speeches during the summer, actively supporting the Greeley and Brown ticket. His speeches generally followed the same line, charging the Grant administration with graft, nepotism, and gross corruption. Robinson had apparently determined to run for office again in the 1872 elections, for he had formulated his own campaign motto by late summer: "Conciliation and reform, peace and prosperity." This theme often appeared in his speeches endorsing Greeley and Brown:

> If we would put an end to corrupt personal government, if we desire peace and Union, a complete restoration of the states on the basis of equality of every citizen before the law, let us vote for Greeley and Brown. Also if we desire to put an end to the shameless bribery and corruption at home which has given our state the name of the "rotten commonwealth," then let us also vote for Greeley and Brown.[23]

The regular Republican party held its state nominating convention first. The delegates met in Topeka on September 4, and, after casting ten ballots, chose Thomas A. Osborn as their candidate for governor. The Democrats and Liberal Republicans scheduled their meetings for the same day, September 11, the Liberals meeting in Union Hall and the Democrats at Representative Hall in Topeka. When the meetings convened, the Liberal Republicans appointed a committee to confer with the Democrats for the purpose of nominating a common ticket. Charles Robinson presided at the joint session, and he reported back to the full convention that an agreement had been reached: the Liberal Republicans would nominate candidates for governor and for two congressional seats, and the Democrats would nominate candidates for lieutenant governor and one congressional seat. The two conventions adopted a joint platform, and they both endorsed Greeley and Brown for president and vice-president. Thaddeus H. Walker of Topeka was given the nomination for governor.

"After the nominations were made," reported the Council Grove *Democrat,* "the two conventions consolidated and inaugurated such measures as were necessary to conduct a joint campaign. . . . There was much enthusiasm and the greatest harmony."[24] The platform that was adopted by the joint convention included planks calling for legislation to protect and build up the agricultural and industrial interests in the state, as well as a denunciation of President Grant's Indian policy. The convention passed a resolution advocating that candidates seeking political office be prohibited from using money and the promise of patronage in order to obtain votes.[25]

Robinson was endorsed as a candidate for the state legislature from Douglas County. The ballot listed him as an Independent candidate. It proved an easy victory at the polls for Robinson, as he was unopposed for the position and thus received all of the 972 votes cast in District 52.[26] This was the first elective political office that Robinson had held since leaving the office of governor in 1863. Thirteen other candidates who had been endorsed by the joint convention in Topeka were elected to the Kansas House, but only two were successful in winning seats in the state Senate. In general, however, with their charges of corruption and their campaign to reform the state government, the Liberal Republicans and Democrats had had little effect upon the voters in Kansas. Republican gubernatorial candidate Thomas Osborn, all three Republican congressional candidates, and the Republican presidential electors all won by a ratio of 2-to-1.

In 1874 Robinson and many of his associates who had been active in the Liberal Republican movement formed the Independent Reform party. Its purpose was to unite the majority of dissatisfied farmers and laborers, who had been hard hit by the Panic of 1873 and the hordes of grasshoppers that invaded Kansas in the summer of 1874. As in 1872, Robinson spoke out for reform and political peace. He was weary of the political war that broke out every two years. "Evidently the Republican party is unequal to the task of conquering permanent peace, and we must have another party to do it," concluded Robinson.[27] Under the leadership of Charles Robinson and Henry Bronson, the movement was centered in the Lawrence area. The effect and strength of their influence was attested to by numerous editorials that appeared in Republican newspapers, imploring the "farmers and workingmen" not to be fooled by the reformers who were trying to use them. One editor sarcastically commented that "if this crowd does not right the wrongs, staunch the wounds, repudiate the bonds, cheapen the transportation, and purify the Augean stables of Douglas County, then it will be of no use for anybody else to try."[28]

The state convention of the Independent Reform party was scheduled for Topeka on August 5, 1874, and Charles Robinson was frequently mentioned as a possible candidate for governor. He was strongly endorsed by the Neodesha *Free Press* in the first week of July, when the editor wrote:

If Charles Robinson would accept the nomination for governor, we have not a doubt he would be elected by an immense majority. The old politicians of the state have so persistently abused and vilified him that the people have learned to regard him as in a special sense the champion of their rights and the uncompromising opponent of political fraud and shystering politicians. The reform party has many good men to choose from, but none better or worthier than Ex-Governor Robinson.[29]

Shortly before the convention, the editor of the *Weekly Kansas Tribune* reported that "from letters, and from conversations with parties south of here, we learn that there is a strong feeling for Gov. Robinson for the head of the ticket."[30]

Delegates to the state convention of the Independent Reform party met as scheduled on August 5, 1874. The platform adopted by the reformers called for more government response to the people on both the state and national levels. It advocated repeal of the national banking laws, reduction of tariffs, state regulation of railroads in order to make them subservient to the public good, and direct election of the president, vice-president, and United States senators. On the second day of the convention, the balloting commenced for the selection of the Independent Reform party's nominees for office. Charles Robinson was one of four candidates for governor, and on the first ballot he finished third. Because no one candidate had received a majority, everyone settled in for a lengthy contest. On the second ballot, the delegates changed their votes so frequently that the secretaries were unable to maintain an accurate record. Before the next ballot was started, Joseph Riggs of Douglas County was instructed to withdraw Robinson's name from the race. He told the delegation that he had received word that "Mr. Robinson was not a candidate and would not accept a nomination."[31] On the third ballot, J. C. Cusey of Miami County received the nomination for governor.

Following the convention, Robinson campaigned diligently for the Independent Reform party. His speeches were devoted largely to a discussion of financial questions and of fiscal abuses by the state and national officials. He clearly outlined his views in a letter that was printed in the *Weekly Kansas Tribune* on August 27, 1874. It read, in part:

> The trouble is not that we have too much currency, but the party in power don't [sic] want a specie basis, and will not have it until forced to by the people. In the first place, the party gives this $20,000,000 of the people's money to the National banks because the money people tells them [sic] to. Second, it contracts the currency to the utmost because it is easier to monopolize a small amount than a large

one, and higher rates of interest can be collected. Third, a return to a specie basis would stop the gold gambling in Wall Street, where, with the aid of $100,000,000 of gold in the United States Treasury, untold sums can be made by party officials and their friends.[32]

Although Robinson had decided not to pursue his candidacy for governor on the Independent Reform ticket, he did consent to become a candidate for state senator from Lawrence. For this position he opposed John Speer of Lawrence, a long-time Lane follower and a leading Republican. The campaign between the two was bitter, and about halfway through the campaign, Robinson wrote his wife that "if I am not defeated, it will be remarkable."[33] Thus, toward the end of the campaign, Robinson made fewer speeches around the state, concentrating his efforts in Douglas County. One of his strongest speeches was given at a rally of the Independent Reform party that was held in Lawrence on October 2, 1874. He warned the people of Douglas County that all Americans were being subjected to a new form of slavery—"that which capital imposes upon labor." He pointed out that Kansas was rapidly approaching a state of bankruptcy, "because the money power is grinding the masses to powder; it is getting possession of the wealth of the people."[34]

The depression resulting from the Panic of 1873 made Robinson's stands on finances quite popular. Throughout the state, the Independent Reform party showed signs of appealing strongly to the people, which caused great concern to the Republican party. Two weeks before the election, Gov. Thomas A. Osborn called a special session of the legislature for the purpose of passing legislation that would alleviate the economic situation in the state. The tactic worked, and Osborn defeated James C. Cusey, the Independent Reform candidate, by a vote of 49,594-to-35,301. Yet, J. R. Goodin, the Independent Reform candidate from the Second District, captured one of the three congressional seats, while Robinson emerged with a narrow victory over John Speer.[35]

The country's monetary system continued to be the main issue of the political reformers in the mid seventies. In 1876 Robinson was the Independent Greenback candidate for state senator from Douglas County.[36] The issues remained the same as in the 1874 campaign. Early in 1876 Robinson addressed a Reform meeting in Topeka. At that time he indicated that he would probably work with "some new party." He argued that the Republican party was "controlled by the money power of the country" and that he was "afraid the Democrats were."[37] Thus, it was no surprise when Robinson listed his party affiliation for the election of 1876 as Independent Greenback. Again Robinson was opposed by John Speer. When the votes were counted, after a hard campaign, Robinson was declared the winner, 1,885-to-1,826. A controversy erupted three weeks after the election, when Robinson received notification that Speer intended to contest the election. The defeated candidate charged that some of the votes cast for Robinson had involved the corrupt use of money and that some of his own votes had not been counted by the election judges.[38] Although the affair received much newspaper publicity, Speer failed to present the required list of illegal voters, and the legislature's investigating committee declared that Robinson had been duly elected.

Even before the Greenback party was officially organized in Kansas in 1877, Robinson was one of its major spokesmen. The issue that prompted the formation of the National Greenback party was the Resumption Act of 1875. One feature of the law, which caused widespread reaction, primarily among farmers and laborers, was the provision for the retirement of $82 million of greenback currency. The retirement of such a large volume of greenbacks, together with the resumption of specie payments, sparked a great reaction among the laboring classes. The circulating medium, which amounted to $52.00 per capita in 1866, had been cut down to $12.28 per capita by 1877. The Greenbackers attributed the country's poor economic condition to the lack of money in circulation. They believed that prosperity could be created by increasing the amount of paper money in circulation through the issuing of additional greenbacks. The party advocated that greenbacks be made legal tender at face value and that all national bank notes be withdrawn.[39]

On May 2, 1878, Charles Robinson called the money question the most important issue in the country:

114

It is only necessary to read the debates in Congress of such men as Henry Wilson, Thad Stevens, and J. G. Blaine, to learn that Congress alone, at the bidding of money dealers, was responsible for the depreciation of the greenback. The issue before the country, and in which the people are interested, is not the price of greenbacks—that can be fixed at any time—but national currency against bank currency. Compared with this, other issues are insignificant.[40]

Two months later the Greenback party met at Emporia and nominated a full slate of candidates for the 1878 elections. Delegates consisted of former members of the Independent Reform party, like Robinson, as well as a number of Democrats who switched to the new cause. Lack of organization, however, kept the party from mounting an effective campaign. The Kansas Greenback party was further hampered when the Republican party of Kansas inserted into its platform a token endorsement for the adoption of greenbacks. None of the Greenback candidates were expected to win, so press reaction toward the party during the campaign was negligible. Charles Robinson was able to maintain his position as state senator for another term. By the end of the 1870s the Greenback movement had run its course in Kansas. Prosperity was beginning to return to the state, and as it did, agitation for greenbacks decreased proportionately.

John P. St. John—a Republican from Olathe, who took office as governor in January, 1879—pointed up another issue. In his initial message to the legislature, St. John stated: "No greater blessing could be conferred by you upon the people of this state than to absolutely and forever prohibit the manufacture, importation and sale of intoxicating liquors as a beverage."[41] This sparked the controversy that became the major political issue in Kansas during the decade of the 1880s. Charles Robinson, who was sitting in the legislature that St. John was addressing, emerged as the leading figure of the forces that then opposed, and continued to fight, the adoption of prohibition in Kansas.

The question of prohibition was not new to the people of Kansas. During the Territorial period the legislature had passed two acts that prohibited the sale of intoxicating liquor to the

Indians. At the Wyandotte constitutional convention a heated discussion occurred on whether or not prohibition should be included in the Kansas Constitution. After much debate, the motion to include it was withdrawn for the sake of expediency.[42]

It was primarily the women who carried the banner for prohibition in the 1860s. An early precedent for the later acts of Carrie Nation was established by the women of Mound City, who, during the Civil War, enforced an unwritten law of that town that no saloon should exist. An enterprising individual decided to open a saloon to serve the troops stationed nearby, but shortly thereafter a wagonload of women carrying hatchets and axes drove into town from the direction of Moneka. Joined by other women from Mound City, they marched to the saloon and proceeded to break every bottle, glass, decanter, and barrel in sight.[43]

During the 1870s the temperance movement in Kansas became more cohesive and better organized. Following the pattern of the crusade throughout the country, churches held temperance revivals, and lecturers of national fame were brought to Kansas to make speeches on the evils of liquor. The first major breakthrough occurred in Kansas in 1874, when the Republican state convention of that year included in its adopted platform an endorsement of temperance principles:

> *Resolved*, That drunkenness is one of the greatest curses of modern society, demoralizing everything it touches, imposing fearful burdens of taxation upon the people, a fruitful breeder of pauperism and crime, and a worker of evil continually. Hence we are in favor of such legislation, both general and local, as experience will show to be the most effectual in destroying this evil.[44]

This was the first recognition of the question in Kansas by a large political organization, and it pledged the Republican party to the cause of prohibition.

In 1878 the prohibitionists found a champion in Gov. John P. St. John. Following his recommendation to the legislature that prohibition measures be enacted into law, numerous bills were introduced in both the House and the Senate. The legislature, however, was sharply divided over the question, and the initial bills were buried in committees. Toward the end of the session a joint resolution was introduced in the Senate, calling for an amendment to the state constitution relative to the manufacture and sale of intoxicating liquors. The wording of the proposed amendment closely followed the governor's recommendation. It passed the Senate after heated debate, but Robinson and other antiprohibitionists were confident that the measure would be killed in the House. On March 5, 1880, the House voted on the resolution; the Topeka *Commonwealth* carried this report on the following day:

> The most exciting and interesting item in the House since the senatorial election was last night during the consideration of senate joint resolution 3, proposing an amendment to the constitution relating to the manufacture and sale of intoxicating liquors. Requiring two-thirds of all the votes of the House to pass it, its passage was stubbornly resisted. At one time the friends of the measure dispaired [*sic*] of their ability to push it through, and began to change their votes, saving the point to move a reconsideration of the vote; but as the members slowly came in and cast their votes in the affirmative, it became apparent that it was possible to pass the resolution. Changes were again made, and finally the vote was announced—yeas 88, nays 34. The friends of the measure then gave way to an expression of their joy at the result, which was only suppressed by the speaker's free use of his gavel.[45]

The resolution provided for a vote on scheduling the amendment in the general election of 1880.

To fight the adoption of the amendment, Robinson joined other antiprohibitionists in forming the People's Grand Protective Union of Kansas. A public campaign was inaugurated in January, 1880, when 125 delegates of the Union met in Topeka and passed the following resolution:

> *Resolved*, That the prohibition amendment of the constitution of the state of Kansas, if adopted, would be a law, in its practical application, far beyond the public sentiment of the people, and would be inoperative; that its adoption

117

would take the whole subject of temperance out of the power of the legislature, leaving the people without remedy. Laws so stringent that they cannot be enforced are destructive of all good, because they teach men not to respect the restraining power of the law. The laws now upon the statutes of the state are as stringent as can be enforced, and may be amended or repealed as the public interest or public sentiment shall demand. The amendment, if adopted, would do what no constitution of any state in this Union now does; it would legalize the manufacture and sale of liquor, unrestricted by law, and the liquor once purchased and in the hands of the purchaser, its use cannot be controlled; thereby offering a premium to falsehood, perjury and intemperance.[46]

Charles Robinson opposed the amendment because he did not believe that it could be enforced. His commitment was also based on his personal philosophy. Robinson was a strong temperance man, but he did not believe in laws decreeing total abstinence. He thought that the man who, of his own volition, was temperate in life reached a higher state of moral development than the man who was forced by law to refrain from harmful practices. Man had to live by the fixed laws of nature in order to progress physically, mentally, and morally; but such laws could not be legislated. "The Creator has given him [man] a body, intellect and a moral nature and made him alone responsible for their use." To pass an amendment that would regulate society's morals would stifle man's progress—for "man is eminently a progressive being."[47]

In the months preceding the 1880 election, Robinson flooded newspapers with letters, and he debated proponents of the prohibition cause at rallies throughout the state. Many of the debates turned into shouting matches, and at least one meeting became so emotional that it had to be adjourned before Robinson had a chance to speak. A reporter for the Lawrence *Standard* vividly described the events at a Prohibition Club meeting held at Valley Grove in May, 1880. The program featured D. L. Hoodley, who spoke in favor of the amendment. Charles Robinson was to provide opposing arguments, but before he was to speak, the following exchange occurred:

Mr. Hoodley: "Mr. President—Before Gov. Robinson opens his batteries I want to make a statement. . . . Governor, you are the best card in the whiskey pack. . . . You are not honest in this opposition business. You are hired by the whiskey men to talk as you do."

Gov. Robinson: "Mr. President. I am over sixty years old, and since my boyhood I have worked for the cause of the people and against their oppressors. The honesty of my motives has never before, to my knowledge, been questioned, and now the charge comes from a man who two years ago had to run away from the county in which he lives to escape the penitentiary!"

Hoodley: "That's a d........d lie. I left on legitimate business." (Intensely dramatic scene)

Gov. Robinson: "It's true. You know it. I can prove it. Perhaps you call running away from the Sheriff and keeping out of the penitentiary a legitimate business." (Great excitement)

Someone at this juncture made a motion for an immediate adjournment.[48]

At another rally a week later, Robinson debated Sidney Clarke before an audience of nearly two thousand people. This time, emotions remained calm, and Robinson was able to make his presentation. As always, he contended that the amendment could not be enforced. He gave statistics from Maine and Massachusetts to point out the failure of other states to enforce similar laws. "These facts," he argued, "show that temperance people . . . are getting too much theology mixed up in temperance and want a vicarious sacrifice, and as the liquor seller seems the most available victim, the sins of liquor drinking are put upon his head, while the drinker is excused."[49] After the election in November, many politicians found themselves in an embarrassing position. Although the amendment had passed by eight thousand votes, the political complications were just beginning to surface.

When it became clear that popular sentiment supported prohibition, those politicians who wished to hold office found that they had to conform to the situation. Leaders in the Republican party were especially affected.[50] During the next four years the radical position on the liquor question, which had developed within the St. John wing of the Republican party, became dominant. During the same period the Democratic party offered itself as the champion of the liquor interests as well as of the "practical" temperance people. Robinson, however, continued to crusade through third-party alignments.

While the legislature attempted to find some effective way to enforce prohibition, Charles Robinson stood firm in his opposition. In speeches and newspaper articles he advocated the adoption of a local-option law, which would prohibit liquor where temperance sentiment was predominant and would merely restrict the traffic in localities where enforcement of prohibition proved impossible.

In 1882 the old Greenback party and the new Union Labor party combined forces as the National Labor Greenback party. Because of his campaign against the prohibition amendment in 1880 and because of his previous reform stands, Robinson was prominently mentioned as a gubernatorial candidate of the new party. When the state convention of the National Labor Greenback party met in Topeka on August 23, 1882, Charles Robinson was nominated on the first ballot. He was joined on the ticket by Sam Wood, his long-time friend and associate, who was the party's nominee for Congress. Initially, most newspaper editors considered the ticket to be a strong one. The editor of the Hiawatha *World* aptly characterized and strongly endorsed both candidates: "When the real history of Kansas pioneers is written, no two men will stand out more strongly for courage, adroitness, sagacity than Charles Robinson, the Puritan, and Sam Wood the Quaker."[51] The platform adopted by the convention contained some concepts that were plainly carried over from the Greenback party, particularly on the matter of currency. But the platform also contained some new and rather radical ideas. Resolutions were adopted supporting the right of labor to combine and calling for the creation of a bureau of labor statistics. Another radical measure protested the alien ownership of public land for purposes of speculation or rent. No mention was made of prohibition, but, as it turned out, the ensuing campaign dealt primarily with that issue.

Robinson's opponents dwelled on his antiprohibition stand, often referring to him as the leader of the free thinkers or as a libertine.[52] Even the newspaper endorsements of Robinson tried to smooth over the prohibition issue. The following article appeared in the Topeka *State Journal* in the middle of the campaign:

> From all parts of the state come expressions of gratification at the nomination of Robinson for governor. . . . Said a prominent business man of Topeka, and a Republican, "I shall vote for Robinson; I have known him for twenty-eight years and I know he is a better temperance man than St. John. He is a temperance man from principle, while St. John makes prohibition a hobby for political purposes."
>
> Said another—one of the "54" boys—"When we had to sleep in tents and out of doors while we built houses to live in, many of the boys thought it absolutely necessary to drink stimulants to keep off the chills, but through cold and wet, thick and thin, Robinson stuck to his temperance principles, and we never could persuade him to touch a drop stronger than water."
>
> A life record of persistent devotion to the principles of temperance is worth more than any amount of bombastic speeches.[53]

Robinson's opponents, however, had only to refer to his previous statements and writings in order to convince the voters that he was a "liquor man." On election day, Robinson garnered only 20,933 votes, while the Democratic candidate, George W. Glick, received 83,237, and the Republican candidate, incumbent John P. St. John, received 75,158.[54] Most Republican experts expected Glick to attract no more votes than Robinson, but on election day he became the first Democratic governor of Kansas. The fact that St. John was making a bid for an unprecedented third term, together with the split in the Republican party over the question of prohibition, probably caused his defeat.

Robinson's defeat did not deter him in the fight against prohibition. In August, 1883, a large prohibition encampment was held at Parsons. Robinson was invited to give an address on his reasons for opposing prohibition. In his speech, Rob-

121

inson reviewed the traditional arguments concerning the problems of enforcing liquor laws. He concluded with a strong statement which clearly summarized his own philosophical arguments on the liquor question:

> Man has been left free by his Creator to roam through the world at will, as in no other way can character be formed. He can investigate all things, use all things, and make all things as he pleases, so he does not trespass on the equal rights of all other men to do likewise. But the prohibitionist says, not so: I, in my wisdom, which is superior to the wisdom of my Creator, have decided that mankind shall not thus be free. . . . If the prohibitionist could re-organize the world according to his own plan, and remove all power to sin by the act of legislature, he would by the same act banish from mankind all virtue, all holiness, all personal liberty, all free agency, all character. Man would thus be reduced to the condition of mere animal, with no soul and no power to acquire one. . . . One word to temperance reformers. The sooner you devote your energies to educating the people to a proper and improper use of intoxicating liquors, and to showing them the evils of intemperance, rather than working in season and out of season to make it physically impossible for man to obtain these liquors, the sooner the world will be reformed and saved from the blighting curse of intemperance.[55]

The opponents of prohibition gained significant support in 1882 and 1883 when the Democratic party came out in favor of resubmitting the liquor question to the people. Governor Glick proposed resubmission in 1883. The proposal was shelved, however, after the prohibitionists staged a convention in Topeka and threatened to defeat any Republican legislator who voted for repeal and resubmission. Robinson was encouraged by the Democrats' stand, and he worked closely with some party members in campaigning for resubmission. This was the first of a series of events that eventually brought Robinson into the folds of the Democratic party.

To emphasize the resubmission issue and also to protest the tariff of 1883, another third party came into being in Kansas. Known as the People's party, the movement was centered in

Douglas County; it was led by Charles Robinson, Judge Solon O. Thacher, and L. F. Green, all of Lawrence. It professed to be an independent, nonpartisan group. The platform favored labor, called for resubmission of the liquor question, and opposed the "protection" tariff of 1883.[56] Some of the same men who composed the People's party then formed the Kansas Anti-Protection League in November, 1883. Edward Russell of Lawrence was president, and Charles Robinson was treasurer, of the organization, which was designed "to call attention to the injustice and inequality of the so-called 'protection' features of the national revenue law, and to seek by all lawful means the immediate reform of the tariff system by removing the burdensome and unnecessary taxes arising from the practice of assisting a few masters of capital and labor at the expense of the entire people."[57]

The tariff conflict arose over action previously taken by the U.S. Congress, which, upon the recommendation of Pres. Chester Arthur, had undertaken a study with a view toward lowering tariffs. A special commission, after studying the subject, recommended that Congress make an average reduction of 20 percent. When the report became the basis for a new tariff measure, the usual process of logrolling began. The result was a measure containing some cuts and many increases; that is, it emerged as essentially a protective act. Southern and Western Democrats had supported lower duties. In Kansas the controversy had the effect of bringing prolabor and antiprotection reformers into closer alignment with the Democratic party.

By early 1884 the Democratic party in Kansas was conducting an all-out effort to enlist the support of the various reform movements. The Democratic Central Committee invited representatives of the Greenback party, the People's party, the Knights of Labor, and antimonopolists to meet with them in Fort Scott. Charles Robinson and S. A. Riggs attended from Douglas County. In August, 1884, Robinson reported to his wife that the Democrats were openly courting the antiprohibitionists and the antiprotectionists and that he had received several letters from the Democrats asking for his assistance.[58] He also stated: "Politics are in a hopeless muddle and no one can predict the future. The Republican party is hopelessly split over prohibition and may be beaten by Gov. Glick again!"[59]

Robinson accepted the Democrats' request for assistance, and the 1884 Democratic platform reflected the coalition of ideas. It actively supported resubmission of the liquor question, it was sympathetic toward labor, and it leaned toward the Greenback fiscal policy. At the convention, Charles Robinson was nominated for state senator from Douglas County on the Democratic ticket.

The Republicans, meanwhile, made an effort to reconcile the split that had developed in their party during the campaign by emphasizing the practical considerations of victory and by appealing to reason on the prohibition question. Candidates urged all Republicans to adopt the single goal of ensuring a Republican victory and to let internal divisions be worked out after the election. The appeal succeeded, and the Republicans swept the elections. Robinson lost in his bid for office by 77 votes. Robinson commented on the tactics of the Republican party in a personal letter to the new governor, John A. Martin, a former antiprohibitionist who was accused of changing his position for the sake of political expediency. Robinson wrote on January 15, 1885:

> Today's mail brings your inaugural and message, both of which I have read with deep interest and gratification. The recommendations are excellent, and your navigation of the *fluids* is worthy of a Columbus. You have dodged both Scylla and Charybdis with consummate skill and I shall now watch the nautical maneuvers of the legislature with . . . great interest.[60]

Charles Robinson continued to work within the Democratic party, and in 1886 his name was again prominently mentioned as a candidate for office. At the Democratic state convention that met in Paola on August 18, 1886, Robinson's name was presented as a candidate for Congress by the Douglas County delegation. At the conclusion of the first ballot, Robinson was declared the Democratic nominee. A reporter from the Lawrence *Daily Journal* described the reaction:

The house at once went wild with cheers, motion after motion being made to make the nomination unanimous, and it carried with three rousing cheers and a tiger. The governor at this stage of the proceedings was practically carried to the platform and again cheer after cheer was proposed and given, giving the governor a very short opportunity to recover. In a fifteen minute speech, he accepted and was followed by Judges Wagstaff and Allen, Salee, and others, closing with three cheers for Robinson.[61]

The Republican candidate was incumbent E. H. Funston of Allen County. Robinson faced a popular opponent, and there were no new issues to bring before the voters. The secretary of the Democratic State Committee, H. Miles Moore, was still confident that Robinson had a good chance of winning. He explained the reasons for his conviction in a letter to Robinson, dated September 18, 1886:

> There are hundreds of the "old guard" of freedom in Kansas and many of them in your District whom I have good reason to believe will take pride and pleasure in casting their votes for you, while they may not vote for any other man on our ticket. . . . If you can hold the Greenbackers level, I believe you can and will be elected. The Democrats I know are, and I think most of the Labor Union, are all in line and will support you.[62]

In the November election, however, the entire Republican ticket was easily elected, and Funston retained his congressional seat. Nationally, the Democrats won with Grover Cleveland, whose election marked the first time that the Democrats had controlled the presidency since 1860. Robinson had supported Cleveland, and when the superintendency of the federally operated Haskell Indian Institute in Lawrence became vacant shortly after Cleveland took office, Robinson became a prime candidate for the appointment.

Robinson may have believed that the appointment would be an opportunity to regain political prestige. He was undoubtedly disappointed by the series of defeats that had been inflicted on him in the previous elections. That he was not ready to step out of politics completely is evidenced by later events. Robinson's interest in education, however, was not motivated by politics alone. Throughout his adult life he had expended great amounts of money and energy in working for a strong educational system in Kansas. At the age of sixty-eight, Charles Robinson, reform politician, became a professional educator.

8

An Educational
and Intellectual Leader

The appointment of Charles Robinson as superintendent of Haskell Indian Institute on January 1, 1887, was the culmination of his many years of activity in the development of education in Kansas. This interest stemmed from his early training in New England, which had stressed the importance of education, and it was promoted by his adoption of a personal philosophy that held that man possessed the ability to advance to a more perfect life by increasing his intellectual capacity. In the twentieth century, education, philosophy, and science have become highly specialized disciplines. During Robinson's formal education they generally were associated with religious inquiry. Early in the nineteenth century, the curriculum in most American colleges focused upon studies in natural and moral philosophy. Natural philosophy included the physical sciences, while courses in moral philosophy encompassed subjects now regarded as the social sciences. After 1820, courses in natural philosophy began to give way to studies in natural science, but the courses in moral philosophy remained. The teachings in the natural sciences developed academic, orthodox, and essentially conservative characteristics, but the concepts of moral philosophy, in several instances, became literary, transcendental, and potentially radical in nature. New liberal theological views, which were expounded by such men as Theodore Parker and Charles Finney, questioned the concepts of authority, tradition, and miracles in religion and looked upon the truth of religion as intuitive. These ideas, while they disturbed many contemporaries, were widely accepted by later generations. It was these teachings that influenced the philosophy of Charles Robinson and promoted his keen interest in education and in man's intellectual development.

Although raised in a traditional New England religious environment, Charles Robinson broke with the Congregational Church early in his adult life. The church opposed the Perfectionist movement, particularly the teachings of John Humphrey Noyes, who was then preaching in the Massachusetts area. Insisting that the transforming grace of Christianity be applied to worldly affairs, Noyes was so confident of the possibility of pure holiness in the world that he founded the Oneida Community.[1] He was an extremist, even among reformers, but his basic philosophy flourished during this period because it articulated what some Americans thought America should be. Robinson sympathized with the teachings of Noyes, and he adopted many of these concepts in developing his own philosophy. In an autobiographical account of his philosophy, written in the 1870s, Robinson stated his beliefs in the following manner:

> Doctor [Robinson] is noted for having but *one* principle, and that applies equally to medicine, politics, and religion, namely, the great fundamental aim in life should be to add as much as possible to the sum total of happiness in the universe. . . . The idea that human life in this world is a commencement of an existence without end, that the body is of secondary importance, merely the tenement that is soon to perish while the soul goes marching on, has never yet been realized to any considerable extent. Seeing these things our Doctor becomes an educator. . . . He endeavors to arouse the people from unconsciousness to thoughtfulness.[2]

Robinson's break with the Congregational Church, which was over the Perfectionist issue, was final; yet he retained a strong interest in philosophy and religion throughout his life. He never again regularly attended any particular church. Occasionally he went to Unitarian services and frequently commented on the sermons that he heard. He was particularly impressed by a Unitarian service in Washington, D.C., that he attended in 1869. In writing about this experience to his wife, Robinson related some of his own beliefs and further pointed up his transcendental learnings:

> I went this morning to hear Dr. Lathrope of Boston preach in the Unitarian Church. This afternoon Mrs. Mott preached at the same place. . . . She looks very old yet speaks very distinctly. Her sentiments were as radical as mine on religious matters. . . . She treated the Bible like any other book and took no stock in form and ceremonies. She said to make one day sacred was to make the others profane. To sanctify the Church was to desecrate other places by comparison. She would make religion consist of everyday life.[3]

He concluded that "man must not only do right, but must study to do good, and a great deal of it. He must live in his intellectual and moral nature. . . . It is his [man's] duty to examine and probe all things for himself. He hears all sides and selects that only which stands the test."[4]

Because he held these beliefs, it was not surprising that Charles Robinson should appear as one of the first promoters of education in Kansas Territory. He was identified with the educational affairs of Kansas from the beginning, and he never lost interest in them. The first school in Lawrence was held in Robinson's back office of the Emigrant Aid Building. The teacher was Edward P. Fitch, and classes commenced on January 16, 1855, less than six months after the arrival of the first group of emigrants from New England. In the summer of 1855, classes were taught by Kate Kellogg in the same building. Her salary was paid by Robinson personally. In 1857 Quincy High School was opened in the Emigrant Aid Building. Shortly after the term began, the high school was moved to the basement rooms of the Unitarian church in Lawrence.[5]

In the fall of 1863, Mary, Charles, and Caroline Chapin arrived in Lawrence and opened a school for girls. Charles Robinson and George W. Deitzler paid the tuition costs for several of the girls. Mrs. Sara T. D. Robinson erplained the school's beginning:

> One day in October, 1863, . . . Mr. Chapin and his sister Mary came up to see us and talk over the matter of their coming to Lawrence, and to learn whether the circumstances . . . would favor the opening of a girls' school in Lawrence. General Deitzler and Governor Robinson were enthusiastic over the matter, and favored the enterprise with all their hearts. They were mindful also that money was needed for the success of the plan, and they each paid the tuition for several of the girls.[6]

By 1863 the town had a good public-school system as well as the private academy for girls. Robinson's main desire for Lawrence, however, was the establishment of a university. He worked toward this goal from the time he first arrived in the Territory. These ambitions were thoroughly supported by Amos A. Lawrence, treasurer of the New England Emigrant Aid Company.

As early as the fall of 1854 Charles Robinson told Amos Lawrence that the citizens of Lawrence would start a college as soon as possible. A plat of the town, which was made at about the same time, showed Mount Oread set aside for the location of a college and churches.[7] The free-state Topeka Constitution of 1855 stated that "the general assembly may take measures for the establishment of a university, with such branches as the public convenience may hereafter demand, for the promotion of literature, the arts, sciences, medical and agricultural instruction."[8] In 1856 Amos A. Lawrence sent Charles Robinson an indeterminable amount of money to lay the foundation of a school building on the northern part of Mount Oread. Robinson began work on the building, but he was forced to abandon the effort when title to the land was disputed.[9] The scarcity of money in Kansas at this time also contributed to the failure. In December, 1856, several prominent citizens held a meeting to consider the matter of establishing a university. Led by Charles Robinson, George W. Deitzler, and the Reverend Ephraim Nute, the gathering adopted a resolution stating that the time had arrived to establish a college in Lawrence. Fifteen trustees were selected to govern the institution; they included Robinson, Nute, Samuel C. Pomeroy, William F. M. Arny of Illinois, Amos Lawrence, and Gov. William Slade of Vermont, a well-known abolitionist.[10]

The college was to be financed by private subscriptions, and Robinson estimated that $100,000 would be necessary to get the school started. This meant that much of the money would have to come from private sources outside the Territory. The promoters had reason to be encouraged, for Amos Lawrence had written to Nute a week before the meeting, outlining his thinking for the proposed school:

> You shall have a college which shall be a school of learning and at the same time a monument to perpetuate the memory of those martyrs of liberty who fell during the recent struggles. . . . It shall be called the "Free-State College," and all the friends of freedom shall be invited to lend it a helping hand.[11]

On February 14, 1857, Amos Lawrence sent Robinson two notes amounting to $10,000, which he held from a loan made to Lawrence University in Appleton, Wisconsin. Accompanying the notes were instructions to Robinson that the interest from these notes be used for the purpose of advancing religion and education in the Territory. Robinson and Samuel C. Pomeroy were named as trustees of this fund.[12] Lawrence's aim was to create a private college, so that when Kansas received an anticipated land grant from Congress for a state university, there would already be a school standing on the ground so that it could receive the grant. Other towns were also attempting to secure the university, notably Manhattan. Nevertheless, on January 13, 1857, Charles Robinson, as Free State governor, signed a bill establishing a university in Lawrence. Little progress was made toward the actual operation of a university, however, due to the divided political situation. The Panic of 1857 cut off the needed outside money, and the proslavery-dominated Territorial legislature of 1857 refused to allow any money for the establishment of a university in a free-state town. The majority of Kansans desired a university, but the division of view-

131

points as to where it should be located and how it should be financed hindered any positive development.

The prospects for state-supported higher education in Kansas improved in 1859, with the writing of the Wyandotte Constitution in July. The parts of the document that related to the creation of a state university were sections 2 and 7 of Article VI:

> Section 2. The legislature shall encourage the promotion of intellectual, moral, scientific and agricultural improvement, by establishing a uniform system of common schools, and schools of a higher grade, embracing normal, preparatory, collegiate and university departments.
>
> Section 7. Provision shall be made by law for the establishment, at some eligible and central point, of a state university, for the promotion of literature, and the arts and sciences, including a normal and an agricultural department. . . .

Providing for a state university in a constitution and creating it by law were two different matters, as evidenced by the struggles in the 1861 and 1862 legislatures. Governor Robinson again faced the problem of the location of the university, but he found no solution to it. Although the legislators seemed to be eager to create a university, a number of local and personal interests frustrated the university movement, delaying its creation for three years after Kansas became a state.

Among the most difficult questions that the legislature of 1861 had to consider were those about where to locate the various state institutions. Second only to the question of where to locate the capital was the issue over placement of the state university. In 1861, Manhattan appeared to have the best claim, because a Methodist institution called Bluemont Central College had already been established there. Its trustees had offered to donate its physical facilities to the state for the state university. Two members of the legislature were appointed to investigate the facilities and the terms of the donation, and then to report their findings to the legislature.[13]

The investigating committee consisted of state Representative William H. Grimes of Atchison and state Senator Otis B. Gunn of Topeka. Their report concluded that the college was

132

almost perfect. Its three-story limestone building had eight rooms on the first two floors which could be used for offices, classrooms, and laboratories; and it had a large hall on the third floor. The college site, according to the report, was "not surpassed in beauty and variety of scenery by any other locality in Kansas."[14]

What the report did not mention was the fact that Bluemont's trustees had made their offer in an attempt to rid themselves of a problem. Bluemont had proved to be a failure. Chartered in 1858 and opened in 1860, it had never really been a college. The only students were preparatory ones. On the same day that the report was presented, Representative Grimes offered a bill to accept the offer of the trustees and to locate the state university at Manhattan. On May 9 the House passed the bill by a vote of 43-to-19 and sent it to the Senate, which passed it on May 23.[15]

Governor Robinson had been watching events with great interest, for he wanted the university to be located in Lawrence. The only avenue open to him was to veto the measure. On May 28 he returned the bill to the legislature with a brief message. To locate the university in Manhattan solely on the basis of the donation of Bluemont College was unfair, he stated. If the University of Kansas were to be located for such a reason, "all portions" of the state should be given the opportunity to make proposals. Robinson's veto was also based on economic factors. "It will be time enough to locate this Institution," wrote Robinson, "when the endowment can be made available, and the question can be fully canvassed before the people." A two-thirds majority was required in order to override the veto. In spite of all their efforts, the supporters of the measure in the House fell short by two votes, and the measure died.

In the second legislature, Manhattan, Emporia, and Lawrence were all strong contestants for the university. The House considered the Manhattan bill first and adopted it 45-to-16. In the Senate, the bill became entangled with the Lane-Robinson controversy. Lane, who was attempting to pack the Senate with his followers in preparation for the impeachment proceedings against Robinson, used the university bill to gain support for expelling four senators, sympathetic to Robinson, who were accused of holding military and political offices simultaneously. The Manhattan men promised to assist Lane on the condition that the new replacements would support the university bill. Lane agreed to this. But when the bill came up for a vote, only one of the four new senators voted in favor of the bill. It was defeated in the Senate, 12-to-11, a severe blow to the Manhattan supporters.[16]

In the spring of 1862 it appeared that the legislature might argue for years over which town should get the university. So far as Lawrence was concerned by 1863, the facilities for higher education amounted to no more than the foundation of a building on a few acres of land. There was no faculty, and no student body. All that existed was the interest from the $10,000 in notes held on Lawrence University in Wisconsin. The hopes of supporters for a university in Lawrence were lifted in 1863, when, under the provisions of the Morrill Act, which had been passed by Congress the year before, a state agricultural college was placed at Manhattan. Emporia and Lawrence were now the key competitors for the state university. Lawrence offered $15,000 in cash and 20 acres of land, whereas Emporia promised 80 acres of land. The money in the Lawrence offer was largely based on the promissory notes that Amos Lawrence agreed to give the town for the purposes of establishing a university. Members of the House Committee on Public Institutions probably knew the conditions and were aware that the Lawrence town fathers did not have the money in hand. So the committee rejected the Lawrence bill and recommended that the Emporia land offer be accepted. A delegation of Lawrence men, led by Charles Robinson, lobbied for passage of their bill despite the committee's disapproval. The Lawrence men succeeded in their efforts. On February 22, 1863, two days after the bill had been signed, Robinson explained to Amos Lawrence that the fund was chiefly responsible for the triumph: "It was with great difficulty that the location was secured here, and nothing saved us but the inducement of your fund."[17]

The struggle for Lawrence citizens was not entirely over, however. The law that was passed said that Gov. Thomas Carney was to appoint three commissioners, who would choose a location for the institution in or near Lawrence on a site of not less than 40 acres. In addition, the citizens of Lawrence were to raise $15,000 for an endowment fund, which they had to deposit with the state treasurer within six months after the site had been given to the state. If the money were not deposited, Emporia would get the university, providing that its citizens donated 80 acres of land.[18]

The three commissioners considered several possible sites in Lawrence, but none compared to the one atop Mount Oread. This land belonged to Charles and Sara Robinson. Because money from any source was scarce, an agreement was reached between the city council and the Robinsons. Through two trades and a small cash payment, the site was made available. In return for 22½ acres, Charles Robinson received half a block of land from the city. Sara exchanged 17¾ acres for 10 acres of land on another part of Mount Oread and a cash payment of $600. With these arrangements completed, Charles and Sara deeded the 40¼ acres of land directly to the state.[19]

Once the site had been selected, the Lawrence residents had until November 1, 1863, to raise the $15,000 in cash. Robinson had been working on this problem since the bill had been passed. On February 22 he wrote to Amos Lawrence to request the use of the money owed by Lawrence University in order to secure the location of the state university at Lawrence. Amos Lawrence agreed, and he offered to bring whatever pressure he could on the college to pay the debt.[20] In spite of their honest intentions, however, the trustees of Lawrence University were unable to raise the money. And after William Quantrill's destructive raid on August 21, 1863, it became impossible to raise the money in Lawrence. Robinson, therefore, again wrote to Amos Lawrence, asking for a gift of $15,000. In return, the people of Lawrence promised to surrender the notes that they held. In October, Amos Lawrence agreed to buy back the notes for $10,000 in cash, if the citizens of Lawrence would raise the additional $5,000. With time running out, several men, including Robinson, agreed to make pledges or sign personal notes. The law, however, demanded cash. Just before the deadline, Governor Carney told

Robinson and his colleagues that he would be willing personally to advance the $5,000 in cash in exchange for the citizens' notes in the same amount. On November 2, 1863, Governor Carney formally announced that Lawrence had met the requirements and that the university would be located there.[21]

At last, the University of Kansas had been permanently placed. The legislature of 1864 passed a charter law, which Governor Carney signed on March 1, 1864. On the following day the Board of Regents was appointed. Charles Robinson was among those named to the first Board of Regents, which had the responsibility of putting the university into operation. They had to find funds to finish building the uncompleted structure, to hire faculty, and to establish a curriculum. To all of these tasks Robinson devoted a great deal of time and effort.

The first Board of Regents consisted of thirteen members, twelve of whom were appointed by the governor for six-year terms. The state superintendent was an ex officio member. When a chancellor was selected in 1865, he also became an ex officio member. An early controversy involving the regents involved the question of coeducation. Despite the provision in the Kansas Constitution that "the legislature, in providing for the formation and regulation of schools, shall make no distinction between the rights of males and females," many doubted the wisdom of applying this provision to the university. The legislature, therefore, inserted a clause into the charter, which stipulated that there should be two branches in the university, a male branch and female branch. The female branch was to be taught exclusively by women, and its facilities were to be separated from those of the male branch. Robinson, a strong advocate of women's education, which is evidenced by his support of the female academy, opposed this segregation, fearing that the quality of the female branch would be inferior to that of the male branch.[22] In taking this stand, he found himself under pressure from Amos Lawrence to alter his views. Lawrence wrote to Robinson on this matter in the spring of 1864:

It seems to me that we are making war against the decrees of Providence and natural laws when we put young

136

women upon the bench to study all day. . . . There is not a strong, child-bearing young woman in a score. They heap up knowledge which they do not want, and contract weaknesses and disease which curse them and their posterity. We shall be forced back to first principles after we have run this channel a while longer. . . . It is plain enough all around: in the country even more than in the city.[23]

Robinson's viewpoint eventually carried, and the regents never put segregated facilities into effect. When Kansas University opened on September 12, 1866, twenty-six of the thirty-five students were women. Undoubtedly, the state's lack of funds aided Robinson in his campaign for a coeducational system.

At the first meeting of the regents in 1865, R. W. Oliver was elected chancellor. Charles Robinson and Solon D. Thatcher were named as the Executive Committee. In this capacity Robinson was instrumental in recruiting and selecting the faculty for the school. A letter that Robinson wrote to F. H. Snow of Boston indicates Robinson's deep concern for a strong faculty. The communication also reflects some of Robinson's views on education:

> I sincerely hope nothing will prevent your acceptance of the professorship in our University. You can preach all you like and there is a wide field of usefulness in that respect. While the institution is not to be sectarian in its government, it is expected that the Professors will be entirely free to cherish their own religious convictions and preach them all they like. The salary, $1,600 per annum, is too small, but it is so regarded by the board, and an early advance will be made, I have no doubt, to at least $2,000. . . . We have one of the most beautiful countries in the world, and a population second to none in stirring enterprise and general intelligence. . . . The location of the University is especially beautiful. When Mr. Pierpont went on the site, he took a long look and exclaimed, "God may have made a more beautiful place than this, but if He has, I have never seen it.". . . We are in the center of the continent geographically, if not morally and intellectually. When we have had you and such as you for our Professors and educators for one generation we hope to be in the latter sense what we are in geographically and in natural beauty.[24]

On July 19, 1866, the first faculty, consisting of D. H. Robinson, E. J. Rice, and F. H. Snow, was formally selected.[25]

From this beginning until 1894, Charles Robinson maintained an active role in the development of Kansas University, serving on the Board of Regents for a total of twelve years. In 1870 he was named chairman of the building committee for the construction of Fraser Hall, the first large building on the campus. He led the financial campaign, in which Lawrence voted a $100,000 bond issue for its construction. During 1870 and 1871 he spent the majority of his time letting contracts and looking after the project. For several months he maintained an office in Lawrence for that purpose alone.[26] After it had been completed, the structure served as the nucleus of the university, housing administrative offices and containing accommodations for over five hundred students.

In recognition for his many years of service to the university, Charles Robinson was awarded the honorary degree of Doctor of Laws by the regents in 1887.[27] In 1890, after leaving his position as superintendent of Haskell Institute, Robinson was reappointed as a member of the Board of Regents. There was no criticism of Robinson's service to the university until the last few months of his life. In 1893 he began to grow impatient with the methods and policies of the university. He felt that the university was growing away from the needs of the people. Thus, in June of 1894, he resigned, giving ill health as his reason. No mention was made of the controversy that existed between Robinson, the chancellor, and the other members of the board. The following resolution was unanimously passed by the board at the time of his retirement:

> The voluntary retirement of Governor Robinson from the Board of Regents at this time gives opportunity in this formal manner to express regret at the severing of relations which has always been pleasant and cordial. The Board has profited by his intimate knowledge of the institution, his patriotism and loyal interest in its aims and objects, and it wishes further to acknowledge for the people of the State of Kansas the indebtedness they owe to him for his wise liberality and active cooperation in every direction calculated to broaden and enlarge the scope of the University.[28]

138

The differences that existed were due to Robinson's philosophy of education. His age may have been an additional factor, for he was then seventy-six years of age. A letter written in 1899 by Charles Scott, who had been secretary of the Board of Regents in 1894, to Frank Blackmar provides some insight into the conflict. In the letter, Scott contends that Robinson, in his last days, could not understand the difference between a college and a university. According to Scott, Robinson insisted that the university should be run along the lines that Williams College had been run on fifty years earlier. Once Robinson had adopted this belief, his pride in and love for the university would not allow him to change his convictions. Scott concluded with the following statement: "He finally resigned, ostensibly on account of ill health, but really, in my judgment, because he found himself unable to change a policy which he was convinced was wrong."[29] Perhaps Robinson, by resigning, recognized that the university had gone beyond his educational philosophy and that his usefulness was past. Education was entering a new age of specialization to which Robinson could not adapt. His concern for the welfare of the university, however, did not waver. Gov. Lorenzo D. Lewelling, a Populist, allowed Robinson to select his own successor to the Board of Regents. He chose Henry S. Clarke, a Lawrence Populist who had been a member of the Lawrence City Council and of the Lawrence Board of Education, as well as sheriff of Douglas County. As a condition of selection, Robinson made Clarke promise that he would resign as a regent if Robinson ever found him negligent of the university's interests.[30]

In his postgubernatorial career, Robinson's interests in educational facilities went beyond those of the University of Kansas. He was involved in a variety of educational institutions. In 1872 and 1873 he served on the Board of Directors for the Quindaro State Normal School. This school for Negroes was established by the Kansas legislature in 1871, and it opened on September 11, 1872, with six students enrolled. The school, which was located just outside of Kansas City, Kansas, was designed to provide educational opportunities for Negro children from all parts of eastern Kansas. In 1873 it had an enrollment of eighty-two students, but the principal's report to the board that year pessimistically stated: "Want of home culture and means renders our work particularly difficult. Students will need preparatory preparation." It was also pointed out that the location was poor, the furniture was inadequate, and the only blackboard was "3 x 6 and faded." The board's report to the legislature recommended changing the location, drawing up a specific plan for school work, and hiring additional qualified teachers immediately.[31] The legislature failed to adopt the recommendation, and the school went out of existence in 1874.

In 1876 Charles Robinson continued his efforts for high educational standards while he was in the state Senate. He sponsored a bill to reform some aspects of the Kansas public-school system and to bring all regulations together. In this bill, the duties of the state and county superintendents were clearly defined; the powers of boards of education were enlarged and their duties defined; school districts were added; and uniform lengths of term were established for schools. The law was comprehensive, and it constituted a major advancement in the organization of the public-school system in the state.[32]

Robinson was associated with another Lawrence school in 1887. Incorporated as the Lawrence Business College and Academy of English and Classics, this private school was designed to serve those who wished to go beyond the public schools but did not want to attend a university. Charles Robinson was one of the incorporators, and he served on its Board of Directors during the first two years of its operation.[33]

In 1887 Robinson became a professional educator when he accepted the appointment as superintendent of Haskell Indian Institute in Lawrence, which was built and operated by the federal government. In 1882 the Forty-seventh Congress appropriated $150,000 for the establishment of Indian training schools. The purpose of these schools, as set forth in the funding bill, was to instruct and "civilize" Indian children west of the Mississippi River. Because of the influence of Congressman Dudley C. Haskell from Lawrence, chairman of the House Committee on Indian Affairs, one of the first schools was located in his city. Work on three buildings began in 1883 on land donated by

Lawrence citizens. By the summer of 1884, two dormitories and a classroom building had been completed. The school opened in the fall of that same year with an enrollment of eighteen boys and five girls.[34]

Dr. James Marvin, a former chancellor of the University of Kansas, was the first superintendent of Haskell Institute. Forced to resign because of ill health in 1885, he was succeeded by Col. Arthur Grabowskii. Grabowskii, who was noted for his strict discipline, ran into considerable difficulty from both faculty and townspeople. According to a report in the Lawrence *Daily Journal*, numerous complaints had been sent to the commissioner of the Bureau of Indian Affairs concerning the management of Haskell Institute. The most serious charges against Grabowskii concerned his cruelty to the Indian children. Finally, the assistant commissioner of the Bureau of Indian Affairs detailed an investigator to look into the situation. According to Grabowskii, who was from Georgia, the whole trouble stemmed from the fact that a Kansas man had not been selected for the position. "On this account alone," said the superintendent, "the local Democracy have antagonized me from the first."[35]

The result of the investigation was that Grabowskii was asked to resign in December, 1886. During the search for a replacement for the superintendent, Charles Robinson's name was prominently mentioned. He had strongly supported both the Democratic party in Kansas and the presidential candidacy of Grover Cleveland in the previous election, and his long involvement in education made him a prime candidate for the position. Robinson was called to Washington in December, 1886, and was asked to consider the job. Upon his return to Lawrence on December 22, he stated to the local press:

> I went to Washington in response to a telegram from Colonel Moonlight concerning some political matters of his. Arriving there I was called upon by a prominent *attache* of the Interior Department, who said he was anticipating my arrival, and that Secretary Lamar wanted to see me at once. . . . After some general conversation the Secretary broached the subject of Haskell Institute, its general affairs, the new buildings to be erected, etc., and in behalf of himself

141

and the President, asked me to accept its superintendency. He said both of the inspectors sent to Lawrence had returned and recommended me as "the only man in Kansas they would choose for the position," and they did not think I would accept it. . . . He made me very generous promises and I expect great successes in the school. I returned by way of the Carlisle School where, by the Secretary's orders, a special exhibition was given for my benefit. My enthusiasm in Indian education was considerably increased thereby.[36]

The same newspaper carried the official press releases from Washington, D.C., announcing Robinson's appointment. Arrangements were swiftly completed, and on January 1, 1887, Charles Robinson took charge of Haskell Institute. The task that was given to him was not an easy one. The school was unpopular among the Indians of Kansas and of the Indian Territory. The only industrial-training subjects were carpentry, cobbling, and a small amount of farming. Parents refused to send their children to the school, and attendance was much below what was expected. Therefore, Robinson made several trips to the Indian Territory in order to recruit students and give Haskell a new image. During his two-year tenure, enrollment increased from 251 to 565.[37]

Superintendent Robinson initiated new programs and changed the emphasis of the institute. One of his first acts was to establish a brass band at the school; the money to purchase instruments was raised among the business leaders. Robinson personally contributed fifty dollars to the fund. According to a Lawrence newspaper article written in 1888, the band played before President Cleveland in Kansas City and "received notice and attention on the part of the President." "The band is now in frequent demand," continued the article. "It plays at many public places and often at the Opera house."[38]

Robinson's major objective when he took the position was to make Haskell a first-rate industrial school. Under his guidance, new training facilities were constructed, including a blacksmith shop, a wagon shop, a harness shop, a tin shop, a printing office, a laundry, and a bakery. In addition, the institute's farm acreage was increased more than 50 percent by Robinson. A large new dormitory and dining hall, completed in 1889, made Haskell Institute the largest and best-equipped Indian industrial school in the United States.[39]

Robinson worked hard at improving the image of the school in the community. Shortly after he took the position, a Lawrence editor noted that no longer were people kept out of the school, "but like the temple of Janus, her doors are ever open to the reception of all who are curious to witness the progress of the children of the Red Man. Visitors are welcome at all times, and are furnished with guides to show them through every department."[40]

The school received much favorable publicity during the two years that Robinson was there as a result of his conscious effort to win over the interest of the townspeople and newsmen. His own public image benefited in the process. One newspaper carried a long story on Robinson entitled "An Over-Worked Man." In this article, the writer expressed concern that Robinson was working so hard, considering his age, and appealed to the Bureau of Indian Affairs to make him slow down. "He is hale, hearty and strong, exceptionally vigorous for a man of his age," said the writer, "but his trips so frequently to the [Indian] Territory and elsewhere and his constant work night and day will tell on him."[41]

Robinson did not excel in all areas of his job as superintendent. He had a difficult time adjusting to federal regulations regarding the purchasing of supplies for the school. After receiving two reprimands from the Bureau of Indian Affairs for violating these regulations, he wrote a lengthy letter to the commissioner in an effort to defend his actions. Robinson viewed the existing regulations as "impracticable and impossible" to observe without great inconvenience. He could not understand the necessity for issuing notices, accepting bids, and letting contracts for all supplies and services. He concluded that the only course he would follow was that of serving the institution to the best of his ability, following the regulations when it was practical.[42] That Robinson continued this practice became evident when he was confronted with a statement showing a disallowance of purchases amounting to over five hundred dollars after his resignation. It took several years to settle the matter, and in the end Robinson paid the government only a small portion of the initial claim.[43]

In September, 1888, Charles Robinson decided to resign and return to his farm to look after personal interests. There was no indication of any other reason for his resigning. Despite the problems over procedural matters with the Bureau of Indian Affairs, Robinson appeared to hold their confidence and trust. The appointment of his successor, Col. O. C. Learnard of Lawrence, was made upon his recommendation. Governor Robinson officially turned over the institution to Learnard on January 1, 1889, thus ending his two years of service as a professional educator.[44]

Charles Robinson was involved in other educational and intellectual organizations during his Kansas career. Recognizing the importance of history, Robinson was associated with early efforts to establish a state historical society. In 1860 he was named chairman of the committee on local history at a meeting of the Historical and Scientific Society, a forerunner of the Kansas State Historical Society. In 1868 Robinson delivered a paper, "Ad Astra per Aspera," before the Kansas Historical Society. In 1873 this was reprinted as an article in the *Kansas Magazine*, the first substantial literary publication in Kansas. The printing of Robinson's article prompted an editorial comment by the publishers, asking whether or not the historical society was still in existence. The Wisconsin Historical Society was given as an example of how such a society might be developed. The editorial closed with an appeal for the creation of a Kansas State Historical Society, adequately financed through legislative appropriation.[45] Such an organization was chartered, and it commenced operation in 1875, although the first appropriations from the state legislature were not granted until 1877. Charles Robinson became active in the new organization in 1877, when he participated in a lecture series sponsored by the society. The following year he was elected to its board of directors, and in 1879 he was elected president of the society for a two-year term. Throughout the 1870s and 1880s Charles Robinson was a frequent contributor to newspapers of articles on Territorial Kansas. Most of the speeches that he gave to Old Settlers' meetings, to the Military Order of the Loyal Legion, and to other organizations were on historical themes relating to the early Kansas struggle.

Another of Robinson's strong interests in the 1870s and 1880s was liberal ideology. Having shown earlier signs of heterodoxy so far as his religious views were concerned, he wholeheartedly embraced reform thought in 1879 by joining the National Liberal League. The National Liberal League had been formed in 1876, having as its objective the effective separation of church and state.[46] In the early 1870s a small group of pious individuals was agitating for an amendment to the Constitution of the United States which would recognize God as the Supreme Being and Christianity as the national religion. Their crusade received little notice in the national press, but in the liberal journals it received a good deal of attention, mostly in the form of ridicule and opposition. Robinson opposed the movement, and in February, 1875, he participated in a "God and the Constitution Convention," which was held in Leavenworth. Appointed to its Resolutions Committee, Robinson was instrumental in writing the following resolution, which was adopted by the Convention:

> Now, if never before, the laymen all over the land have a vital interest in the question "Who or what is God?" This question, I, as a citizen of this Republic, ask of those who propose to supplant Republicanism with Theocracy. He [God] is a spirit and would have all worship Him in spirit and truth. He is not a peevish, jealous or envious God, is not opposed to the acquisition of knowledge. . . . He wants no display of fasting, almsgiving or praying and needs no plaudits or endorsements from his creatures.[47]

By 1879 the National Liberal League claimed to have more than two hundred local auxiliaries in Kansas alone. It opposed the use of the Bible in public schools, the public support of sectarian schools and charitable institutions, the official recognition of religious holidays, and the judicial oath. In 1882, to this

145

list of positions it added advocacy of the repeal of all laws on observance of the Sabbath.[48]

In the fall of 1879 the league sponsored a camp meeting at Bismarck Grove, north of Lawrence.[49] Robinson was one of the chief promoters of the encampment, which was open to all interested citizens. In a public letter that was used to draw attention to the meeting, he was perhaps overly optimistic about the results that were expected from the encampment:

> The old time theological barricades erected around the most ignoble of superstitions is fast crumbling to dust. A decade more and they will all have vanished from before the advancing footsteps of enlightened civilization, and in place of the altar of sacrifices to unknown Gods or a triumverate of Gods and Deities, will be erected a monument to the most beautiful of all faculties, Reason![50]

The meeting, which was held September 5–10, received extensive coverage in the eastern Kansas press. There was general surprise at the number of eminent men and women who were identified with the liberal, or "Free Thinkers," movements. Included among the active participants were D. R. Anthony, Leavenworth publisher; Sol Miller, editor of the Troy *Kansas Chief*; F. P. Baker, editor of the Topeka *Commonwealth*; Mr. and Mrs. Frank Doster of Marion County; Annie L. Diggs (later an important Populist agitator); and George F. Peck, an attorney for the Santa Fe Railroad. The five-day meeting was devoted largely to speeches against church control over secular life. One critic of the meeting, commenting on the program, stated that thirteen prominent men who spoke were from eight states and delivered twenty-two addresses. Many different philosophies, including atheism, materialism, spiritualism, and universalism, were represented; yet all attacked the Christian religion.[51]

On September 9 the Kansas Liberal League was organized, and these officers were selected: Charles Robinson, president; W. H. T. Wakefield, secretary; and Mrs. Frank Doster, treasurer. A committee of seven was then named to draft a declaration of principles. Charles Robinson was chairman of the committee, which had the difficult problem of producing a document to meet all the divergent views that were represented. Before the convention adjourned, a platform and a series of resolutions had been adopted. The platform, which was heavily influenced by Robinson's own philosophy, provided a theoretical base for the Liberal League's activities in Kansas. The final product began:

Whereas, Advancing civilization has changed our conditions, and more general education has enlarged our views, given us a greater comprehension of natural law; and

Whereas, the teachings of the remote past have been found incompatible with modern science, and positive knowledge has been substituted for the assumptions of ignorance; and

Whereas, We, a body of free American citizens, wishing to unite for mutual aid, encouragement, advancement, and protection, with no desire to abridge any person's honest thought or free expression of the same, to the end that all mankind may know our sentiments, do solemnly agree;

1. That the universe is governed by fixed and unchanging laws.
2. That inspiration is as widely diffused as mind.
3. That each individual is responsible for his own acts, and must suffer for his own wrong-doing.
4. That change and progression is the universal law of nature.
5. That man now occupies a higher plane, morally, socially, and intellectually, than at any other period since he has been an occupant of this earth.
6. That we hail with delight the dawning of a brighter day for humanity, when, absolved from enslavement to delusive creeds and barbarous deities, the race can emerge into the full light of illumined truth.
7. That freedom, fellowship, toleration and character shall be our watchwords.[52]

In addition to the general platform, the league adopted a series of resolutions which dealt specifically with contemporary issues. Although the organization decided not to form a political party based on the right of religious freedom, they voted in favor of a resolution to recommend and assist only political candidates who upheld their objectives as they are stated above. Another important resolution gave recognition to women, calling for their equal rights "on the rostrum, in the pulpit, at the polls, in all our educational departments and professions, as well as avenues of business and labor." The same resolution also advocated equal pay for equal services performed by men and women. Other resolutions called for the abolition of conflict between capital and labor, and for the continuance of a strong separation between church and state.[53]

The entire affair was regarded as a great success by those present. All financial obligations were met, attendance was good, and there were no disturbances to mar the proceedings.[54]

Members of the Liberal League returned again to Bismarck Grove in 1880. The question of holding evening sessions was discussed, those in favor arguing that many people would come at night who would be ashamed to be seen in the daytime. As a result, evening sessions were held. The 1880 meeting, however, was not peaceful. On the last day, Col. W. G. Coffin, upset at the insults to the Bible, attempted to interrupt the program in order to defend the Bible. The program chairman, G. W. Brown, announced that the program had already been made out and that it could not be interrupted. Both men became very excited. Brown called Coffin a puppy and a fanatic. Coffin countered by calling Brown a knock-kneed monkey. The Kansas City *Times* reported that prospects were very good for a row when the meeting was hastily adjourned.[55]

Subsequent meetings of the Liberal League were nearly all held in Ottawa or Valley Falls and were practically ignored by the press except for criticism of individuals who participated in them. The Lawrence *Daily Journal* severely chastised Robinson in 1884, when it was observed that he went so far as to

> applaud and laugh at the rantings of a speaker at the Liberal Convention at Ottawa, who denounced Mary, the mother of Christ, as a prostitute, and no better than any other prostitute. Such demonstrations may in the Governor's judgment be very smart and cunning, but it was certainly not in very good taste for an ex-Governor of the young state of Kansas to make such a spectacle.[56]

By the early 1890s the Liberal League ceased to function as anything more than a loosely knit intellectual society with exchanges of correspondence between a few members. Letters written and received by Robinson, however, continued to discuss radical religious ideas on much the same basis as discussions at previous encampments of the league.[57]

No identifiable long-term effects resulted from the activities of the Kansas Liberal League. Yet its existence indicates that there was a significant number of intellectual individualists in Kansas in the last quarter of the nineteenth century. Charles Robinson, as one of the organizers of the league and one of the formulators of its doctrines, played a significant role in liberal intellectual circles. For him, such an involvement was an expression of philosophical principles stressing the importance of education and thought in man's progressive nature.

9

The Final Years

The years from 1889 to 1894 were ones of political turmoil in Kansas. Charles Robinson, after his retirement from Haskell Institute, had intended to spend the remainder of his life in writing and in looking after his large estate. He found his plans altered, however, when he became involved in the farmers' movement that swept through Kansas in 1889 and 1890.

After he left the governor's chair in 1863, Charles Robinson practiced farming. He was successful in this occupation, and by 1889 he had no financial worries. The Robinson farm, Oakridge, was located four miles north of Lawrence and consisted of over sixteen hundred acres of Kansas River Valley land on which wheat, corn, and other farm crops grew in abundance. In addition, Robinson had other land holdings in the immediate vicinity of Lawrence.[1] As a farmer, he was widely recognized for both his practical and theoretical knowledge of agriculture. He was active in several agricultural and horticultural societies in Kansas, and he frequently made speeches at meetings on methods for improved and more productive farming. He was also an active leader in early farmers' organizations in Kansas. In 1873 he participated in a farmers' state convention in Topeka, which attempted to unite the numerous local and county organizations around the state into a strong pressure group. In a major address to the convention, Robinson extolled the benefits of such an organization and suggested a plan for putting it into effect. He advocated that county and state organizations be formed in all agricultural states as auxiliaries to a national organization. A national headquarters should be established. Through correspondence with all auxiliaries, it would fix prices for all farm products, thereby placing farmers on the same footing with dealers in wool, cotton, or iron. "We can then obtain laws, regulate railroads, and [influence] the price of every commodity bought by the farmer," concluded Robinson. He did not advise forming a political party, but he urged the farmers to vote for candidates who promised to assist them in obtaining stricter controls on railroad and commodity prices. During the following two days of the convention, the Farmer's Cooperative Association of the State of Kansas was created along the lines suggested by Robinson.[2] Sixteen years later the Kansas Farmers' Alliance followed a similar pattern of organization. Charles Robinson was also a member of the state Grange organization, and in the 1870s he served on its transportation committee. In this capacity, he publicly urged both the higher taxation of railroads and the state regulation of freight and passenger rates.[3]

These and similar farmers' organizations thrived during the depression years of the mid 1870s, but they became much less active in the period of prosperity that immediately followed. The years 1877 to 1881 were marked by good crops, high market prices for farm products, and increased property values. Agricultural prosperity, however, was only a by-product of the national industrial expansion, which fostered rapid urban development. Land values skyrocketed; but the speculators and promoters focused on towns rather than on agricultural land. The prosperity of the farmers did not have a sound base. When the boom began to subside after 1881 and land values started to decline, farmers were particularly hard hit. An end came to the noticeable lack of concern over agricultural issues and problems that farmers had exhibited during the boom years, and such organizations as the Grange were revived.[4]

Even before the collapse of the boom in the 1880s, dissatisfaction was apparent among Kansas farmers. Prices for farm products declined steadily after 1881. Corn sold for 83 cents per bushel in 1881, and 28 cents a bushel in 1890; wheat dropped from $1.19 in 1881 to 49 cents per bushel in 1894. Similar declines affected livestock and "all farm products." The sharp drop in prices for farm crops sparked a corresponding decline in land values. The result of the situation was the development of an overwhelming indebtedness, both private and public. The census of 1890 reported that the total mortgage debt of Kansas was more than 27 percent of the actual value of all Kansas real estate. In Kansas, 60 percent of all taxed acreage carried a mortgage, a figure that was unmatched in any other state. The state auditor's *Report* for 1890 established the assessed value of all property in Kansas at $348,457,943 and the total public and private indebtedness at $706,181,627.[5] A diary for the years 1887–1891, kept by Leon Riddle, a farmer in Marion County, provides a close look at the economic effects of the depression in Kansas. Two entries will suffice to show the local conditions that gave rise to the political protest movement that erupted in 1890.

[July 30, 1887] I am harder up for money than I ever was in my life. I stood around the streets all day wondering what kind of turn I could make to raise some money. The crop prospects are so blue & there is no confidence in Real Estate. You can't sell anything.

[February 12, 1890] There is a great deal of complaint of very hard times. Everything the farmer has to sell is so cheap. Corn about 12¢, oats 15, Hay 2.50 delivered in town, Eggs 10¢ all winter. And wheat about 50¢ per bus[hel]—and of course when this is the case the hard times are sure to be close.[6]

Charles Robinson, as a farmer and a reformer, sympathized with the plight of the small landholder who was struggling to make a living. He was an active member of the Douglas County Grange in the 1870s and 1880s. He was also involved in the formation of the Kansas Farmers' Alliance in 1889, a movement designed to organize the "reformers and farmers and laborers of Kansas" into a massive pressure group.[7] Initially, the alliance was not intended to become directly involved in politics; rather, its members decided "to support only those candidates who coincide with their views and adopt their principles."[8] It became apparent to some leaders, however, that the alliance, composed as it was of Republicans, Democrats, and old third-party men, could not continue to function as a pressure group only, for making independent endorsements would soon cause splits in the organization. Thus, a movement to create a separate political party based on support from the alliance began to attract widespread interest.[9]

One of the first indications of a shift toward more active political participation came at a meeting of Douglas County farmers, which was held at the courthouse in Lawrence on March 5, 1890. The first topic of discussion concerned withholding products from market until the prices were better. As the meeting progressed and accounts of economic injustices were given, the resentment of the farmers mounted. At the end of the meeting, the farmers of Douglas County declared that they were determined to find the real reasons for the depression and "to find out and apply the remedy."[10] Charles Robinson must have had mixed emotions about the possibility of forming a new party. Although he was involved and active in the alliance movement, he had been closely associated with the Democrats for more than five years. He could only wait to see what specific course of action a new party would adopt.

Similar meetings were held around the state in the following months, and by early summer the majority of the membership of the alliance believed that the benefits to be gained as a separate party outweighed the risks of entering politics. Since the machinery of the two major parties was controlled by town dwellers and was connected to railroads and corporations, the members naturally concluded that the best way out of their troubles was through an independent political movement. Accordingly, Benjamin Clover, president of the alliance, called for a meeting of all reform organizations at Topeka on June 12, 1890, to determine the appropriate action to follow in the political campaign. Joining the alliance delegates in Topeka were representatives of the Knights of Labor, members of the

Union Labor party, and former leaders of the Greenback party. The Knights of Labor had gained significant strength in Kansas in the 1880s among miners and railroad men, who hoped to combat the importation of Italian contract laborers and to win disputes over wages and over safety in the mines. The Knights were antimonopoly; they favored land reform and policies promoting inflation; and they believed that primary producers, whether agricultural or mechanical, had the same interests.[11]

The Union Labor and Greenback elements had been involved in the alliance movement from the beginning; they had contributed valuable ideas as well as leaders. Many of Robinson's friends and colleagues from this previous involvement with the Union Labor and Greenback parties emerged as leaders of the alliance. They included W. H. T. Wakefield, who had been the Union Labor vice-presidential candidate in 1888, and W. F. Rightmire, who was a former Union Labor candidate for state attorney general. But Charles Robinson did not attend the meeting. His close association with the Democrats, together with rumors that he was favored by many leaders of the Democratic party as their choice for gubernatorial candidate, raised doubts about his loyalty among some leaders of the alliance.[12] The assembled delegates at the alliance convention unanimously decided that a full slate of nominations should be entered in the 1890 election. It was determined, however, that it would be better to create an organization that would be separate from the Farmers' Alliance in order to keep the alliance from becoming entirely partisan. The assembled delegates decided that the name of the new party would be the People's party. A state nominating convention was scheduled to meet in Topeka on August 13, 1890. One of the final acts of the June convention was the adoption of a resolution that clearly stated that the delegates were not interested in combining forces with any other party. In light of the rumor that Robinson might be a Democratic candidate, it was significantly pointed in its wording and appeared to have been aimed directly at Robinson. It read: "We will not support for any office any member of our organization who will accept a nomination from either of the old parties, but will consider such a member a traitor to our cause."[13]

While Charles Robinson generally favored the principles of the platform adopted by the National Alliance at St. Louis in December, 1889, he was determined to make prohibition a key issue in the Kansas election.[14] In an open letter that Robinson wrote to the *Kansas Democrat* in July, 1890, he advocated the open saloon, saying:

> If the opening of original package saloons will only open the eyes of the people, it will be a blessing to the community, for their temperance work will take the place of prohibition talk. . . . One thing they will do . . . is discard the policeman's club as a moral agent. And another thing they ought to do and that is to set in motion the usual things that were discarded in 1881. . . . Good Templar's organizations, temperance melodies, festivals and talks as they existed before attempted prohibition . . . will do more to save young men and old people from intemperance than all the prohibiting laws ever enacted.[15]

In the late spring and early summer, Robinson was mentioned by non-Republican elements of the press as the logical candidate for governor of the new party. Some even went so far as to suggest that the People's party would be wise to combine with the Democrats in supporting him. Robinson's attitude was that he would accept the nomination of the People's party if it were offered, but that he would stand on his own convictions. On August 9, 1890, he wrote to W. H. T. Wakefield, an active leader of the People's party who was campaigning for Robinson's selection, explaining that he would not run if a narrow platform were adopted. In that letter, Robinson warned Wakefield that, should the platform be narrowed down to attract only a man who was a "republican, a prohibitionist, or a man devoid of convictions," he would have to ask that his name be withheld from the convention. Robinson's letter was in reaction to a remark made by William A. Peffer, editor of the *Kansas Farmer*, in which he had stated that no man should head the ticket who had been so publicly identified with any particular social, political, or religious movement that he had become "obnoxious to large classes of people." Whether or not Peffer was referring to anyone specifically, Robinson took it as a direct affront. "So you see I am a most complete outcast," said Robinson to Wakefield, "and I do not want to disturb him [Peffer] in his convictionless fight, led by a prohibition republican who never entertained a conviction unless it was first found to be popular."[16] Nevertheless, Robinson was reported to be a leading contender for the Populist nomination for governor one day prior to the convention. According to one newspaper observer, he had the entire delegations of Douglas and Shawnee counties behind him.[17]

John F. Willits, president of the Jefferson County Alliance, called the state nominating convention to order on the morning of August 13, 1890. There were 250 delegates from the Farmers' Alliance, the Citizens' Alliance, the Union Labor party, the Knights of Labor, and other reform groups.[18] The combination of the numerous special interest groups prompted a wide range of discussion on political issues. The question of resubmitting the prohibition amendment, however, received little attention. "Ignore the whole question. We have something of more importance to talk about," was the prevailing attitude among the delegates.[19] The plan was to straddle the issue and make no commitment at all in order to attract votes from both sides of the issue. This strategy hurt the chances of Robinson's nomination, for his views on resubmission were well known. Following a flurry of nominations, the field eventually came down to three men: John Willits, Charles Robinson, and William Peffer. Each was asked to make a few remarks before the balloting began. Robinson stated that he would accept the nomination if the delegates thought that he could win. He told them that the People's party would be assured of a victory by joining with the Democrats. This last statement, even more than his stand on resubmission, ended his chances of getting the nomination. It was understood that Robinson was the man the Democrats wanted and that if he were nominated by the People's party, the Democrats would endorse the ticket. The convention, however, was determined to make its own stand and to avoid all bargaining or fusion. Willits received the nomination on the first ballot with 397 votes. Robinson finished second with 101, while William Peffer received only 15 votes.

Robinson was disappointed and somewhat annoyed by the

selection of Willits. The same people who defeated him at the convention were the ones who, prior to the convention, had urged that they be allowed to present his name for the nomination. He believed that they had done this for the purposes of uniting the various factions in opposition to the Republican party. As a result of this maneuver, however, Robinson concluded that the leaders of the Democratic party would never support Willits, noting that some of them had always opposed fusion, but that now they all were opposed to it.[20] No less shocked than Robinson was the editor of the Topeka *Democrat*, who was quoted in the Topeka *Daily Capital* as saying:

> The curtain is lifted. We know now where we are. . . . The democracy have no mud to throw at the alliance, but the door has been rudely slammed in their face, and they have no intention of again asking for admission into a political domicile in which they are not wanted. . . . The democracy and resubmission republican can win next November without any aid from the surly prohibs in the Farmers' alliance.

The article ended with the prophetic observation that "it is war along the line now in Kansas."[21]

The Republicans, confused as to what new issues they could present in order to disrupt the Populists, met on September 2. They renominated the 1888 ticket headed by incumbent Governor Lyman Humphrey. The platform that they adopted was broad enough to offer the radicals anything they wanted, such as a new system of property assessment, the abolition of child labor, the abolishment of railroad passes for state officials, and a popularly elected railroad commission.

The Democrats and the Resubmissionists met in separate convention on September 9, 1890, in Wichita. Following the completion of the temporary organization of the Democratic convention, it was announced the Resubmission convention had appointed a conference committee to meet with the Democrats. A similar committee was appointed by the Democratic chairman. This conference issued a joint report, which stated that the Resubmission convention was ready to endorse the full Democratic ticket, provided that its nominee for lieutenant governor was endorsed by the Democrats. A motion was made and unanimously adopted to that effect. When it was declared that nominations for governor were in order, Charles Robinson's was the only name presented. He was unanimously nominated by acclamation.[22]

The platform adopted by the Democrats did not vary from the Populist platform a great deal, except on the question of prohibition. Three out of the fifteen articles in the platform dealt with this question: one called for resubmission of the prohibition amendment, one called for abolishment of testimony of paid informers in court cases involving prohibition violations, and one "emphatically" endorsed a local-option system of liquor control. The remainder of the platform—which included reduction of tariffs, enactment of new fiscal laws, free coinage of silver, and regulation of railroads—agreed with that of the Populists. Similarly, both contained strong repudiations of incumbent Republican Senator John J. Ingalls. Thus, the principal difference in the platforms of the three parties came down to the questions concerning prohibition, with the Democrats calling for resubmission. The Republicans endorsed Ingalls, while the Democrats and the Populists asked the voters to repudiate him.

The initial reaction to Robinson's candidacy was favorable in most Democratic papers and even in a few Republican ones. According to the Wyandotte *Herald*, Charles Robinson was a platform in himself. "His public and private life has been such as to commend him to the better element of all parties."[23] John Martin, editor of the Atchison *Champion*, a leading Republican paper, also had some kind words to say about Robinson:

> The nomination of Hon. Charles Robinson for governor, on the democratic state ticket, is one of the very best nominations ever made during the entire history of Kansas. While not agreeing with Gov. Robinson politically, the *Champion* as an act of common justice feels moved to say that his nomination is a strong one. . . . The democratic party is to be congratulated upon the wisdom shown in this nomination.[24]

There was a general belief that the campaign would be a bitter and arduous one; therefore, some concern was expressed at the beginning about how well Robinson, now seventy-two years of age, would hold up physically. When asked this question on one occasion, he replied that he had never felt better in his life: "All I want is a fair amount of sleep every twenty-four hours and I will keep up with the campaign to the very letter."[25]

Robinson's initial campaign plans were to concentrate on economic issues and specifically to attack the McKinley tariff bill. This issue he believed to be the greatest question before the people, and one that the Republicans in Kansas were trying to ignore. He argued that this particular measure, which would raise duties on all imports, was framed in the interest of Eastern manufacturers at the expense of Western farmers.[26] Once the campaign had started, however, Robinson expanded his speeches to cover three main issues: the tariff, resubmission, and the free coinage of silver. As the campaign became more heated, he was occasionally ridiculed in Republican papers for his presentation. In mentioning a Democratic rally in Topeka, the Ottawa *Daily Republican* advertised Robinson's appearance in the following manner: "Be in time! Be in time! Great three-ring circus under one tent! Positively the last appearance of the wonderful three horse straddler, Charles Robinson! Come one, come all."[27]

Robinson had promised to canvass the state thoroughly if he received the Democratic nomination. In the two months' campaign he spoke in every major town in Kansas, from Leavenworth to Dodge City, and from Pittsburg to Wichita. Through this widespread public exposure of Robinson, the Democrats were undoubtedly counting on Robinson's personal popularity to win the election.

The tactics of the two opposing parties took different courses. Burdened with nominees who were relatively unknown, the Populists' strategy was to get out large crowds and use forceful speakers, such as Mary E. Lease and "Sockless Jerry" Simpson. Their most prominent speaker from out of state was Leonidas Polk, who was the president of the National Farmers' Alliance. He came from North Carolina to Kansas to campaign for the Populist party during the summer, and he remained through

159

the autumn. These Populist orators were denounced by Republican papers as "calamity howlers." The Topeka *Capital* ran an editorial for several consecutive days under the heading "Who Is Polk?" He was denounced as the chief of the "calamity howlers," and even more significantly, it was pointed out that he had been an officer in the Confederate Army during the Civil War. This was sufficient ammunition for the Republicans to wave the "bloody shirt," a tactic that had never failed to bring a victory to the Republicans in Kansas. Charges against the personal character of the Populist candidate for governor also proved effective for the Republicans.[28] Only on one occasion in the early stages of the campaign did Robinson come under fire from the Republicans. Mention was made of his impeachment in 1862, but the matter was not pursued. The Republicans either considered Robinson out of the race, or they feared that personal attacks on the "grand old man" of Kansas would do them more harm than good.[29]

On election day the Republican party was shocked. Populists were elected to five of the seven seats in the U.S. House of Representatives and to ninety-one of the one hundred and twenty-five positions in the Kansas House. Willits, who received nearly 101,000 votes, lost to the Republican incumbent by less than 8,000 votes, while Robinson, who received over 70,000 votes, finished third. Nevertheless, he had run some 15,000 votes ahead of his party, making significant inroads into both the Republican and the Populist votes. Willits ran about 9,000 votes behind other Populist candidates. Had the Populists nominated Robinson rather than Willits, the outcome, in all probability, would have been a larger victory for the Populists.[30]

The advantages of a fusion became obvious to the leaders of the Democratic and the Populist parties as they evaluated the election of 1890 and prepared for the campaign of 1892.[31] In rejecting Robinson as their candidate in 1890, the Populists lost two years in their struggle to elect a governor who was committed to solving the agricultural problems.

Though defeated, Robinson was praised by the Democrats for his efforts. "No one will say that Governor Robinson was not an ideal leader," wrote the editor of the *Kansas Democrat*, "the

160

campaign made by him, under the circumstances, was little short of marvelous."[32] Charles Robinson, in his final political effort, had indeed conducted a hard and tedious campaign for a man over seventy years of age. His participation significantly altered the future course of action of the Democratic and the Populist parties, for in 1892 they did form a coalition, which enabled them to defeat the Republicans.

Until his death, Robinson continued to write articles advocating the adoption of the policies that he had campaigned for in 1890. In 1893 he wrote an article for the *New Kansas Magazine* entitled "Remonetization or Demonetization, Which?" He contended that the gold "base" standard was the cause of the economic problems then existing. The remedy, he concluded, was for the government to decide upon a proper volume of currency and then to have no other "standard" or "base." Gold, silver, and any other legal tender could then be used equally, without fear of money dealers getting control of a system based on a single standard.[33] Articles written by Robinson on similar issues periodically appeared in Lawrence and Topeka newspapers.[34] Because of this sustained activity, Robinson was often urged to seek political office again. When Cleveland was reelected president in 1892, James F. Legate, a prominent leader in the Kansas Democratic party, urged Robinson to consider seeking an appointment as secretary of agriculture.[35] Robinson, however, decided that his position was simply one of serving in the ranks. He answered Legate's letter and other similar requests with the same reply. He urged that his name not be used in connection with any political office. "I am a back runner in personal politics because of age," concluded Robinson, "and because there is no work that I could do that there are not plenty of younger men . . . who would do as well as I could, if not better. So leave me out of all calculations so far as office and let me serve as a private in the ranks."[36] Robinson used the same arguments in denying rumors that he would run for governor in 1894.

A major portion of Robinson's efforts following the 1890 campaign was devoted to the completion of *The Kansas Conflict* —a personal account of the Kansas Territorial struggle—in which

Robinson defended the course of action of the Topeka movement and the free-state cause. Admitting that his book was not an attempt at a complete historical account of the early period, he used it as a vehicle to counter the charges against him and to imply that the actions of James Lane and John Brown, the alleged Kansas heroes, had been detrimental to Kansas. As a result, the book received widespread notice as well as a great amount of reaction from Kansans who sympathized with Lane and Brown. Most of the newspaper notices of the book after it appeared in 1892 were favorable. A typical review appeared in the Kansas City *Times*:

> Gov. Charles Robinson's book, "The Kansas Conflict," is out and will be the literary sensation of the season along the Missouri and Kaw rivers. . . . The chapters of the book which will be most discussed are those relating to Lane and John Brown. . . . Gov. Robinson shows that Brown's actions were injurious and unjustifiable and that Lane provoked a great deal of the bitterness which colored the events in which he was engaged.[37]

To ensure wide distribution of the book, Governor Robinson publicly offered to provide a free copy to any public library in Kansas that would write to him at Lawrence.

The leading critic of the Robinson book was Daniel W. Wilder, a well-known Kansas writer. Wilder wrote Robinson a personal letter soon after the book had been published, to inform the author that he was glad that the book had been written. "But I am decidedly on the other side in the main part of your version or perversion," wrote Wilder. "Your wife's book is better than yours."[38] Thus, even in his final years, Charles Robinson's life was marked by political involvement and controversial viewpoints.

Throughout the spring and summer of 1894 Charles Robinson was in poor health, suffering from chronic bladder and stomach trouble. In July he journeyed to Excelsior Springs, Missouri, where he hoped to alleviate his condition at the hot springs. After two days of treatment, he wrote to his wife that he did not know "what effect the water will have in my case. . . .

So far no injury has resulted, and if I ever get comfortably cool I can enjoy the place very well."[39] He returned home in early August, and on August 10 became severely ill. He died on August 17, 1894, at the age of seventy-six. Simple and brief funeral services were conducted at Plymouth Congregational Church in Lawrence on the following Sunday afternoon.

Notice of Robinson's death appeared as a major story in nearly every Kansas newspaper. The stories consisted of glowing tributes and lengthy biographical sketches. Feature articles on Robinson also were carried in the New York *Times* and in various papers in New England. One of the most glowing tributes was the following poem in the Lawrence *Gazette*, written by Henry M. Greene:

CHARLES ROBINSON

Fallen at length, is the Nestor of our time,
Founder and savior of our infant State,
The lofty life to Freedom dedicate—
The Champion ever mailed to challenge crime,
And make the people's rustic cause sublime.
Peer of the commonwealth he did create,
His strength hath known no weakness, no abate,
From this strange stillness back to youth's rich prime.
And is he fallen? Nay; a wiser thought
Follows the spirit as it slow withdrew,
Leaving the fields on which he grandly fought.
The writhing wrongs his prowess overthrew,
And lo! amidst the zenith stars inwrought,
We speed the newest orbed. Hail, and adieu.[40]

Although it was not so poetic, an editorial in the Lawrence *Daily Journal* contained a more accurate assessment of Robinson's life:

Among the names Kansas has given to history, none are more prominent than his. . . . His history has been a part of the history of Kansas and the country. . . . His life was a constant warfare. Even in peace his aggressive disposition led him into controversies, and his antagonistic nature caused him to make war upon whatever seemed to him to be wrong or leading into error. During the later years of his

163

life he appeared to try and shake off this natural tendency.
. . . But he could not. . . . To the very last his dominant
passion prevailed, and his eagerness to be in the midst of the
battle, and in the very heat of the struggle, was over-
powering.[41]

Had the editor who wrote this summary of Robinson's life
had an additional ten years' perspective, he might well have
carried the association of Robinson with controversy even beyond
his death. The discussion that Charles Robinson began by
writing *The Kansas Conflict* increased in intensity and expanded
in scope after his death. Sara Robinson, motivated by a desire
to make a hero of her late husband in the annals of Kansas history, ably carried on the Lane-Brown-Robinson dispute. She and
Robinson's friends began the campaign by getting the Kansas
legislators to enact a law which provided one thousand dollars
to place a bust of Robinson at the University of Kansas in
memory of his services and of the large bequest that he left to
the school at the time of his death.[42] The committee that was
selected to make arrangements for the bust commissioned Lorado
Taft to do the sculpture, which was dedicated on February 22,
1898. The use of public funds for this project sparked new
controversy about Robinson. As attacks were made by critics,
Sara Robinson replied to them in a bitter and defensive manner.
While many of Robinson's colleagues encouraged her attacks on
the critics of her husband, others advised that Robinson's place
in history was secure and that she would be better off making
no replies. Unfortunately, for both herself and her cause, she
paid no attention to this advice. In 1898 she paid three hundred
dollars to secure a version of Robinson's biography that would
meet with her approval for inclusion in the *National Cyclopedia
of Biography*.[43]

A year after the death of her husband, Sara Robinson
began an active effort to publish an approved biography of him.
The task was assigned to Frank W. Blackmar, who was furnished
both money and material by Mrs. Robinson.[44] Frank Blackmar
was professor of history and sociology at the University of Kansas
from 1889 until 1897. In that year he was appointed dean of
the university's graduate school. He also served as an adminis-

trator of the Robinson estate. Although he was very favorable to the Robinson view of Kansas history, Blackmar did not make fanciful claims for his subject, as some biographers of John Brown and James Lane have done. Nevertheless, publication of his book in 1901 renewed the Robinson-Lane-Brown controversy.

The leading critic of Robinson was William E. Connelley, who was encouraged and supported in his efforts by D. W. Wilder. Connelley moved to Topeka from Bonner Springs in 1899 in order to take charge of the book department of Crane and Company publishing house. He wrote a number of books about Kansas history, including a biography of James Lane in 1899 and a full-length biography of John Brown in 1900. Both books were highly partisan and contained statements derogatory to Charles Robinson. When he applied to Sara Robinson in 1900 for permission to see her collection of materials for a possible biography of Charles Robinson, he was refused access and was informed that a biography was already being prepared. From that point, Connelley led the attack on Robinson.[45]

When Blackmar's book failed to silence the critics, Sara Robinson undertook to finance the publication of two books written by George W. Brown, who was formerly an editor of a free-state newspaper in Lawrence during the Territorial struggle. Both books, *False Claims of Kansas Historians Truthfully Corrected* and *Reminiscences of Governor R. J. Walker*, were published in 1902, and both were aimed primarily at William Connelley's interpretation of John Brown.[46] At this stage of the controversy, tempers flared on both sides. Upon receipt of *False Claims Corrected*, Connelley wrote a long and violent letter to Brown, which illustrated the climate of the controversy as well as the fact that Connelley believed that history was a peculiarly personal matter. Connelley wrote, in part:

> Your book came, and I have glanced through it. I do not blame you for trying to bolster up your former leader, and Robinson's cause. Both need it, God knows. . . . You bawl "Liar! Liar!" You are the liar. . . . You condemn John Brown and Jim Lane because their lives were not without sin! Great God! Holy man art thou! I believe a man should be as clean as you and Robinson pretend to be. . . . Did you

ever read of the men who threw stones at the woman, thou holy man? I believe you and Robinson would have refrained from throwing on an entirely different ground from that set out in the holy writ, and would have followed the woman home.[47]

A few months later Connelley wrote *Appeal to the Record*, the most vicious attack upon Robinson ever printed. In the preface, Connelley asked for public support to carry on the fight "for decency and justice to Kansas pioneers." He claimed that he was a poor man and that he could not stand alone against the Robinson estate, and so he asked for financial assistance for his writings, which defended "the men who fought to make Kansas free and great from the defamation heaped upon them by Robinson, G. W. Brown, and the money which Robinson left at Lawrence."[48]

The controversy, which had extended over the previous five years, was rapidly losing its appeal to newspapers and publishers. Following the appearance of *Appeal to the Record*, G. W. Brown decided that he would no longer argue with Connelley. Sara Robinson, however, continued until the time of her death to write occasional letters to newspapers, making public her low opinion of Connelley, Wilder, and others who criticized Robinson. The controversy was unfortunate for Sara's image. A poem sent anonymously to the Kansas State Historical Society was widely distributed by Connelley after he became executive secretary of that institution in 1912:

THE OLD WOMAN WHO DIDN'T LIVE IN A SHOE

There lives an old lady in Lawrence town,
Who keeps a red rag and she calls it "John Brown."
Who mocks at a goblin that drives her insane,
And the name of that monster is *Lane*, Jim Lane.
And her favorite black beast, for she keeps them in order,
Is fear of the "Red Legs," who raided the border.

She once had a husband, our first Governor,
She didn't love him, and he didn't love her.

He is dead, praise the Lord! And she'll die, more's the praise!
And somewhere or other old hades they'll raise.

She is old; she is rich; so, we leave her alone,
Though her rabies so rank would melt a mad-stone.

There's a reverence for years, there's beauty in age,
When the sunset of life has illumined the page,

When the folly of youth into wisdom has turned,
And the sacrifice incense on Time's altar has burned.

All the incense she knows is the venom of hate
In these pitiful years when her candle burns late.

So we'll leave her till Gabriel calls her, alack!
But we'll welcome the noise when the hearse comes back!

A KAW SQUAW.[49]

Sara Robinson died on November 16, 1911, at the age of eighty-four. Since she had no immediate heirs, the bulk of the remainder of the Robinson estate, including Oakridge, was left to the University of Kansas. With her passing, the campaign to create a hero out of Charles Robinson came to a close. The last seventeen years of her life had been devoted to perpetuating a heroic image of Charles Robinson. In the long run, her attempts served only to cloud his image. Writers of Kansas history in the first four decades of the twentieth century paid little attention to Charles Robinson's role in Kansas history, while James Lane and John Brown continued to be recognized as the leaders of the antislavery struggle in Kansas. Only in the last thirty years has Charles Robinson's role in the free-state cause been assessed in a favorable view.[50]

In retrospect, it can be said that Robinson's Kansas career had two distinct phases. The first phase occurred from 1854 to 1862, the second from the time that he left office as governor until his death. Both were exciting and controversial. In his first six years in Kansas he became the leader of the free-state cause, received national attention for his courageous stand against pro-slavery forces in 1856, and was elected the first governor of Kansas in 1860. Within two years, as a result of the controversy with James Lane, Robinson found himself being ignored by the Lincoln administration in Washington and facing impeachment charges by the state legislature. Although he was not convicted, Robinson left politics for nearly a decade, and the Republican party for the rest of his life. In abandoning the Republican party, Robinson destroyed an opportunity to become the leading politician in Kansas. "Had he been content to bide his time, the death of Lane would have vindicated him," wrote Sol Miller in 1894, "and he would have been the leader and pride of Kansas for a quarter of a century after his unscrupulous antagonist was mouldered to dust."[51] Robinson's character and philosophy, however, would not allow him to follow this course. He became an agitator and a fighter who supported policies that opposed injustice and supported the common good. He fought both for and against certain issues at different times during the thirty years of his postgubernatorial career, but the Republican party was his constant foe.

Had Charles Robinson remained a Republican, his contributions to Kansas history could not have been any more significant. From 1864 until his death, Robinson consistently championed educational and reform measures which contributed to the state's welfare and progress. He was a leading spokesman for both woman and Negro suffrage. He strongly supported and contributed to higher education in Kansas. He fought for the improved conditions of farmers and laborers, and he served as an agitator against policies that he deemed to be unfavorable to the common man. On many issues, such as religion, Robinson was considered a radical. But all his causes and actions were based on careful reasoning and calm judgment. His major weakness was that once he had made a decision or judgment, he showed little patience with people or groups who disagreed with him, thus alienating potential support on other issues. This was the major reason that Robinson did not obtain the necessary political strength to be elected to a major office between 1863 and 1894. In spite of his defects as a political leader, the force of Charles Robinson's personality helped to influence and guide the development of Kansas in the nineteenth century. There can be little doubt that his concern for the betterment of Kansas and its citizens was a genuine personal commitment.

Notes

These acronyms are used throughout the notes:

KHC   *Kansas Historical Collections*
KHQ   *Kansas Historical Quarterly*
KSHS   Kansas State Historical Society, Topeka, Kansas

CHAPTER 1

1. S. T. D. Robinson, "Notes on Charles Robinson," ms., Robinson Collection, Kansas City, Kansas, Public Library.
2. John Speer, untitled ms. on James Lane and Charles Robinson, p. 2., Connelley Collection, KSHS.
3. S. T. D. Robinson, "Notes" ms.
4. Charles Robinson, "True Doctor," ms., Robinson Papers, KSHS.
5. Charles Robinson, *The Kansas Conflict* (New York: Harper & Brothers, 1892), p. 28; see also Frank W. Blackmar, *The Life of Charles Robinson* (Topeka; Kan.: Crane & Co., 1902), p. 40; George Washington Brown, *The Rescue of Kansas from Slavery* (Rockford, Ill.: G. W. Brown, 1902), p. 176.
6. For a detailed summary of the trip to California by Robinson, see Louise Barry, comp., "Charles Robinson—Yankee '49er: His Journey to California," *KHQ* 34 (1968):179–88.

7. Robinson, *Kansas Conflict*, p. 31. Although no diary now exists, many of his entries were printed in a pamphlet, *Nebraska and Kansas: Report of the Massachusetts Emigrant Aid Company* (Boston, 1854). Other entries appear in Robinson, *Kansas Conflict*.

8. Barry, "Charles Robinson—Yankee '49er," p. 184.

9. Robinson, *Kansas Conflict*, pp. 36–37.

10. Ibid., p. 38.

11. Josiah Royce, "An Episode of Early California Life: The Squatter Riot of 1850 in Sacramento," in his *Studies of Good and Evil* (New York: D. Appleton & Co., 1898), pp. 323–29.

12. Ibid., p. 326.

13. J. H. McKune to Mary Robinson, November 9, 1895, Robinson Papers, KSHS.

14. Ibid.; Letter from N. McKinney to Charles Robinson, August 14, 1890, Robinson Papers, KSHS.

15. Royce, "An Episode of Early California Life," p. 347.

16. Alberta Pantle, ed., "The Connecticut Kansas Colony: Letters of Charles B. Lines to the New Haven (Conn.) *Daily Palladium*," *KHQ* 22 (1956):20.

17. Robinson, *Kansas Conflict*, p. 67.

18. In the spring of 1855 a new charter was obtained, and the name of the company was changed to the New England Emigrant Aid Company.

19. Statement of T. S. Huffaker, Council Grove, Kans., October 30, 1905, *KHC* 9 (1905–1906):129n.

20. Webb Scrapbooks, vol. 1, p. 75, KSHS.

21. Eli Thayer, *The New England Emigrant Aid Company* (Worcester, Mass.: F. P. Rice, 1887), p. 13; Samuel A. Johnson, *The Battle Cry of Freedom* (Lawrence: University of Kansas Press, 1954), p. 10.

22. Quoted from William H. Carruth, "The New England Emigrant Aid Company as an Investment Society," *KHC* 6 (1897–1900):93.

23. Quoted in Johnson, *Battle Cry of Freedom*, p. 55.

24. For a breakdown of numbers and names within each of the six Emigrant Aid Company parties of 1854, see Louise Barry, "The Emigrant Aid Company Parties of 1854," *KHQ* 12 (1943):115–55.

25. Carruth, "The New England Emigrant Aid Company as an Investment Society," p. 94.
26. Robinson, *Kansas Conflict*, p. 81.
27. For a full descriptive account of the conflict, see William G. Cutler, ed., *History of the State of Kansas* (Chicago: A. T. Andreas, 1883), p. 75; Robinson, *Kansas Conflict*, pp. 78–83.
28. Leverett W. Spring, *Kansas: The Prelude to the War for the Union* (Boston: Houghton, Mifflin & Co., 1885), pp. 33–35.
29. Sara T. L. Robinson, *Kansas: Its Interior and Exterior Life* (1st ed.; Boston: Crosby, Nichols & Co., 1856), p. 13.

CHAPTER 2

1. New York *Daily Times*, May 27, 1854.
2. Elmer Leroy Craik, "Southern Interest in Territorial Kansas, 1854–1858," *KHC* 15 (1919–1922):342, 344.
3. Ibid., p. 346; Spring, *Kansas*, p. 43.
4. Charles Robinson, "On Human Slavery," ms., Robinson Papers, KSHS.
5. James C. Malin, "The Topeka Statehood Movement Reconsidered: Origins," in *Territorial Kansas: Studies Commemorating the Centennial* (Lawrence: University of Kansas Publications, Social Science Studies, 1954), pp. 40–41, 49.
6. Robinson, *Kansas Conflict*, p. 121.
7. At that time, free-state men were elected in all the protested districts except Leavenworth, where again there was evidence of fraudulent voting.
8. *Brunswicker*, Brunswick, Missouri, April, 1855; quoted from Cutler, *History of the State of Kansas*, p. 98.
9. Quoted in Blackmar, *Charles Robinson*, pp. 132–33.
10. See Robinson, *Kansas: Its Interior and Exterior Life*, and Blackmar, *Charles Robinson*, for the best examples of this argument.
11. Robinson, *Kansas Conflict*, p. 169.
12. Robert W. Richmond, "The First Capitol of Kansas," *KHQ* 21 (1954–1955):323.
13. Robinson, *Kansas: Its Interior and Exterior Life*, p. 70.
14. Cutler, *History of the State of Kansas*, p. 106.

15. Letter from S. C. Smith to S. T. D. Robinson, February 12, 1899, Robinson Papers, KSHS.
16. Joel K. Goodin, "The Topeka Movement," *KHQ* 13 (1913–1914):128.
17. *Kansas Free State*, Lawrence, August 20, 1855.
18. William E. Connelley, *James Henry Lane: The "Grim Chieftain" of Kansas* (Topeka, Kans.: Crane & Co., 1899), p. 46.
19. *Herald of Freedom*, Lawrence, January 19, 1856.
20. John J. Ingalls, "Kansas—1541–1891," *Harpers Magazine* 86 (1893):702.
21. *Daily Conservative*, Leavenworth, July 3, 1865; Albert D. Richardson, *Beyond the Mississippi: From the Great River to the Great Ocean* (Hartford, Conn.: American Publishing Co., 1867), pp. 44–45.
22. John James Ingalls, *A Collection of the Writings of John James Ingalls* (Kansas City, Mo.: Hudson-Kimberly Publishing Co., 1902), pp. 454–55.
23. Cutler, *History of the State of Kansas*, p. 239.
24. Milton W. Reynolds, in the Kansas City *Times* (1885), quoted in William E. Connelley, *A Standard History of Kansas and Kansans* (Chicago: Lewis Publishing Co., 1918), 1:426.
25. Malin, "The Topeka Statehood Movement," p. 43; see also *Kansas Free State*, Lawrence, September 10, 1855; *Herald of Freedom*, Lawrence, September 1 and 8, 1855.
26. Cutler, *History of the State of Kansas*, p. 110.
27. See Goodin, "The Topeka Movement," pp. 122–249, for a complete transcript of the meetings and correspondence of the Executive Committee of Kansas Territory.
28. Cutler, *History of the State of Kansas*, p. 111.
29. For a complete printing of the text of the Topeka Constitution, See Daniel W. Wilder, *The Annals of Kansas, 1541–1885* (Topeka, Kans.: T. Dwight Thatcher, Kansas Publishing Co., 1886), pp. 91–106.
30. All amendments had to originate in the legislature, to pass two successive annual legislatures by a two-thirds vote of both houses, and then to be referred to the people for a

referendum. No amendment could be introduced before 1865, and only one in every five years thereafter.

31. A free-state account of the Dow murder and the Branson rescue was published in the New York *Daily Tribune*, December 8, 1855. A proslavery account can be found in the Cincinnati *Gazette*, December 5, 1855.

32. Quoted in Spring, *Kansas*, p. 90.

33. Robinson, *Kansas Conflict*, p. 203; Stephenson, *Political Career of James H. Lane*, p. 57.

34. Robinson, *Kansas Conflict*, p. 220.

35. Ibid.

CHAPTER 3

1. *Congressional Globe*, 34th Cong., 1st sess., pp. 296–98.

2. Letter from Amos A. Lawrence to Charles Robinson, January 31, 1856, Robinson Papers, KSHS.

3. Goodin, "The Topeka Movement," pp. 171–72.

4. Jay (James) Monaghan, *Civil War on the Western Border, 1854–1865* (Boston: Little, Brown & Co., 1955), p. 48.

5. Quoted in James C. Malin, *John Brown and the Legend of Fifty-six* (Philadelphia: American Philosophical Society, 1942), p. 46.

6. The assailant was not identified until twenty-five years later, when it was discovered that Jones had been shot by J. F. Filer, a tramp printer. See Spring, *Kansas*, pp. 108–10.

7. Robinson, *Kansas: Its Interior and Exterior Life*, p. 201.

8. *Squatter Sovereign*, Atchison, April 29, 1856.

9. Webb Scrapbooks, vol. 12, p. 59, quoted in Malin, *John Brown and the Legend of Fifty-six*, p. 49.

10. Quoted in Johnson, *Battle Cry of Freedom*, p. 158.

11. The following account of Robinson's capture and return to Leavenworth is based on a manuscript by Sara Robinson entitled "A Long Look Backward," Robinson Collection, Kansas City, Kansas, Public Library.

12. Quoted in ibid.

13. Robinson, *Kansas: Its Interior and Exterior Life*, p. 300.

14. Quoted in George W. Martin, "The First Two Years of Kansas," *KHC* 10 (1907–1908):139.

15. One of the best studies of John Brown's Kansas career is Malin's *John Brown and the Legend of Fifty-six*. This is not a biography of John Brown but rather a history of the Brown legend. After evaluating what contemporaries had to say about Brown and after examining his Kansas activities, Malin suggests that Brown's crusade in 1856 was little more than highway robbery and outlawry under the cloak of the free-state cause, which dared not expose him. According to Malin, Brown was a man who had little influence in either making or marring Kansas history, and his reputation was based solely on legend. A recent study, which is more sympathetic to Brown, is Stephen B. Oates, *To Purge This Land with Blood* (New York: Harper & Row, 1970). According to Oates, while Brown was not a saint, he was a sincere crusader against slavery.

16. Quoted from Malin, *John Brown and the Legend of Fifty-six*, pp. 26–27; see also a letter from J. Blood to Charles Robinson, November 29, 1879, Robinson Papers, KSHS.

17. Quoted in Monaghan, *Civil War on the Western Border*, p. 63.

18. Letter from John C. Fremont to Charles Robinson, March 17, 1856, Robinson Papers, Spencer Library, University of Kansas, Lawrence.

19. Marvin Ewy, "The United States Army in the Kansas Border Troubles, 1855–1856," *KHQ* 32 (1966):382; see also W. Stitt Robinson, Jr., "The Role of the Military in Territorial Kansas," in *Territorial Kansas: Studies Commemorating the Centennial* (Lawrence: University of Kansas Publications, Social Science Studies, 1954), pp. 89–90.

20. Letter from Charles Robinson to Messrs. Allen, Blood, Hutchinson, and others, August 16, 1856, Robinson Papers, KSHS.

21. Robinson, *Kansas: Its Interior and Exterior Life*, pp. 340–41.

22. Letter from Thomas Webb to S. T. D. Robinson, October 10, 1856, New England Emigrant Aid Company Records, KSHS.

23. Robinson, *Kansas Conflict*, pp. 337–40.

24. Letter from Charles Robinson to Sara Robinson, January 15, 1857, Robinson Papers, KSHS.

25. Ibid.

26. Walker's speech was aimed at calming the aroused emotions of the two opposing forces. His arguments reflected a common view among moderate proslavery sympathizers that if slavery were economically feasible in Kansas, the question would be resolved by the need for large forces of cheap labor to fully utilize the natural climate and geography. If slavery did thrive in the climate, the settlement of the area would soon reflect it. In either case, they believed, popular sovereignty should be allowed to follow a natural course, unhindered by strong emotional feelings. See Franklin B. Sanborn, "Some Notes on the Territorial History of Kansas," *KHC* 13 (1913–1914):252–53.

27. *Republican*, Lawrence, June 11, 1857.

28. Sanborn, "Some Notes on the Territorial History of Kansas," p. 255.

29. Robinson, *Kansas Conflict*, p. 357; Spring, *Kansas*, pp. 216–17.

30. Sanborn, "Some Notes on the Territorial History of Kansas," p. 256.

31. For a full discussion of the Lecompton Constitution, see Robert W. Johannsen, "The Lecompton Constitutional Convention: An Analysis of Its Membership," *KHQ* 23 (1957): 226 ff.

32. Letter from Charles Robinson to Sara Robinson, September 13, 1857, Robinson Papers, KSHS.

33. Letter from Schuyler Colfax to Charles Robinson, April 23, 1857, Robinson Papers, KSHS.

CHAPTER 4

1. George L. Anderson, "Some Phases of Currency and Banking in Territorial Kansas," in *Territorial Kansas: Studies Commemorating the Centennial* (Lawrence: University of Kansas Publications, Social Science Studies), pp. 103–4.

2. Letters from John J. Ingalls to his father, March 29, 1859, and April 3, 1860, quoted in "Some Ingalls Letters," *KHC* 14 (1915–1918):113, 116.

3. Quoted from Paul Wallace Gates, "Land and Credit Problems in Underdeveloped Kansas," *KHQ* 31 (1965):43–44.

4. Homer E. Socolofsky, "Wyandot Floats," *KHQ* 36 (1970): 244.

5. Charles J. Kappler, *Indian Affairs, Laws and Treaties*, 2d ed. (Washington, D.C.: Government Printing Office, 1904), 2:681.

6. *Chindowan*, Quindaro, May 23, 1857.

7. *Chindowan*, Quindaro, May 13, 1857.

8. Alan W. Farley, "Annals of Quindaro: A Kansas Ghost Town," *KHQ* 22 (1956):311; George W. Veale, "Coming in and Going Out," *KHC* 11 (1909–1910):6–7.

9. Letter from Charles Robinson to Amos A. Lawrence, November 12, 1859, Robinson Papers, KSHS; contract between Charles Robinson and Alfred Gray, August 14, 1857, Gray Papers, KSHS.

10. Lela Barnes, ed., "An Editor Looks at Early-Day Kansas: The Letters of Charles Monroe Chase," *KHQ* 26 (1960): 269–70.

11. Abelard Guthrie diary, Guthrie Papers, KSHS.

12. O. B. Gunn, "Quindaro," ms., Robinson Collection, Kansas City, Kansas, Public Library.

13. Paul Wallace Gates, *Fifty Million Acres: Conflicts over Kansas Land Policy, 1854–1890* (Ithaca, N.Y.: Cornell University Press, 1954), p. 115.

14. Contract between Charles Robinson and the Kansas Land Trust, January 31, 1857, Robinson Papers, KSHS.

15. Letter from Charles Robinson to J. Lyman, September 14, 1857, Robinson Papers, KSHS.

16. Letter from Charles Robinson to Sara Robinson, October 3, 1857, Robinson Papers, KSHS.

17. Letter from James Denver to his wife, January 4, 1858, Denver Papers, KSHS.

18. Quoted from Anderson, "Some Phases of Currency and Banking," p. 107.

19. Quoted from *Herald of Freedom*, Lawrence, May 7, 1859.

20. Robinson, *Kansas Conflict*, pp. 418–19.

21. James C. Malin, "Notes on the Writing of General Histories of Kansas," *KHQ* 21 (1954–1955):336.

22. Letter from Charles Robinson to Sara Robinson, January 6, 1859, Robinson Papers, KSHS.
23. Gates, *Fifty Million Acres*, p. 117.
24. Legal documents of title dated September 1, 1862, June 5, 1868, April 25, 1871, and September 2, 1873. Items are in the William H. Sears Collection, KSHS, and in the Robinson Papers, KSHS.
25. Ibid.
26. Cutler, *History of the State of Kansas*, p. 178.
27. Letter from Charles Robinson to Sara Robinson, October 1, 1860, Robinson Papers, KSHS.
28. Letter from Charles Robinson to Sara Robinson, October 20, 1890, Robinson Papers, KSHS.
29. Cutler, *History of the State of Kansas*, p. 179.
30. Charles Robinson, running on the Republican ticket, defeated Samuel Medary, the nominee of the Democratic party, by a vote of 7,908 to 5,395; *Republican*, Lawrence, January 19, 1860. The elections were held prior to admission of Kansas as a state, with the understanding that the office would not be conferred until Kansas' admission as a state.
31. Letter from Charles Robinson to Sara Robinson, July 4, 1859, Robinson Papers, KSHS.

CHAPTER 5

1. O. E. Learnard, "Organization of the Republican Party," *KHC* 6 (1897–1900):314.
2. *Herald of Freedom*, Lawrence, May 28, 1859; *Republican*, Lawrence, May 26, 1859.
3. G. Raymond Gaeddert, *The Birth of Kansas* (Lawrence: University of Kansas, 1940), p. 20.
4. The Wyandotte constitutional convention was the fourth such convention held. After the defeat of the Topeka Constitution, the proslavery officials submitted to Congress, in January, 1858, the Lecompton Constitution without the approval of the people of Kansas. The United States Senate passed a bill by a vote of 33-to-25 to admit Kansas under the Lecompton Constitution. The House of Representatives, however, adopted a substitute bill by a vote of 120-to-112. A compromise was reached in the form of the English bill,

which ordered another vote by the Kansas citizenry. The voting was held on August 2, 1858, and the Lecompton Constitution was soundly defeated. The Territorial legislature of 1858, which was controlled by the Free State party, authorized the drafting of the Leavenworth Constitution. It was completed in May, 1858, and was presented to Congress on January 5, 1859. Congress took no action on it. An election in March, 1859, upheld the Territorial legislature in issuing a call for yet a fourth constitutional convention.

5. *Chief*, White Cloud, May 12, 1859.

6. Rosa M. Perdue, "The Sources of the Constitution of Kansas," *KHC* 7 (1901–1903):130–51.

7. Cutler, *History of the State of Kansas*, p. 175; Gaeddert, *Birth of Kansas*, p. 78.

8. Letter from H. Wilson to Charles Robinson, August 15, 1859, Robinson Papers, KSHS.

9. *Tribune*, Topeka, October 22, 1859.

10. *Herald of Freedom*, Lawrence, October 15, 1859.

11. *Chief*, White Cloud, January 26, 1860.

12. *Kansas State Record*, Topeka, July 14, 1860.

13. Stephenson, *The Political Career of General James H. Lane*, pp. 98–99.

14. Louise Barry, ed., "A Chronology of Kansas Political and Military Events, 1859–1865," *KHQ* 25 (1959):287; *Republican*, Lawrence, January 26, 1861; Gaeddert, *Birth of Kansas*, pp. 88–91.

15. *Republican*, Lawrence, January 31, 1861.

16. E. C. Manning, "In at the Birth," *KHC* 7 (1901–1902):204.

17. *Republican*, Lawrence, January 31, 1861.

18. *News*, Emporia, February 9, 1861.

19. *News*, Emporia, February 9, 1861.

20. Letter from Thomas Ewing, Jr., to Charles Robinson, November 22, 1860, Ewing Papers, KSHS.

21. Letters from Charles Robinson to Sara Robinson, December 19 and 20, 1860, Robinson Papers, KSHS.

22. Letter from Sara Robinson to Charles Robinson, December 30, 1860, Robinson Papers, KSHS.

23. Letter from Thomas Ewing, Jr., to Hugh Ewing, January 17, 1861, Ewing Papers, KSHS.
24. Letter from Charles Robinson to Sara Robinson, January 11, 1861, Robinson Papers, KSHS.
25. *News*, Emporia, February 9, 1861.
26. Letter from Charles Robinson to Sara Robinson, January 11, 1861, Robinson Papers, KSHS.
27. Letter from Marcus Parrott to Alfred Gray, March 12, 1861, Gray Papers, KSHS.
28. David E. Ballard, "The First State Legislature," *KHC* 10 (1907–1908):234; *Border Sentinel*, Mound City, December 17, 1869; *Daily Capital*, Topeka, December 23, 1945.
29. *News*, Emporia, February 16, 1861.
30. *Daily Missouri Republican*, St. Louis, Missouri, February 4, 1861, quoted in Joseph G. Gambone, "Samuel C. Pomeroy and the Senatorial Election of 1861, Reconsidered," *KHQ* 37 (1971):22.
31. Gaeddert, *Birth of Kansas*, p. 106.
32. Robinson, *Kansas Conflict*, p. 432.
33. *Republican*, Lawrence, April 4, 1861; *Kansas State Journal*, Lawrence, April 4, 1861; *News*, Emporia, April 6, 1861.
34. Letter from George Deitzler to Charles Robinson, April 16, 1861, Robinson Papers, KSHS.
35. Kansas, *Senate Journal*, 1861, p. 228.
36. Quoted in Stephenson, *The Political Career of General James H. Lane*, p. 104.
37. See Edgar Langsdorf, "Jim Lane and the Frontier Guard," *KHQ* 9 (1940):24–25.
38. Kansas, *House Journal*, 1861, pp. 460, 494, 509, 510, 539; Clifford S. Griffin, "The University of Kansas and the Years of Frustration," *KHQ* 32 (1966):18–19.
39. *Compiled Laws of Kansas*, 1862, pp. 449–51, 465, 466, 612–13; Gaeddert, *Birth of Kansas*, pp. 123–25.
40. Gaeddert, *Birth of Kansas*, pp. 124–28.
41. *Journal*, Topeka, January 2, 1909.
42. *Conservative*, Leavenworth, April 26, 1861.
43. *Daily Conservative*, Leavenworth, May 13, 1861.
44. Executive Correspondence of the Governors of Kansas, 1861, KSHS.

45. *Republican*, Lawrence, May 30, 1861.
46. Stephenson, *The Political Career of General James H. Lane*, p. 106; Gaeddert, *Birth of Kansas*, p. 147.
47. Monaghan, *Civil War on the Western Border*, p. 196.
48. Spring, *Kansas*, p. 278.
49. *Daily Conservative*, Leavenworth, October 9, 1861.
50. *Daily Conservative*, Leavenworth, October 15, 1861.
51. *Chief*, White Cloud, January 22, 1862; *News*, Emporia, January 23, 1862.

CHAPTER 6

1. *Herald of Freedom*, Lawrence, November 30, 1883, in Kansas Scrap Book 4, p. 74, KSHS.
2. Samuel James Reader, "The Letters of Samuel James Reader, 1861–1863," *KHQ* 9 (1940):34.
3. Quoted in Robinson, *Kansas Conflict*, p. 437.
4. *Republican*, Lawrence, January 23, 1862.
5. *Daily State Record*, Topeka, January 18, 1862; Stephenson, *The Political Career of General James H. Lane*, pp. 135–36.
6. Kansas, *House Journal*, 1861, p. 446.
7. *Republican*, Lawrence, February 20, 1862.
8. *Proceedings in the Cases of the Impeachment of Charles Robinson, Governor; John W. Robinson, Secretary of State; and George S. Hillyer, Auditor of the State of Kansas* (Lawrence: Kansas State Journal, 1862), p. 256, hereafter cited as *Impeachment Proceedings*.
9. *Impeachment Proceedings*, pp. 20–22, 256.
10. *Impeachment Proceedings*, pp. 157–59, 200.
11. *Impeachment Proceedings*, pp. 173, 256–259.
12. Gaeddert, *Birth of Kansas*, p. 166.
13. *Impeachment Proceedings*, pp. 256–57.
14. *Impeachment Proceedings*, p. 261.
15. Cortez A. M. Ewing, "Early Kansas Impeachments," *KHQ* 1 (1932):311–12.
16. S. T. Robinson, ms. on Charles Robinson, Robinson Collection, Kansas City, Kansas, Public Library.
17. Floyd P. Baker, "Retiring Address," *KHC* 3 (1885):103–6.
18. Letter from John J. Ingalls to his father, February 23, 1862, Ingalls Papers, KSHS.

19. Baker, "Retiring Address," p. 104; *Republican*, Lawrence, February 20, 1862.
20. *Conservative*, Leavenworth, February 15, 1862.
21. Ewing, "Early Kansas Impeachments," pp. 314–15.
22. Baker, "Retiring Address," p. 105.
23. James H. Lane et al., "Citizens of Kansas Protest," April 6, 1862, Robinson Papers, KSHS.
24. Ibid.
25. Letter from Charles Robinson to Sara Robinson, April 17, 1862, Robinson Papers, KSHS.
26. Letters from Charles Robinson to Sara Robinson, April 29, May 4 and 8, 1862, Robinson Papers, KSHS.
27. *Chief*, White Cloud, February 27, 1862.
28. Ewing, "Early Kansas Impeachments," p. 319; *Impeachment Proceedings*, pp. 251 ff., 344–49; Gaeddert, *Birth of Kansas*, p. 187.
29. Gaeddert, *Birth of Kansas*, p. 187.
30. Ewing, "Early Kansas Impeachments," p. 324; Senators Curtis and Lambdin voted against Robinson on the first article, and Senator Ersick voted against him on the fifth article.
31. *News*, Emporia, June 21, 1862.
32. *Kansas State Journal*, Lawrence, June 26, 1862.
33. Secretary of State John Robinson, contending that the special legislative session called to hold the impeachment trials was illegal, took the matter to the state Supreme Court. When the court ruled against him, he vacated the office; see Ewing, "Early Kansas Impeachments," p. 318; *Daily Conservative*, Leavenworth, June 28 and July 13, 1862; S. T. D. Robinson, ms. on Charles Robinson, Robinson Collection, Kansas City, Kansas, Public Library.
34. Stephenson, *The Political Career of General James H. Lane*, pp. 127, 128; Spring, *Kansas*, p. 283.
35. Letter from Frederick P. Stanton to James H. Lane, August 23, 1862, Executive Correspondence of the Governors of Kansas, 1862, KSHS.
36. Letter from Charles Robinson to E. M. Stanton, August 20, 1862, Robinson Collection, Kansas City, Kansas, Public Library.

37. Letter from T. B. Eldridge to Charles Robinson, August 28, 1862, Robinson Collection, Kansas City, Kansas, Public Library.
38. Letter from E. M. Stanton to Charles Robinson, August 28, 1862, Robinson Collection, Kansas City, Kansas, Public Library.
39. Robinson, *Kansas Conflict*, p. 463; Spring, *Kansas*, p. 283; Gaeddert, *Birth of Kansas*, p. 156.
40. Letter from Charles Robinson to Amos A. Lawrence, June 27, 1863, Robinson Papers, KSHS.
41. Quoted in Gaeddert, *Birth of Kansas*, p. 157.
42. Quoted in Stephenson, *The Political Career of General James H. Lane*, p. 136.
43. *Kansas State Journal*, Lawrence, October 16, 1862.
44. *Kansas State Journal*, Lawrence, October 2, 1862.
45. *News*, Emporia, October 4, 1862.
46. *News*, Emporia, October 4, 1862; Gaeddert, *Birth of Kansas*, p. 197.
47. *Chief*, White Cloud, November 13, 1862.
48. Robinson, *Kansas Conflict*, p. 446.
49. *Kansas Chief*, Troy, January 10, 1889.

CHAPTER 7

1. Charles Robinson, "True Doctor" ms., Robinson Papers, KSHS.
2. Letter from C. H. Langston to Charles Robinson, December 17, 1863, Robinson Papers, KSHS.
3. Letter from Charles Robinson to C. H. Langston and members of the Colored Citizens Committee of Leavenworth, December 25, 1863, Robinson Papers, KSHS.
4. Ms. in Miscellaneous Writings of Charles Robinson, Robinson Papers, KSHS.
5. Letter from Charles Robinson to Sara Robinson, November 13, 1865, Robinson Papers, KSHS.
6. For a full discussion of Lane's suicide and the scandal that preceded the event, see Stephenson, *The Political Career of General James H. Lane*, pp. 157–60.
7. Letter from S. C. Smith to Charles Robinson, August 5, 1866, Robinson Papers, KSHS.

8. Letter from Charles Robinson to S. N. Wood, November 9, 1866, Wood Papers, KSHS.
9. *News*, Emporia, January 4, 1867.
10. Sister Jeanne McKenna, " 'With the Help of God and Lucy Stone,' " *KHQ* 36 (1970):14–15.
11. "A Circular Letter of S. N. Wood," April 5, 1879, Women's Suffrage Papers, KSHS.
12. *News*, Emporia, June 7, 1867.
13. Letters from Charles Robinson to S. N. Wood, April 6 and 15, 1867, Women's Suffrage Papers, KSHS.
14. *News*, Emporia, June 7, 1867.
15. *Weekly Reader*, Topeka, May 9, 1867.
16. *News*, Emporia, October 4, 1867.
17. *News*, Emporia, November 15, 1867.
18. *News*, Emporia, November 22, 1867.
19. Letter from Charles Robinson to Susan B. Anthony, November 20, 1867, Women's Suffrage Papers, KSHS.
20. Letter from Charles Robinson to Elizabeth Cady Stanton, December 5, 1867, Women's Suffrage Papers, KSHS.
21. Letter from Charles Robinson to Sara Robinson, January 23, 1868, Robinson Papers, KSHS; Minutes of the Women's Suffrage Movement, 1867–1875, p. 53, Women's Suffrage Papers, KSHS.
22. Letter from Charles Robinson to Sara Robinson, August 31, 1870, Robinson Papers, KSHS.
23. Charles Robinson's notes for speeches, 1872, Robinson Papers, KSHS.
24. *Democrat*, Council Grove, September 12, 1872.
25. *Democrat*, Council Grove, September 12, 1872.
26. Wilder, *Annals of Kansas*, p. 555.
27. *Weekly Kansas Tribune*, Lawrence, October 15, 1874.
28. *Weekly Kansas Tribune*, Lawrence, October 16, 1873.
29. *Weekly Kansas Tribune*, Lawrence, July 9, 1874.
30. *Weekly Kansas Tribune*, Lawrence, August 6, 1874.
31. *Weekly Kansas Tribune*, Lawrence, August 13, 1874.
32. *Weekly Kansas Tribune*, Lawrence, August 27, 1874.
33. Letter from Charles Robinson to Sara Robinson, October 5, 1874, Robinson Papers, KSHS.
34. *Weekly Kansas Tribune*, Lawrence, October 8, 1874.

35. Mark A. Plummer, *Frontier Governor: Samuel J. Crawford of Kansas* (Lawrence: University Press of Kansas, 1971), p. 148.

36. The independent party in the 1876 elections was called the Independent National party, although it is often referred to as the Greenback party. The name Greenback party was formally adopted after the elections.

37. *Weekly Kansas Tribune*, Lawrence, February 10, 1876.

38. John Speer, Formal Protest of Election, December 9, 1876, Robinson Papers, KSHS.

39. Karl A. Svenson, "The Effect of Popular Discontent on Political Parties in Kansas" (Ph.D. dissertation, University of Iowa, 1948), p. 34.

40. *Weekly Kansas Tribune*, Lawrence, May 2, 1878.

41. Quoted in Clara Francis, "The Coming of Prohibition to Kansas," *KHC* 15 (1919–1922):214.

42. Ibid., pp. 200–201.

43. Grant W. Harrington, "The Genesis of Prohibition," *KHC* 15 (1919–1922):228–31.

44. Francis, "The Coming of Prohibition to Kansas," p. 209.

45. *Commonwealth*, Topeka, March 6, 1880.

46. Quoted in Francis, "The Coming of Prohibition to Kansas," p. 224.

47. Robinson, "True Doctor" ms. in Robinson Papers, KSHS.

48. *Standard*, Lawrence, May 20, 1880.

49. *Standard*, Lawrence, May 26, 1880.

50. James C. Malin, "Was Governor John A. Martin a Prohibitionist?" *KHQ* 1 (1931–1932):63–73.

51. *Daily State Journal*, Lawrence, September 26, 1882.

52. *Daily State Journal*, Lawrence, October 19, 1882.

53. *State Journal*, Topeka, September 26, 1882.

54. Cutler, *History of the State of Kansas*, p. 230.

55. Jas. C. McGinnis, ed., "Ex-Governor Charles Robinson on Prohibition," pamphlet (St. Louis, Mo., 1883).

56. *Weekly Gazette*, Lawrence, October 25, 1883.

57. *Gazette*, Lawrence, November 15, 1884.

58. Letter from Charles Robinson to Sara Robinson, August 4, 1884, Robinson Papers, KSHS.

59. Letter from Charles Robinson to Sara Robinson, August 20, 1884, Robinson Papers, KSHS.
60. Letter from Charles Robinson to John A. Martin, January 15, 1885, Executive Correspondence of the Governors of Kansas (Martin), KSHS.
61. *Daily Journal,* Lawrence, August 20, 1886.
62. Letter from H. Miles Moore to Charles Robinson, September 18, 1886, Robinson Papers, KSHS.

CHAPTER 8

1. Robinson, "Notes on Charles Robinson" ms., Robinson Collection, Kansas City, Kansas, Public Library.
2. Robinson, "True Doctor" ms., Robinson Papers, KSHS.
3. Letter from Charles Robinson to Sara Robinson, January 17, 1869, Robinson Papers, KSHS.
4. Robinson, "True Doctor" ms., Robinson Papers, KSHS.
5. Blackmar, *Charles Robinson,* pp. 334–35; Cutler, *History of the State of Kansas,* p. 323.
6. Quoted in Blackmar, *Charles Robinson,* p. 336.
7. Griffin, "The University of Kansas and the Years of Frustration, 1854–1864," p. 6; Johnson, *Battle Cry of Freedom,* pp. 17, 33.
8. Quoted in Clyde L. King, "The Kansas School System—Its History and Tendencies," *KHC* 11 (1909–1910):444.
9. Wilson Sterling, ed., *Quarter-Centennial History of the University of Kansas, 1866–1891* (Topeka: Crane & Co., 1891), p. 42.
10. Clifford S. Griffin, *The University of Kansas: A History* (Lawrence: University Press of Kansas, 1974), pp. 14–15.
11. Letter from Amos A. Lawrence to the Reverend E. Nute, December 16, 1856, quoted from Sterling, *History of the University of Kansas,* pp. 42–43.
12. Letter from Amos A. Lawrence to Charles Robinson and S. C. Pomeroy, February 14, 1857, Robinson Papers, KSHS.
13. Kansas, *House Journal,* 1861, pp. 112–13, 151, 178–79; Gaeddert, *Birth of Kansas,* p. 120.
14. Kansas, *House Journal,* 1861, pp. 271–73.
15. Ibid., pp. 274, 296, 311, 349, 354–55; Griffin, *University of Kansas,* p. 19.

16. Kansas, *Senate Journal*, 1862, pp. 155, 191–92; Griffin, "University of Kansas and the Years of Frustration," p. 20.
17. Letter from Charles Robinson to Amos A. Lawrence, February 22, 1863 (copy), Robinson Papers, KSHS.
18. Kansas, *General Laws*, 1863, pp. 115–16.
19. Blackmar, *Charles Robinson*, pp. 343–44; Griffin, "University of Kansas and the Years of Frustration," p. 20.
20. Letters from Charles Robinson to Amos A. Lawrence, February 22 and March 17, 1863 (copies), and R. Z. Mason to Charles Robinson, March 30, 1863, Robinson Papers, Spencer Library, University of Kansas, Lawrence.
21. Griffin, *University of Kansas*, p. 28.
22. King, "Kansas School System," p. 445.
23. Letter from Amos A. Lawrence to Charles Robinson, March 26, 1864, Robinson Papers, Spencer Library, University of Kansas, Lawrence.
24. Letter from Charles Robinson to F. H. Snow, July 25, 1866, Robinson Papers, Spencer Library, University of Kansas, Lawrence.
25. Griffin, *University of Kansas*, p. 33.
26. Letter from Charles Robinson to Sara Robinson, June 20, 1870, Robinson Papers, KSHS; Sterling, *History of the University of Kansas*, p. 92.
27. Letter from Frank H. Hodder to George Martin, November 10, 1906, Hodder Papers, Miscellaneous Collections, KSHS.
28. Letter from Charles F. Scott to Charles Robinson, June 5, 1894, Robinson Papers, Spencer Library, University of Kansas, Lawrence.
29. Letter from Charles F. Scott to Frank W. Blackmar, July 21, 1899, Robinson Papers, Spencer Library, University of Kansas, Lawrence.
30. Griffin, *University of Kansas*, p. 186.
31. *Annual Reports of the Kansas Superintendent of Public Instruction*, 1872, 1873; Cutler, *History of the State of Kansas*, p. 224.
32. *Laws of Kansas*, 1876, chap. 22; Nina Swanson, "The Development of Public Protection of Children in Kansas," *KHC* 15 (1919–1922):246.
33. *Weekly Journal*, Lawrence, June 9 and July 7, 1887.

34. *Daily Journal,* Lawrence, June 28, 1888; *Star,* Kansas City, October 16, 1934; Geneva Goddard, "A Study of the Historical Development and Educational Work of Haskell Institute" (Master's thesis, Kansas State Teachers College, Emporia, 1930), pp. 2, 4, 5, 7.
35. *Daily Journal,* Lawrence, August 12, 1886.
36. *Weekly Journal,* Lawrence, December 23, 1886.
37. *Daily Capital,* Topeka, August 8, 1888.
38. Robinson Clippings Scrapbooks, vol. 5, pp. 186–87, Robinson Papers, Spencer Library, University of Kansas, Lawrence.
39. Ibid.; Blackmar, *Charles Robinson,* p. 352.
40. *Gazette,* Lawrence, February 24, 1887.
41. *Daily Journal,* Lawrence, March 16, 1887.
42. Letter from Charles Robinson to J. D. Atkins, September 12, 1887, Robinson Papers, KSHS.
43. Letters from Charles Robinson to John A. Gorman, September 15, 1892, and from Charles F. Meserve to Charles Robinson, December 8, 1892, Robinson Papers, KSHS.
44. *Daily Capital,* Topeka, May 23, 1889.
45. *Kansas Magazine* 3 (May, 1873):483; Malin, "Notes on the Writing of General Histories of Kansas," pp. 411–12.
46. See James C. Malin, *A Concern about Humanity: Notes on Reform, 1872–1912, at the National and Kansas Levels of Thought* (Lawrence, Kan.: James C. Malin, 1964), p. 65.
47. Draft of the resolution passed during the "God in the Constitution Convention," Robinson Papers, KSHS.
48. A. B. Bradford, *An Exposition of Liberalism and a Defense of the Demands of the National Liberal League* (Enon Valley, Pa.: Pittsburg Liberal League, 1879), pp. 1–14; Malin, *Concern about Humanity,* p. 66.
49. Bismarck Grove, an enterprise of the Kansas Pacific Railroad, was located on the north side of the Kansas River outside of Lawrence. It contained facilities for large meetings and conventions. It was advertised nationally by the Union Pacific Railroad, and virtually hundreds of meetings were held there annually on a year-around basis. Charles Robinson served as president of the board of directors of Bismarck Grove in the early 1880s. For further information on the history of the facility, see Jim L. Lewis, " 'Beautiful Bis-

marck'—Bismarck Grove, Lawrence, 1878–1900," *KHQ* 35 (1969):225–56.

50. Malin, *Concern about Humanity*, pp. 66–67.
51. Ibid.; Michael J. Brodhead, *Persevering Populist: The Life of Frank Doster* (Reno: University of Nevada Press, 1969).
52. Malin, *Concern about Humanity*, p. 71.
53. Ibid.
54. Lewis, " 'Beautiful Bismarck,' " p. 232.
55. *Times*, Kansas City, September 6, 1880; *Tribune*, Topeka, September 6, 1880.
56. *Daily Journal*, Lawrence, October 28, 1884.
57. Letters from Ruth [?] to Charles Robinson, June 2 and September 8, 1890, Robinson Papers, KSHS.

CHAPTER 9

1. Although the census records for 1870 indicated that Charles Robinson owned only seventy-seven acres of improved land, the census reports for 1875 showed that he had in excess of 1,200 acres of fenced land and that he employed four people. Less than ten years later, his land holdings were reported at 2,100 acres of improved land, and he was regarded as one of the richest men in the state. United States Bureau of the Census, *Ninth Census of the United States, 1870* (Douglas County, Grant Township); *Daily Journal*, Lawrence, October 28, 1884.
2. *Spirit of Kansas*, Lawrence, March 29, 1873; *State Journal*, Topeka, October 19, 1882.
3. *Spirit of Kansas*, Lawrence, August 9, 1873.
4. James C. Malin, *Winter Wheat in the Golden Belt of Kansas: A Study in Adaption to Subhumid Geographical Environment* (Lawrence: University of Kansas Press, 1944), pp. 248–49.
5. W. P. Harrington, "The Populist Party in Kansas," *KHC* 16 (1923–1925):408.
6. Quoted from Brodhead, *Persevering Populist*, p. 40.
7. Harrington, "Populist Party in Kansas," pp. 405–6; Blackmar, *Charles Robinson*, pp. 309–10.
8. *Daily Journal*, Lawrence, March 19, 1890.

9. Peter H. Argersinger, "Road to a Republican Waterloo: The Farmers' Alliance and the Election of 1890 in Kansas," *KHQ* 33 (1967):449.

10. Ibid., p. 450; *Daily Journal*, Lawrence, March 4, 1890.

11. Harrington, "Populist Party in Kansas," p. 411; Argersinger, "Road to a Republican Waterloo," p. 456.

12. On June 16, 1890, Robinson received a letter from Democratic party leader John Martin of Topeka, urging him not to "discourage the efforts or dampen the ardor of your friends in the movement to nominate you for Democratic governor in 1890." Letter from John Martin to Charles Robinson, June 16, 1890.

13. Harrington, "Populist Party in Kansas," p. 411.

14. The seven principal demands of the alliance as presented in the St. Louis Platform were: (1) Abolition of national banks and substitution of legal-tender notes, (2) legislation to suppress speculators in grain futures, (3) free and unlimited coinage of silver, (4) prohibition of alien ownership of and railroad restrictions on land, (5) equal taxation, (6) issuance of fractional paper currency, and (7) government ownership of the means of communication and transportation. Charles Robinson advocated all of these financial policies in a paper read before the Seminary of Historical and Political Science at the University of Kansas on May 2, 1890, Robinson Papers, Spencer Library, University of Kansas, Lawrence.

15. *Kansas Democrat*, Topeka, July 11, 1890.

16. *Kansas Democrat*, Topeka, August 14, 1890.

17. *Kansas Democrat*, Topeka, August 10, 1890.

18. Membership in the Farmers' Alliance was limited to citizens living in rural areas. Thus a Citizens' Alliance, or town auxiliary, was formed in 1890, so that townspeople interested in a third party could identify with the agrarian movement.

19. *Kansas Democrat*, Topeka, August 13, 1890.

20. *Journal-Tribune*, Lawrence, August 15, 1890.

21. *Daily Capital*, Topeka, August 15, 1890.

22. *Gazette*, Lawrence, September 11, 1890.

23. *Herald*, Wyandotte, September 18, 1890.

24. *Kansas Democrat*, Topeka, September 11, 1890.

25. *Times*, Kansas City, September 20, 1890.

26. *Dickinson County News,* Abilene, September 18, 1890.
27. *Daily Republican,* Ottawa, September 23, 1890.
28. Harrington, "Populist Party in Kansas," p. 414; *Daily Capital,* Topeka, October 1, 1890.
29. *Kansas Democrat,* Topeka, October 4, 1890.
30. See Argersinger, "Road to a Republican Waterloo," p. 468.
31. Letter from R. M. Jones to Charles Robinson, April 28, 1892, Robinson Papers, KSHS. Jones wrote to Robinson, informing him of a joint Democrat-Populist effort in 1892: "Such arrangement, I am assured, the People's party generally desire. . . . The sensible element is now in control."
32. *Kansas Democrat,* Topeka, November 14, 1890.
33. Charles Robinson, "Remonetization or Demonetization, Which?" *New Kansas Magazine* 4 (1893):23–24.
34. After the Pullman strike of 1894, Robinson wrote an article, which was widely printed in eastern Kansas newspapers, entitled "Corporate Power." In this article he attributed the strikes and lockouts to the country's high protective tariff; Strikes Clippings, vol. 1, KSHS.
35. Letter from James F. Legate to Charles Robinson, November 25, 1892, Robinson Papers, KSHS.
36. Letter from Charles Robinson to H. Miles Moore, November 25, 1892, Moore Papers, KSHS.
37. *Times,* Kansas City, May 19, 1892.
38. The other book that Wilder referred to was Sara Robinson's *Kansas: Its Interior and Exterior Life,* a contemporary account of the free-state struggle; letter from D. W. Wilder to Charles Robinson, April 27, 1892, Robinson Papers, KSHS.
39. *Tribune,* Lawrence, August 17, 1894; letter from Charles Robinson to Sara Robinson, July 26, 1894, Robinson Papers, KSHS.
40. *Gazette,* Lawrence, August 17, 1894.
41. *Daily Journal,* Lawrence, August 17, 1894.
42. Robinson left a bequest of $200,000 to the University of Kansas; *Dickinson County News,* Abilene, August 30, 1894; *Gazette,* Lawrence, August 30, 1894.
43. Malin, *John Brown and the Legend of Fifty-six,* p. 457.
44. Letters from Sara Robinson to Frank W. Blackmar, November 19 and December 18, 1896, Robinson Papers, Spencer

Library, University of Kansas, Lawrence. An extensive file of correspondence between Sara Robinson and Blackmar exists in the archives at Kansas University. It encompasses the years 1895 to 1908. She wrote frequent letters to Blackmar, providing him with information that she wished to have him include in the biography of her late husband. In many cases the information appeared verbatim in Blackmar's book on Robinson.

45. Malin, *John Brown and the Legend of Fifty-six*, p. 459.
46. Ibid., p. 461. Not only did Mrs. Robinson finance these publications, she provided money for G. W. Brown's care in his old age.
47. Letter from William E. Connelley to G. W. Brown, January 21, 1903 (copy), Connelley Collection, KSHS.
48. Quoted from a letter printed on the inside cover of William E. Connelley's *An Appeal to the Record* (Topeka: William E. Connelley, 1903).
49. Miscellaneous Writings file, Connelley Collection, KSHS.
50. James Malin's *John Brown and the Legend of Fifty-six* was the first major publication on Kansas history since the early part of the twentieth century that carefully examined Robinson's leadership and contained a favorable interpretation of his activities. Subsequent works, notably Samuel Johnson's *Battle Cry of Freedom*, support and augment Malin's interpretation.
51. *Chief*, Troy, August 22, 1894.

Bibliography

In doing the research on this book, I found that some manuscript sources were particularly useful. The most important manuscript material on Charles Robinson is in the private papers of Charles and Sara T. D. Robinson that are located at the Kansas State Historical Society in Topeka, Kansas. This collection consists of correspondence, papers written by Charles and Sara, diaries, business records, and numerous clippings spanning his life in Kansas. The earliest material is from 1834, but there are few papers until 1855. Robinson's activities in the fight for a free Kansas are covered both by letters that he wrote and by others that he received. After the early statehood period (1861–1863), materials in the collection deal chiefly with personal, family, and business matters, though such subjects as the construction of the University of Kansas, local and national politics, and his personal philosophy are also covered, and speeches are included. Unfortunately, there is little on the elections of the 1870s and 1880s. Following Charles Robinson's death in 1894, all correspondence and documents center around Sara's activities.

Information about Robinson's business and political activities in the Territorial period was also found in the papers of the New England Emigrant Aid Company and in the personal papers of Amos A. Lawrence, Samuel N. Wood, Thomas Ewing, Jr., and Abelard Guthrie (all of which are in the Manuscript Division of the Kansas State Historical Society). Other valuable information for his post-Territorial careers was found in the papers of John J. Ingalls, George W. Brown, and James W. Denver, and in the collections of William E. Connelley and William H. Sears (Manuscript Division, Kansas State Historical Society). Valuable manuscript material on Charles Robinson is contained in the subject files entitled Women's Suffrage, University of Kansas, and the Executive Correspondence of the Governors of Kansas, 1859–1894, at the Kansas State Historical Society.

An important source for information on Robinson's early life is the Charles and Sara Robinson Collection at the Kansas City, Kansas, Public Library. It contains several unpublished manuscripts written by Sara Robinson, recounting her knowledge of her husband's family, his youth and educational training, and his California experiences. Other important materials in this collection are letters received by Sara from people associated with her husband during his life who recount their own knowledge of the events of the period. The letters of S. C. Smith to Sara Robinson were an outstanding source of information for the late Territorial and early statehood periods.

The story of Charles Robinson's relationship with the University of Kansas is covered in the Robinson papers in the Spencer Library at the University of Kansas in Lawrence. Valuable information was also derived from this collection pertaining to Sara's activities after her husband's death, particularly in the correspondence between Sara and Frank Blackmar of the University of Kansas.

MANUSCRIPTS AND ARCHIVES

Adams, Zu. Papers, Kansas State Historical Society, Topeka, Kansas (hereafter cited as KSHS).

Blood, James. Papers. KSHS.

Brown, George Washington. Papers. KSHS.

Connelley, William E. Collection. KSHS.

Crawford, George A. Papers. KSHS.

Denver, James W. Papers. KSHS.

Ewing, Thomas, Jr. Papers. KSHS.

Executive Correspondence of the Governors of Kansas, 1859–1894. Collection. KSHS.

Bibliography

Gray, Alfred. Papers. KSHS.

Guthrie, Abelard. Papers. KSHS.

Hodder, Frank. Papers. Miscellaneous Collections. KSHS.

Hudson, Joseph Kennedy. Papers. KSHS.

Ingalls, John J. Papers. KSHS.

Kansas Miscellaneous Collections. Spencer Library, University of Kansas, Lawrence, Kansas.

Lane, James H. Papers. KSHS.

Lawrence, Amos A. Papers. KSHS.

Moore, H. Miles. Papers. KSHS.

New England Emigrant Aid Company. Records. KSHS.

Robinson, Charles and Sara. Collection. Kansas City, Kansas, Public Library.

Robinson, Charles and Sara. Papers. KSHS.

Robinson, Charles and Sara. Papers. Spencer Library, University of Kansas, Lawrence, Kansas.

St. John, John P. Records. KSHS.

Sears, William H. Collection. KSHS.

Strikes Clippings. KSHS.

Women's Suffrage. Collection. KSHS.

Wood, Samuel N. Papers. KSHS.

NEWSPAPERS
(From Kansas unless otherwise noted)

Abilene, *Dickinson County News*, 1890–1894.

Atchison, *Freedom's Champion*, 1859.

Atchison, *Squatter Sovereign*, 1856.

Concordia, *Cloud County Blade*, 1879–1880.

Council Grove, *Democrat*, 1872–1873.

Emporia, *Kansas Greenbacker*, 1877–1880.

Emporia, *News*, 1861–1862, 1866–1868.

Junction City, *Union*, 1872.

Kansas City, Mo., *Star*, 1894.

Kansas City, Mo., *Times*, 1880, 1890–1894.

Lawrence, *Daily Journal*, 1884–1887.

Lawrence, *Gazette*, 1883–1894.

Lawrence, *Herald of Freedom*, 1855–1859.

Lawrence, *Journal*, 1892.

Bibliography

Lawrence, *Journal-Tribune*, 1890.
Lawrence, *Kansas Free State*, 1855.
Lawrence, *Kansas State Journal*, 1861–1864.
Lawrence, *Republican*, 1857–1862.
Lawrence, *Spirit of Kansas*, 1873–1874.
Lawrence, *Standard*, 1880.
Lawrence, *Tribune*, 1894.
Lawrence, *Weekly Journal*, 1884–1887.
Lawrence, *Weekly Kansas Tribune*, 1874–1878.
Leavenworth, *Daily Conservative*, 1861–1865.
Leavenworth, *Herald*, 1856, 1860.
Leavenworth, *Times*, 1877.
Liberty, Mo., *Democratic Platform*, 1854.
Mound City, *Border Sentinel*, 1869.
Ottawa, *Daily Republican*, 1890.
Parsons, *Sun*, 1871.
Quindaro, *Chindowan*, 1857–1860.
Topeka, *Daily Capital*, 1888–1894, 1934.
Topeka, *Daily Commonwealth*, 1868–1872, 1880–1882.
Topeka, *Daily State Record*, 1862.
Topeka, *Journal*, 1909.
Topeka, *Kansas Democrat*, 1889–1891.
Topeka, *Kansas State Record*, 1860.
Topeka, *State Journal*, 1882.
Topeka, *Tribune*, 1880.
Topeka, *Weekly Leader*, 1867.
Troy, *Chief*, 1894.
Troy, *The Kansas Chief*, 1889.
White Cloud, *Chief*, 1862.
Wyandotte, *Herald*, 1890.

SCRAPBOOKS AND PAMPHLETS

Anonymous. *The People's Choice for Governor, Honorable Charles Robinson.* Topeka, 1890.
Biographical Scrapbooks. R., vol. 4. KSHS.
Bradford, A. B. *An Exposition of Liberalism and a Defense of the Demands of the National Liberal League.* Enon Valley, Pa.: Pittsburgh Liberal League, 1879.

Bibliography

Collected Biography Clippings. Vol. 1. KSHS.

Guthrie, Abelard. *To the Public.* Quindaro, Kans.: Abelard Guthrie, 1860.

Haskell Institute Clippings. Vol. 1. KSHS.

Kansas Governors Clippings. Vol. 4. KSHS.

Kansas Political and Biographical Scrapbooks, 1872–1896. Compiled by W. C. Webb. KSHS.

McGinnis, James C., and Robinson, Charles. *Prohibition: It is in Violation of the Reserved Rights of the Citizens; Is Not Sanctioned by the Teachings of the Bible; and Is Impracticable and Delusive as a Temperance Expedient, Together with an Address by Ex-Governor Charles Robinson of Kansas.* St. Louis, Mo.: Woodward & Tiernan Printers, 1884.

Nevins, Allan. *Kansas and the Stream of American Destiny.* Lawrence: University of Kansas Press, 1954.

Populist Party Clippings. Vol. 1. KSHS.

GOVERNMENT PUBLICATIONS

United States:

Bureau of the Census. *Ninth Census of the United States,* 1870. Washington, D.C., 1872.

Congressional Globe. 34th Cong., 1st. sess.

House of Representatives. *Miscellaneous Documents,* Report No. 1017. 35th Cong., 2d sess., 1858–1859, vol. 2.

House of Representatives. *Report of the Special Committee Appointed to Investigate the Troubles in Kansas; With the Views of the Minority of Said Committee.* Report No. 200. 34th Cong., 1st sess., 1856.

State of Kansas:

Compiled Laws of Kansas, 1862, 1863, 1876.

House Journal of the Legislative Assembly of the State of Kansas, 1861–1879.

Kansas State Census, 1875, 1885.

Proceedings in the Cases of the Impeachment of Charles Robinson, Governor; John W. Robinson, Secretary of State; and George S. Hillyer, Auditor of the State of Kansas. Lawrence: Kansas State Journal, 1862.

Bibliography

Report of the Adjutant General of the State of Kansas, 1861–1865. Vol. 1. Topeka, 1896.

Reports of the Kansas Superintendent of Public Instruction, 1872–1873.

Senate Journal of the Legislative Assembly of the State of Kansas, 1861–1880.

BOOKS

Bartlett, Irving H. *The American Mind in the Mid-Nineteenth Century.* New York: Thomas Y. Crowell Co., 1967.

Blackmar, Frank W., ed. *Kansas: A Cyclopedia of State History.* 2 vols. Chicago: Standard Publishing Co., 1912.

———. *The Life of Charles Robinson.* Topeka, Kan.: Crane & Co., 1902.

Brewerton, George Douglas. *Wars of the Western Border: Or New Homes and a Strange People.* New York: Derby & Jackson, 1858.

Bright, John D., ed. *Kansas: The First Century.* 4 vols. New York: Lewis Historical Publishing Co., 1956.

Brodhead, Michael J. *Persevering Populist: The Life of Frank Doster.* Reno: University of Nevada Press, 1969.

Brown, George Washington. *False Claims of Kansas Historians Truthfully Corrected.* Rockford, Ill.: George Washington Brown, 1902.

———. *The Rescue of Kansas from Slavery.* Rockford, Ill.: George Washington Brown, 1902.

Castel, Albert. *A Frontier State at War: Kansas, 1861–1865.* Ithaca, N.Y.: Cornell University Press, 1958.

Clugston, William George. *Rascals in Democracy.* New York: R. R. Smith, 1940.

Columbian History of Education in Kansas. Topeka: Kansas State Historical Society, 1893.

Connelley, William E. *An Appeal to the Record.* Topeka, Kans.: William E. Connelley, 1903.

———. *James Henry Lane: The "Grim Chieftain of Kansas."* Topeka, Kans.: Crane & Co., 1899.

———. *A Standard History of Kansas and Kansans.* 5 vols. Chicago: Lewis Publishing Co., 1918.

197

Bibliography

Cordley, Richard. *A History of Lawrence, Kansas.* Lawrence, Kans.: Lawrence Journal Press, 1895.

Crawford, Samuel J. *Kansas in the Sixties.* Chicago: A. C. McClurg & Co., 1911.

Cutler, William G., ed. *History of the State of Kansas.* Chicago: A. T. Andreas, 1883.

Filler, Louis, ed. *Late Nineteenth-Century American Liberalism.* Indianapolis, Ind.: Bobbs-Merrill Co., Inc., 1962.

Gaeddert, G. Raymond. *The Birth of Kansas.* Lawrence: University of Kansas, 1940.

Gates, Paul Wallace. *Fifty Million Acres: Conflicts over Kansas Land Policy, 1854–1890.* Ithaca, N.Y.: Cornell University Press, 1954.

Giles, Frye W. *Thirty Years in Topeka: A Historical Sketch.* 2d ed. Topeka, Kan.: Capper Special Services, Inc., 1960.

Gleed, Charles S., ed. *The Kansas Memorial: A Report of the Old Settlers' Meeting Held at Bismarck Grove, Kansas, Sept. 15th and 16th, 1879.* Kansas City, Mo.: Ramsey, Millett & Hudson, 1880.

Griffin, Clifford S. *The University of Kansas: A History.* Lawrence: University Press of Kansas, 1974.

Howes, Charles C. *This Place Called Kansas.* Norman: University of Oklahoma Press, 1952.

Ingalls, John James. *A Collection of the Writings of John James Ingalls.* Kansas City, Mo.: Hudson-Kimberly Publishing Co., 1902.

Johnson, Samuel A. *The Battle Cry of Freedom.* Lawrence: University of Kansas Press, 1954.

Kappler, Charles J. *Indian Affairs, Laws and Treaties.* 2d ed., vol. 2. Washington, D.C.: Government Printing Office, 1904.

McNeal, Thomas A. *When Kansas Was Young.* New York: MacMillan Co., 1922.

Malin, James C. *A Concern about Humanity: Notes on Reform, 1872–1912, at the National and Kansas Levels of Thought.* Lawrence, Kans.: James C. Malin, 1964.

―――. *John Brown and the Legend of Fifty-six.* Philadelphia: American Philosophical Society, 1942.

―――. *On the Nature of History: Essays about History and Dissidence.* Lawrence, Kans.: James C. Malin, 1954.

Bibliography

————. *Winter Wheat in the Golden Belt of Kansas: A Study in Adaption to Subhumid Geographical Environment.* Lawrence: University of Kansas Press, 1944.

Monaghan, Jay (James). *Civil War on the Western Border, 1854–1865.* Boston: Little, Brown & Co., 1955.

Nelson, Maidee T. *California: Land of Promise.* Caldwell, Idaho: Caxton Printers, Ltd., 1962.

Nevins, Allan. *Ordeal of the Union.* Vol. 2: *A House Dividing, 1852–1857.* New York: Charles Scribner's Sons, 1947.

Oates, Stephen B. *To Purge This Land with Blood.* New York: Harper & Row, 1970.

Owen, Jennie Small. *The Annals of Kansas, 1886–1925.* 2 vols. Topeka: Kansas State Historical Society, 1954, 1956.

Paige, Lucius. *History of Hardwick, Massachusetts.* Boston: Houghton, Mifflin & Co., 1883.

Plummer, Mark A. *Frontier Governor: Samuel J. Crawford of Kansas.* Lawrence: University Press of Kansas, 1971.

Porter, Kirk H., and Johnson, Donald Bruce, comps. *National Party Platforms, 1840–1960.* 2d ed. Urbana: University of Illinois Press, 1961.

Potter, Don. *1854–1954: Lawrence—100 Years of History Significant to Kansas.* Lawrence, Kans.: Don Potter, 1954.

Randall, James G., and Donald, David. *The Civil War and Reconstruction.* 2d ed. Boston: D. C. Heath & Co., 1961.

Richardson, Albert D. *Beyond the Mississippi: From the Great River to the Great Ocean.* Hartford, Conn.: American Publishing Co., 1867.

Robinson, Charles. *The Kansas Conflict.* New York: Harper & Brothers, 1892.

Robinson, Sara T. L. *Kansas: Its Interior and Exterior Life.* 1st ed. Boston: Crosby, Nichols & Co., 1856.

Spring, Leverett W. *Kansas: The Prelude to the War for the Union.* Boston: Houghton, Mifflin & Co., 1885.

Stephenson, Wendell H. *The Political Career of General James H. Lane.* Vol. 3 of *Publications of the Kansas State Historical Society.* Topeka, Kans.: State Printer, 1930.

Sterling, Wilson, ed. *Quarter-Centennial History of the University of Kansas, 1866–1891.* Topeka, Kans.: Crane & Co., 1891.

Bibliography

Thayer, Eli. *A History of the Kansas Crusade: Its Friends and Its Foes.* New York: Harper & Brothers, 1889.

——. *The New England Emigrant Aid Company.* Worcester, Mass.: F. P. Rice, 1887.

United States Biographical Dictionary: Kansas Volume. Chicago: S. Lewis & Co., 1879.

University of Kansas. *Territorial Kansas: Studies Commemorating the Centennial.* Lawrence: University of Kansas Publications, Social Science Studies, 1954.

White, William A. *The Changing West: An Economic Theory about Our Golden Age.* New York: MacMillan Co., 1939.

Wilder, Daniel W. *The Annals of Kansas, 1541–1885.* Topeka: T. Dwight Thatcher, Kansas Publishing Co., 1886.

Zornow, William F. *Kansas: A History of the Jayhawk State.* Norman: University of Oklahoma Press, 1957.

HISTORICAL COLLECTIONS

Kansas Historical Collections. Known also as *Transactions of the Kansas State Historical Society.* 17 vols. Published biennially, with some omissions, from 1881 until 1929. Topeka, Kans.

ARTICLES

Anderson, George L. "Some Phases of Currency and Banking in Territorial Kansas." In *Territorial Kansas: Studies Commemorating the Centennial,* pp. 103–47. Lawrence: University of Kansas Publications, Social Science Studies, 1954.

Argersinger, Peter H. "Road to a Republican Waterloo: The Farmers' Alliance and the Election of 1890 in Kansas." *Kansas Historical Quarterly* 33 (1967):443–69.

Baker, Floyd P. "Retiring Address." *Kansas Historical Collections* 3 (1881–1884):101–9.

Ballard, David E. "The First State Legislature." *Kansas Historical Collections* 10 (1907–1908):232–37.

Barnes, Lela, ed. "An Editor Looks at Early-day Kansas: The Letters of Charles Monroe Chase." *Kansas Historical Quarterly* 26 (1960):113–51, 267–301.

Bibliography

Barry, Louise, comp. "Charles Robinson—Yankee '49er: His Journey to California." *Kansas Historical Quarterly* 34 (1968):179–88.

———. "The Emigrant Aid Company Parties of 1854." *Kansas Historical Quarterly* 12 (1943):115–55.

[———, ed.] "A Chronology of Kansas Political and Military Events, 1859–1865." *Kansas Historical Quarterly* 25 (1959): 283–300.

Blackmar, Frank W. "Biography the Basis of History: Charles Robinson." *Kansas Historical Collections* 6 (1897–1900): 187–202.

———. "A Chapter in the Life of Charles Robinson." *Annual Report of the American Historical Association* (1894), pp. 213–26.

———. "Sara T. D. Robinson." *Graduate Magazine* 10 (1912): 134–40.

Bumgardner, Edward. "The First Kansas Band." *Kansas Historical Quarterly* 5 (1936):278–81.

Carruth, William H. "The New England Emigrant Aid Company as an Investment Society." *Kansas Historical Collections* 6 (1897–1900):90–96.

Craik, Elmer Leroy. "Southern Interest in Territorial Kansas, 1854–1858." *Kansas Historical Collections* 15 (1919–1922): 334–450.

Denton, Charles Richard. "The Unitarian Church and 'Kansas Territory,' 1854–1861." *Kansas Historical Quarterly* 30 (1964):307–38, 455–91.

Dolbee, Cora, "The Fourth of July in Early Kansas, 1854–1857." *Kansas Historical Quarterly* 10 (1941):34–78.

Ewing, Cortez A. M. "Early Kansas Impeachments." *Kansas Historical Quarterly* 1 (1931–1932):307–25.

Ewy, Marvin. "The United States Army in the Kansas Border Troubles, 1855–1856." *Kansas Historical Quarterly* 32 (1966):385–400.

Farley, Alan W. "Annals of Quindaro: A Kansas Ghost Town." *Kansas Historical Quarterly* 32 (1956):305–20.

Francis, Clara. "The Coming of Prohibition to Kansas." *Kansas Historical Collections* 15 (1919–1922):192–227.

Fry, Mabel S. "Charles Robinson, First Governor of Kansas."

Bibliography

Bulletin of the Shawnee County Historical Society 35 (1961): 21–24.

Gambone, Joseph G. "Samuel C. Pomeroy and the Senatorial Election of 1861, Reconsidered." *Kansas Historical Quarterly* 37 (1971):15–32.

Gates, Paul W. "A Fragment of Kansas Land History: The Disposal of the Christian Indian Tract." *Kansas Historical Quarterly* 6 (1937):227–40.

———. "Land and Credit Problems in Underdeveloped Kansas." *Kansas Historical Quarterly* 31 (1965):41–61.

Glick, George W. "The Drought of 1860." *Kansas Historical Collections* 9 (1905–1906):480–84.

Goodin, Joel K., ed. "The Topeka Movement." *Kansas Historical Collections* 13 (1913–1914):122–249.

Griffin, Clifford S. "The University of Kansas and the Sack of Lawrence: A Problem of Intellectual Honesty." *Kansas Historical Quarterly* 34 (1968):409–26.

———. "The University of Kansas and the Years of Frustration, 1854–1864." *Kansas Historical Quarterly* 32 (1966):1–32.

Harrington, Grant W. "The Genesis of Prohibition." *Kansas Historical Collections* 15 (1919–1922):228–31.

Harrington, W. P. "The Populist Party in Kansas." *Kansas Historical Collections* 16 (1923–1925):403–50.

Hickman, Russell K. "Speculative Activities of the Emigrant Aid Company." *Kansas Historical Quarterly* 4 (1935):235–67.

Holliday, Cyrus K. "The Presidential Campaign of 1856—The Fremont Campaign." *Kansas Historical Collections* 5 (1889–1896):48–60.

Howes, Cecil. "Pistol-Packin' Pencil Pushers." *Kansas Historical Quarterly* 13 (1944–1945):115–38.

Ingalls, John J. "Kansas—1541–1891." *Harper's Magazine* 86 (1892–1893):697–713.

———. "Some Ingalls Letters." *Kansas Historical Collections* 14 (1915–1918):94–122.

Jarrell, Arch W. "Kansas Portraits—Charles Robinson." *Jayhawk* 2 (January, 1929):15–16.

Johannsen, Robert W. "The Kansas-Nebraska Act and Territorial Government in the United States." In *Territorial Kansas: Studies Commemorating the Centennial*, pp. 17–32.

Bibliography

Lawrence: University of Kansas Publications, Social Science Studies, 1954.

———. "The Lecompton Constitutional Convention: An Analysis of Its Membership." *Kansas Historical Quarterly* 23 (1957):225–43.

King, Clyde L. "The Kansas School System—Its History and Tendencies." *Kansas Historical Collections* 11 (1909–1910): 424–55.

Langsdorf, Edgar. "Jim Lane and the Frontier Guard." *Kansas Historical Quarterly* 9 (1940):13–25.

Learnard, O. E. "Organization of the Republican Party." *Kansas Historical Collections* 6 (1897–1900):312–16.

Lewis, Jim L. " 'Beautiful Bismarck'—Bismarck Grove, Lawrence, 1878–1900." *Kansas Historical Quarterly* 35 (1969): 225–56.

Lindquist, Emory. "Religion in Kansas during the Era of the Civil War." *Kansas Historical Quarterly* 25 (1959):313–33, 407–37.

McKenna, Sister Jeanne. " 'With the Help of God and Lucy Stone.' " *Kansas Historical Quarterly* 36 (1970):13–26.

Malin, James C. "An Introduction to the History of the Bluestem-Pasture Region of Kansas: A Study in Adaptation to Geographical Environment." *Kansas Historical Quarterly* 11 (1942):3–28.

———. "Judge Lecompte and the 'Sack of Lawrence.' " *Kansas Historical Quarterly* 20 (1952–1953):465–94, 553–97.

———. "Notes on the Literature of Populism." *Kansas Historical Quarterly* 1 (1931–1932):160–64.

———. "Notes on the Writing of General Histories of Kansas." *Kansas Historical Quarterly* 21 (1954–1955):184–223, 264–87, 331–78, 407–44, 598–643.

———. "The Topeka Statehood Movement Reconsidered: Origins." In *Territorial Kansas: Studies Commemorating the Centennial*, pp. 33–69. Lawrence: University of Kansas Publications, Social Science Studies, 1954.

———. "Was Governor John A. Martin a Prohibitionist?" *Kansas Historical Quarterly* 1 (1931–1932):63–73.

Manning, E. C. "In at the Birth, And—." *Kansas Historical Collections* 7 (1901–1902):202–5.

Bibliography

Martin, George W. "The First Two Years of Kansas." *Kansas Historical Collections* 10 (1907–1908):120–48.

Miller, Raymond C. "The Background of Populism in Kansas." *Mississippi Valley Historical Review* 11 (1924–1925):469–89.

Pantle, Alberta, ed. "The Connecticut Kansas Colony: Letters of Charles B. Lines to the New Haven (Conn.) *Daily Palladium*." *Kansas Historical Quarterly* 22 (1956):1–50, 138–88.

Perdue, Rosa M. "The Sources of the Constitution of Kansas." *Kansas Historical Collections* 7 (1901–1902):130–51.

Reader, Samuel James. "The Letters of Samuel James Reader, 1861–1863." *Kansas Historical Quarterly* 9 (1940):26–57, 141–74.

Richmond, Robert W. "The First Capitol of Kansas." *Kansas Historical Quarterly* 21 (1954–1955):321–25.

Robinson, Charles. "Ad Astra per Aspera." *Kansas Magazine* 3 (1873):389–93.

———. "Remonetization or Demonetization, Which?" *New Kansas Magazine* 4 (1893):22–24.

Robinson, W. Stitt, Jr. "The Role of the Military in Territorial Kansas." In *Territorial Kansas: Studies Commemorating the Centennial.* Lawrence: University of Kansas Publications, Social Science Studies, 1954.

Royce, Josiah. "An Episode of Early California Life: The Squatter Riot of 1850 in Sacramento." In his *Studies of Good and Evil*, pp. 298–348. New York: D. Appleton & Co., 1898.

Sanborn, Franklin B. "Some Notes on the Territorial History of Kansas." *Kansas Historical Collections* 13 (1913–1914):249–65.

Sears, Gen. William H. "The Robinson Rifles." *Kansas Historical Quarterly* 2 (1933):309–20.

Socolofsky, Homer E. "Wyandot Floats." *Kansas Historical Quarterly* 36 (1970):241–304.

Spring, Leverett Wilson. "The Career of a Kansas Politician." *American Historical Review* 4 (1898–1899):80–104.

Swanson, Nina. "The Development of Public Protection of Children in Kansas." *Kansas Historical Collections* 15 (1919–1922):231–78.

Bibliography

Veale, George W. "Coming in and Going Out." *Kansas Historical Collections* 11 (1909–1910):5–12.

Walker, Edith, and Leibengood, Dorothy. "Labor Organizations in Kansas in the Early Eighties." *Kansas Historical Quarterly* 4 (1935):283–90.

UNPUBLISHED WRITINGS

Goddard, Geneva. "A Study of the Historical Development and Educational Work of Haskell Institute." Master's thesis, Kansas State Teachers College, Emporia, 1930.

McKenna, Sister Jeanne (Mary Berard). "Samuel N. Wood: Chronic Agitator." Ph.D. dissertation, St. Louis University, 1968.

Svenson, Karl A. "The Effect of Popular Discontent on Political Parties in Kansas." Ph.D. dissertation, University of Iowa, 1948.

Index

Index

Index

Index

Index

son, 70, 93, 100, 168; in Liberal League, 146
Missouri (state), 18, 82
Missouri Compromise, 17–18
Missouri River, 58
Moore, H. Miles, 125
Mound City, Kansas, 116
Mount Oread, 135

National Labor Greenback party, 120
National Liberal League, 145
Negroes: exclusion of by Free State party, 19, 32; Kansans' views towards, 29; Robinson's views on, 101–2; suffrage of, 104–6, 108. *See also* Quindaro State Normal School; Slavery
Neodesha *Free Press*, 111
Ne Plus Ultra (steamboat), 4
New England Emigrant Aid Company: motives, 12, 22; and Robinson, 13, 16, 42, 48. *See also* Emigrant Aid Company
New Kansas Magazine, 161
Noyes, John Humphrey, 128
Nute, Reverend Ephraim, 130, 131

Oakridge farm, 167
Oliver, Mordecai, 39
Oliver, R. W., 137
Osawatomie, Kansas, 68
Osborn, Thomas A., 109, 111, 113
Ottawa, Kansas, 148
Ottawa *Daily Republican*, 159

Panic of 1857, 59, 61
Parrott, Marcus J., 31, 53, 75, 99, 109
Parsons, Kansas, 121
Pate, Henry C., 45
Patronage, political and military, 75, 78, 87, 96–97
Peffer, William F., 155, 156
People's Grand Protective Union of Kansas, 117
People's party (1883), 122
People's party (1889), 154, 155, 156. *See also* Populist party
Pierce, Franklin, 30, 36, 37, 45, 46
Polk, Leonidas, 159–60

Pomeroy, Samuel C.: appointed general agent for Emigrant Aid Company, 13; sketch, 13–14; as railroad promoter, 60; elected U.S. Senator, 75–76; and bond scandal, 88–89; named, 104, 131
Popular sovereignty, 17, 18
Populist party, 156, 158, 159, 160, 161
Pottawatomie massacre, 44
Pratt, Caleb S., 72
Prohibition: as a political issue, 116–21; Robinson's views on, 118–19, 122; and the Republican party, 116–17. *See also* Antiprohibition; Resubmission question
Proslavery party: organized, 33; activities of, 33; and the Lecompton Constitution, 53

Quantrill's raid, 135
Quindaro, Kansas, 58–60
Quindaro *Chindowan*, 58
Quindaro State Normal School, 139–40

Railroads, in Kansas: Robinson's interest in, 60–63; promotion of, 60–62; Leavenworth, Pawnee and Western, 60, 63–64; Quindaro, Parkville, and Grand River, 62; and Lawrence, 63; Union Pacific, 64, 187n49; Atchison, Topeka and Santa Fe, 65
Reeder, Andrew H., 20, 21, 30, 31, 39
Republican party: and the Kansas statehood movement, 45, 46; organized in Kansas, 67–68; and Robinson, 68, 100, 102, 168; division of, 76; opposed by third-party movements, 108–16; and prohibition, 116–24; campaign of 1890, 157; mentioned passim
Resubmission question, 122–24, 156
Resumption Act of 1875, 114
Rice, E. J., 138
Riggs, Joseph, 112
Rightmire, W. F., 154
Robinson, Charles: ancestry, 1–2; birth of, July 21, 1818, 2; educa-

Index

tion of, 2–3; religious attitudes of,
2, 3, 127–29, 145–48; first marriage
of, 3; journeys to California, 4–5;
and California land issue, 6–9;
elected to California legislature, 9;
returns to Massachusetts, 9–10;
second marriage of, 10; journey to
Kansas of, 11; his attitude toward
slavery, 13, 19, 21, 32–33; and New
England Emigrant Aid Company,
13, 16, 22, 42, 48; and free-state
movement, 21, 54; and Free State
party, 22, 25–27, 35; Fourth of July
address of, 23; description of, 28;
named treasurer of Executive Committee of Kansas Territory, 31; his
role in Wakarusa War, 34; nominated for governor under Topeka
Constitution, 35; and the "Fabian
policy," 37; his inaugural address
of 1855, 38; a target of proslavery
wrath, 41; indicted for treason, 41;
his attempt to flee Kansas, 42;
urges Fremont to run for president, 45; resigns as agent of New
England Emigrant Aid Company,
48; plots to secure statehood with
Geary, 49; resigns as Free State
governor, 49; addresses Grasshopper Falls Convention, 52; and land
speculation, 57; and Quindaro,
Kansas, 58–60; and railroad development in Kansas, 60–64; as agent
for Kansas Land Trust, 61; property of, 64, 150, 188n1; and Republican party, 67–69, 100, 102,
168; as Republican candidate for
governor, 69–70, 177n30; seeks office of Commissioner of Indian
Affairs, 72–74; takes office as governor, 72; and conflict with Lane, 76,
78, 80–84, 86, 89–90, 92–100; views
on state government, 77; impeachment of, 87–96; attitude toward
Lincoln, 97; leaves office, 100; reform philosophy, 101; attitude toward Negroes, 103; involvement in
woman-suffrage movement, 103–8;
as candidate for state legislature,
110, 113; organizes Independent
Reform party, 111; joins Greenback
party, 113–14; opposes prohibition,
117–25, 156; candidate for governor
in 1882, 120; views on tariff of, 123;
joins Democratic party, 124; as
candidate for Congress in 1886,
124; his views on education, 127–
28, 129, 139–40; donates land for
university, 135; as a member of
University of Kansas Board of Regents, 136–39; appointed superintendent of Haskell Indian Institute,
141–42; resigns from Haskell, 144;
Liberal League activities of, 145–
49; agricultural interests of, 150–
51; and Farmers' Alliance, 152; and
People's party, 155–56; as Democratic candidate for governor in
1890, 158–60; his impact on the
election of 1890, 160–61; retires
from politics, 161; publishes *The
Kansas Conflict*, 161–62; death of,
August 17, 1894, 163; summary of
his career, 167–68

Robinson, D. H., 138

Robinson, Huldah (mother of
Charles), 2

Robinson, J. W., 70, 88–89, 91, 92–95

Robinson, John, 1

Robinson, Jonathan (father of
Charles), 2

Robinson, Martha (sister of Charles),
2, 64

Robinson, Sara T. D. (wife of
Charles): on Robinson ancestry, 1;
on Robinson's boyhood, 2; description of, 10; education of, 10; arrival
in Kansas, 15; speaks on behalf of
free-state cause, 42; her dislike of
Kansas, 65–66; encourages husband
to seek Washington position, 73;
her interest in education, 130; donates land for university, 135; au-
thorizes biography of Charles Robinson, 164, 190n44; attacks critics
of her husband, 164–67; death of,
167. *See also* Lawrence, Sara T. D.

Root, J. P., 70

212

Index

Index

Weer, William, 93

Whitfield, J. W., 31, 39

Wilder, Daniel W., 68, 162, 165

Willits, John F., 156–57, 160

Wilson, Henry, 69, 115

Woman suffrage: Robinson's views on, 103, 104; campaign for in 1867, 105–8; defeat of, 107

Wood, J. N. O. P., 24

Wood, Samuel N.: presides at Lawrence town meeting, 33; Sheriff Jones tries to arrest, 40; indicted for treason, 41; escapes from Territory, 42; urges Robinson to run for political office, 104; and woman-suffrage movement, 105–8; nominated for Congress, 120

Wyandot Indians, 57, 58

Wyandot land floats, 57

Wyandotte, Kansas, 59

Wyandotte Constitution, 68–69, 70, 71, 177–78n4